Ask Seek Knock

To Ask Is The Secret

By Larry Lyons

Ask Seek Knock
by Larry Lyons

Printed in the United States of America

Library of Congress Card Number: 00-111517
ISBN 9781612154831

www.xulonpress.com

PURPOSE

The purpose of this writing is to bring Honor and Glory to the Most High God. To lift up the Name above all names, the Name of Jesus, our Lord and Savior. He Who is "Emmanuel": for "God is with us!"

FOREWARD

This writing is not meant to stand in and of itself. If anyone reads these words herein, it is our hope that the reader will be drawn closer to Jesus, be inspired to read His Word, The Word Of God, The Holy Scriptures, and to accept Jesus as the Lord And Savior — — — — to be saved!

Our hope and prayer is that you may come to know Jesus personally, to love Him fully, in this life and to be with Him in heaven for all eternity.

If you are in Scriptures, it is our hope that you will stay there. If you are not in Scriptures, it is our hope that these words will lead you there.

INTRODUCTION

There is no more important happening in our existence than to be secure in Heaven with the Lord. If we miss that, we have missed everything. If we arrive in Heaven as our final home for all eternity, we have gained everything.

Jesus said, "No eye has seen, no ear has heard, nor has it entered into the heart of any man, what the Father has in store for those who love Him."

Sounds like a great place doesn't it? If we bring to mind all the desires we might have that could make us happy, it isn't even close, compared to Heaven.

Jesus said, "In My Father's house there are many mansions; if it were not so, I would have told you. I go to prepare a place for you. And if I go to prepare a place for you, I will come again, and receive you unto Myself; that where I am, there you may be also."

To be in Heaven is to gain everything.

To not be there is to lose everything.

The choice is ours.

Accept Jesus and be victorious.

Reject Jesus and lose.

WHY THIS WRITING?

During the years I have been asked to give testimonial talks at Christian gatherings such as Full Gospel Businessmen's breakfasts and dinner meetings. It seems like after each meeting a person would come up and say something like, "You ought to write a book." I would pass it off, being thankful to the Lord that He helped me share something that helped one of His people in their spiritual walk.

In my thinking, there are already too many books: the world does not need another book! I feel that what we need is to read the important BOOK, The Bible: the "Instruction Book For Life."

And yet, the thought kept coming to mind. Each time I was asked to consider writing a book, the idea became stronger. Maybe I should at least write something for my family, whom I love very much. Maybe the inspiration given to me and the experiences of some of my encounters with The Lord Jesus would be of value to them, as they would walk with Jesus through their human life into eternal life.

For some time, the inspiration kept building that I should write these thoughts down until one day I decided to take my wife Elayne to lunch to discuss this with her. Often times

The Good Lord has spoken to me through Elayne, for He sees us as one in our marriage. Sometimes when faced with a most difficult decision, I'll ask Him to speak to me through Elayne when I bring the situation up for discussion. Whether or not to put these thoughts down in book form was such a decision. So, on May 6, 1988, I took Elayne to a special lunch to explain my problem. Almost immediately, she stated that she felt in her heart that it should be done. This confirmed to me that I should get going. She also added that we should include personal family examples that would show that we have always "been there" for each other throughout our marriage, while at the same time, we needed to be supportive and available to each of our children, their spouses, and their children, whenever we were needed. Family is important to The Lord. Family should be important to us as well.

DEDICATION

Of course the first dedication is to The Good Lord Jesus, Who has blessed us so richly. To You, Lord Jesus, Our love, honor, and commitment.

To my parents William and Katherine, who are now deceased, but did the best they could under the circumstances of life. They agreed with God to give nine of us brothers and sisters the gift of life. To my wonderful brothers and sisters, each of whom I love very much; Marianne, Katherine, Julie, William, Robert, Lambert, Michael, and Angelice. To my life-partner, Elayne, my good and faithful wife, who is my answer to prayer from The Lord, the one The Lord had in mind when He said, "It is not good for man to live alone."

By Elayne saying yes to me in marriage, and yes to The Lord in her life, we have been blessed with ten wonderful children - each a gift from The Lord: Christopher, Maria, Carla, Peter, Daniel, Laura, Anna, Felicia, Paul and Anita. Each different and each loved in a special way. Our love to each of our children, their spouses, and at the time of this writing, twenty-seven grandchildren and five great grandchildren.

CONTENTS

1

AGATHA – CONCERN FOR A FRIEND

"The Lord is not slack concerning His promise, as some men would count slackness; but is longsuffering toward us, not willing that any should perish, but that all should come to repentance."

(1Peter3:9)

Early evening, one Saturday night, while I was working in the garage on one of the family vehicles, I received a phone call from a friend. Dick asked if I would make the time in the near future to go over to the Americana Nursing Home, in Davenport, Iowa, to see an elderly friend of his. Agatha was in her 80's and Dick didn't know how long she would live. More importantly, he didn't know where she stood in her relationship with The Lord, and thought maybe I would have a chance to pray with her.

I didn't want to go since I had a lot of other things to do, but the longer I thought about it, the more I realized that I should go. I went over that same evening. When I came into the nursing home, I asked the first person I met in the hallway, a nurse I guess, "Where can I find Agatha?" The nurse answered, "Go down the hall to the first corner, make a sharp left and you'll run right into her room." No one stopped me or questioned me. When I came into Agatha's room, I found it to be not much larger than the bed she was lying in. She was staring up at the ceiling lying on her back. I thought at first that she was dead, since she was so very thin and pale. When I leaned over her bed-rail and called "Agatha." she slowly turned her head toward me to acknowledge my presence. I told her that I was a friend of Dick's. She nodded with a weak smile.

While driving over to see Agatha, thoughts ran through my mind as to what I would say to her, or for that matter, if she would even be responsive to me. I felt so inadequate. I did ask The Lord for help. Almost immediately, without any fore-thought, I surprisingly asked her, "Agatha, have you ever asked Jesus into your heart as your personal Lord and Savior?" Simply, she answered, "No." Then, I asked her if she would like to, and she answered, "Yes!" I asked her to pray with me by repeating the words after me. If she meant the prayer from her heart, Jesus would come in.

So we prayed together: "Lord Jesus, forgive me for I am a sinner. I believe You Lord Jesus died for me and Your precious blood will cleanse me from all my sin. By faith, I now receive you into my heart as my Lord and Savior, trusting You only for my salvation. Lord Jesus, help me to do Your will each day, In Jesus name I pray."

Tears came down the sides of her eyelids. I told her she was a good person and to keep her eyes fixed on Jesus. It was about five months after my visit that Dick informed me of her death. I never did see her again, but my hope is to meet Agatha in the Kingdom, for it is truly The Lord's will that not one should perish.

2

ANGELS TO THE RESCUE

*"And call upon Me in the day of trouble: I will deliver
thee, and thou shalt glorify Me."*
(Psalms 50:15)

Our daughter, Anna and her husband, Hal, who live in
the Chicago area, asked my wife Elayne and I, to come
up to Chicago to look over a house that they might purchase.
It was in the depth of winter. We had a six to eight inch snow
fall the day before we were to leave, so that evening; I drove
over part of Interstate 80 to see if the roads were cleared
sufficiently to drive on. In Iowa, the roads were fine. So, we
called Anna and Hal the night before we were to leave to
confirm a meeting at 11:00 a.m. the next day.

In order to allow for weather conditions, we left at 6:00
a.m. Since it was winter, it was still dark out. On the Iowa
part of Interstate 80, the road was cleared of snow, however,
as soon as we crossed the Mississippi River bridge, to enter
into Illinois, we found that the highway conditions changed
immediately. The road was covered with six to eight inches
of hard-packed ice and snow. We considered turning back,
but it was as difficult to get off the highway, as it was to keep
going, so we thought we would keep going for a while to

see if the conditions would improve. After a discussion, we decided to stay on Interstate 80, rather than take the toll-road, as Interstate 80 would be more traveled by trucks, so the chances would be better of the road conditions improving.

We were traveling about forty-five mph. between the toll road exit and the Illinois Interstate 80 cloverleaf turn around, when we encountered an experience we will remember for life.

First of all, what we did that was important happened in our own driveway before we left home that morning. Elayne and I held hands and we prayed that The Lord Jesus would protect us on the trip, both going and coming – in Jesus name we prayed.

We were driving in the right hand lane of a two-lane highway, in our 1985 Chevy Celebrity. This was the first car we owned that had front-wheel drive, so I was not familiar with how it would handle on ice and snow. We let all the traffic pass us by. All of a sudden, the back end of the car started to swerve to the right. Immediately, I tried to correct by turning the steering wheel. Then the back end swerved to the left, and I pushed the shifting lever into neutral in an attempt to bring the car under control. At that point, the back-end started toward the ravine, while heading backwards. Just before the car would have left the high-way, it continued turning until it lined up with the highway, so that we were traveling down the highway going backwards. I held a tight grip on the steering wheel and didn't touch anything. Since it was dark out, we had our headlights on. We could see a truck approaching us from the rear. The driver of the truck probably wondered why our headlights were pointed at him, when he was going the proper direction.

We traveled backwards for about eight to ten seconds in complete silence. Neither Elayne nor I said a word during this time. Then, at the same exact instant, we both spoke out loud in normal pitched voices. Elayne said, "Jesus save us!" I said," Lord help us!" I of course still held a tight grip on the steering wheel. In less than a second, immediately after we both spoke, it felt as if the car was wrenched quickly. The car turned sideways, perpendicular to the direction of the highway, skidding down the middle of the highway. The car skidded for about two hundred feet. The tires bit into the ice and snow, slowing the car down. When the car had slowed down considerably I turned the steering wheel a little and we were going frontward again, in the proper direction. The shifting lever was back in "drive" again; even though I am certain that I had put it into neutral earlier.

We had experienced a miracle. The enemy's plan was to kill us. Elayne told me later that she had a scene go through her mind, while we were heading toward the ravine, that the car tumbled and caught on fire, killing both of us. But of course, that didn't happen, because the Lord is kind and merciful, and He has written in His word:

> *"And call upon Me in the day of trouble: I will deliver you, and you will glorify Me."*

He did, and we are! We continued on into Chicago. Along the way, we counted thirth-one vehicles off the road. How fortunate we had been to avoid a serious accident.

As I look back on that incident, I feel that angels must have grabbed our car, to turn it sideways, when we spoke out to call on the name of The Lord. We realized later that each of us had prayed for The Lord to save "Us," and to help "*us*" rather than saying, "*me*." This helped us to see the unity in our marriage as The Lord says:

> *"For this reason, a man leaves his parents, and cleaves to his wife, and the two become one flesh."*
> (Genesis 2:24)

With Jesus first in each of our lives, we have become one in our marriage.

3

WORD IN TIME OF NEED

*"So shall My Word be that goeth forth out of My
mouth: It shall not return to Me void, but shall
accomplish that which I please, and it shall prosper
in the thing whereto I sent it."*

(Isaiah 55:11)

O ut of customer loyalty, I usually purchased all the gasoline I needed for our car from one particular service
station. Very seldom did I go to another station, unless we
were on a trip out of town. Even then, I would always try to
get back into town to go to my favorite station.

Early one morning, I had a breakfast appointment in
Illinois. When coming back across the bridge from Illinois
into Iowa, I noticed a sudden lurch in the vehicle. I looked
down at the gas gauge to see that I was in trouble. The gas
tank gauge was sitting on empty. So, I knew I had to get to
a gas station quickly and it had to be the nearest one. Just
across the bridge, in Bettendorf, Iowa, there was an Amoco
station, and I pulled in.

After pumping the gas I needed, I went into the station
to pay the bill. As soon as I opened the door to the office,
I could hear the loud voice of a customer, who was hol-

22

lering and shouting profanity at the owner of the station. The owner was behind the counter, somewhat subdued, taking the verbal abuse without responding to the customer. The man appeared to be about age forty to forty-five. One of the other station attendants waited on me. As I was signing the credit-card voucher, the one-sided argument continued. As I glanced at the man, I noticed that his neck veins were protruding. It was hard to figure out the problem, but my feeling was that this man was out of control, and I wanted out of there as quickly as I could. When the attendant handed me the receipt, the thought came to my mind that I should give the man one of the ASK witness cards that I usually carry with me. The ASK card contains The Lord's Word. It doesn't indicate where it was printed, nor is any denomination mentioned, only the Lord's Word. It is written in the first person, so that the reader can make a personal affirmation if he or she agrees with the written word. A second thought immediately came to mind; I don't like fights, and he would probably throw it away anyway, so maybe I should just leave quickly. Then as quickly came the thought, "If this were his last day on earth, you would not give him a card?"

Not being real brave, I interrupted him by tapping his shoulder. When he turned to his left to face me I said, "This is for you sir, have a good day!" As I got into my car, I noticed that he had Wisconsin plates. My guess was that he was a traveling salesman, in town on business. Happy that I was obedient and in one piece, I took off to the post office nearby.

When finished at the post office, I started to my next appointment in Geneseo, Illinois. To get there, I had to travel up the Iowa side of the Mississippi River to get to the Interstate 80 bridge, which crossed over the river near LeClaire, Iowa. At the east edge of Bettendorf, Iowa, traveling on State Street, I came to the large Alcoa Aluminum plant located there. While passing the plant, I noticed a car in the right-hand lane going very slowly. As I approached the car to pass, I looked over at the driver, and to my amazement, it was the customer from Wisconsin, who just minutes before, was chewing on the owner of the gas station. The man didn't even look up. He was holding the ASK card in his left hand while steering the car with his right hand. He didn't even notice me as I continued to my appointment. He was reading the small print side of the card, which is The Lord's Word – The Good News – the salvation message of Jesus Christ. I thanked The Lord for letting me see how He works in the lives of others, while working through imperfect people to accomplish His purpose.

As I traveled, I prayed for him that The Word would penetrate his heart, and that he would be able to make a free decision for The Lord Jesus, without any encumbrance from the enemy. Then, as I thought about him, I wondered what he would tell his wife when he got home that evening. Maybe something like: "You won't believe it! Here I was, in this gas station, making a fool out of myself, cussing out this station owner, when a complete stranger came up and..."

4

NEVER TOO LATE

"Train up a child in the way he should go; when he is old, he will not depart from it."
(Proverbs 22:6)

When I heard that an elderly friend of mine was in the hospital, I decided to go visit him at my earliest opportunity. His vital signs were failing, so he was not expected to live very long.

At his bedside, we talked about anything and everything that was on his mind. Mostly, he talked and I listened. He was near age ninety, so I wanted to be kind to him and show him love and concern. I knew him to be a godly man as he went to church every Sunday, and conducted his life and business affairs with rigid discipline. He came from a traditional church background, attending private religious schools when young. Therefore, I knew he had heard a lot about Jesus, but what I didn't know was if he had made a commitment to Jesus with a personal relationship. When he would die, did he know that he would be in heaven with The Lord! His grandson was also concerned, as he told me about his grandfather being in the hospital.

Before going to see him in the hospital, I had asked The Lord to give me a humble heart, to be a good listener, and to say the words he needed to hear. After a long visit, it was really time for me to go as I had other commitments. When I made a motion toward leaving, by saying, "Well, it's so good to see you, and ..."

He interrupted me by asking, "Larry, would you pray for me before you go?"

I said, "Why don't we pray together?"

He followed with, "You pray, I'll listen." I simply asked him if he would like to ask Jesus into his heart, and he said, "Yes!"

We prayed together, him repeating after me:

"Lord Jesus, forgive me for I am a sinner. I believe You Lord Jesus died for me and Your Precious Blood will cleanse me from all my sins, By faith, I now receive You Lord Jesus, into my heart as my Lord and Savior, trusting You only for my salvation. Lord Jesus, help me to do Your Will each day, in Jesus Name, I pray."

He thanked me with tears in his eyes. Going down the hospital hallway, I thought, here is a godly man, who knew a lot about Jesus, but until this day, he had not made a personal commitment to The Good Lord. Now, later in life, he knows Jesus in a personal way. God never gives up on anyone, but hopes that each person will come to a saving knowledge of His Son, Jesus Christ. Each one of us has to make that choice. My friend made that decision only when he could, during his earthly life. Shortly after that meeting with him in the hospital, his earthly life ended, but now his eternal life is just beginning.

Some months after the meeting with this man in the hospital, I had breakfast with his grandson. The grandson mentioned to me his concern about his grandfather's relationship with the Lord before he died. I was able to relate to him what happened. The grandson's prayers for his grand-father were answered.

5

NOW IS THE DAY

"Behold, now is the acceptable time; behold, now is the day of salvation."

(2Corinthians 6:2)

When I was a much younger man, there was a popular song that hit the spotlight. The title was, "Enjoy Yourself." The words went something like this:

Enjoy yourself; it's later than you think.
Enjoy yourself, while you're still in the pink.

The years go by, as quickly as a wink,
Enjoy yourself, enjoy yourself,
It's later than you think!

Often I wondered about the real message of that song. Was it the world speaking? Saying, eat, drink, and be merry, for tomorrow you will die? Is it the world saying things are going to get worse? Why enjoy now? Is something going to change? There is a deeper message here. It requires of us a decision; we either accept or reject the world or The Lord Jesus Christ. We can't accept both. We are free to choose our life style, as each of us has a free will, however, we cannot choose the consequences, as these are pre-set by the God who made each of us, as well as everything we see around us.

The Lord's message would be: "Prepare Yourself," rather than enjoy yourself. Real joy is to be with The Lord Jesus when our earthly bodies are transformed into heavenly bodies. Every person, I believe, is rewarded. Some get our reward here – enjoy yourself, and some get our reward in Heaven – prepare yourself.

Some years ago, when I had an office in the Davenport Bank Building in downtown Davenport, Iowa, I met a man in the elevator who became a friend. He was a rather successful architect, both professionally as well as financially. Without judging him, I did observe him to be quite materialistic. He would never discuss things of a religious or spiritual nature, although one of his greatest sources of business income came from designing churches.

One day, when we were at lunch, he remarked that one has to go after the things he wants in life. He said I wasn't aggressive enough. To emphasize his point, he said, "If what I wanted was across that street (pointing to Third Street in downtown Davenport, Iowa) and there were bodies in the street, I'd walk over them to get it!" That statement hurt me, as it showed the great difference in our thinking. There didn't seem to be any way I could reach him, and I really tried to be his friend.

When I moved my office away from downtown Davenport, to a Bettendorf, Iowa location, I didn't see him much in over two years. At our home one morning, I received a phone call from him. He was at his sister's home in Rock Island, Illinois. He was crying over the phone. I learned that he was at his sister's home recuperating from major surgery. I was able to calm him down, telling him that I would stop to see him sometime. He gave me his sister's address. As

I was leaving home for the office, I noticed two Christian books on one of our bookshelves. Since I had two of the same book I took one with me to give to him. As I thought about it, I decided to see him that very morning. His sister felt he would recuperate better at her house than by himself, since he lived alone. The sunroom was made into a bedroom for him. The furnishings were warm and beautiful. He had a full view of the backyard and could watch the squirrels at the feeder. What a perfect place to recover. He explained his complicated surgery to me. It involved his genital urinary system. I told him that he looked great for having gone through such a complex surgery only six days earlier. As he sat in his easy chair, I handed him the Christian book I had brought for him. I told him it was his to keep as I had an extra copy. I told him the book helped me quite a bit, and now with time on his hands, maybe it could be of help to him. He thanked me, and then set the book down on the end table, telling me that he would look at it sometime.

Immediately, he started telling me all the details of his surgery, and how bitter he was that his regular physician did not catch the problem in his office visit some weeks previous. Now, he had surgery, which involved the removal of some of his vital organs. The surgeon told him that a simple test of his urine, some weeks previous, could have caught the problem at an early stage, most probably eliminating the need for surgery. He cursed his doctor by name, and then said, "I am going to get a piece of his business," meaning, I'm sure, that he was going to sue him. He related that a urine sample was given during his earlier doctor's office visit, but since the doctor went on vacation, apparently the nurse did not perform the necessary test, which would have shown the problem. I asked him to look at the good side of things. "The doctor isn't God," I said. "Try to be thankful for the successful surgery," I continued, "Look at the speedy recovery, with a return to health!" He simply stated, "No, I'm going to get a piece of that (curse) doctor's business."

After leaving, I prayed for him that he could see the truth, and be able to make a free decision. How badly I felt for his attitude, though nothing I said had seemed to change his mind.

When I saw him, it was a Tuesday morning. His recovery was remarkable, for only a few days after our visit, on a Friday evening, he went shopping with his sister and his fiancé. I learned from his fiancé, that they returned to his sister's home about 9:00p.m. He said he was somewhat tired from the outing, so he went to bed early, while his sister and his fiancé watched television for another hour or so. The next morning, on Saturday, they found the architect lying in bed, with his hands folded across his chest. A telephone was by his side. He died in his sleep without any sign of apparent distress.

Often I have wondered; what were his last thoughts? Did he ever look at the book I gave him to read? Was he thinking about his upcoming marriage? Was he still planning to get "a piece of that doctor's business?" Or, was he reconciling with The Good Lord? I sure hope so. He had plenty of time for that, or did he?

When The Lord says in His Word, "Now is the day of salvation," I believe this means that when we are thinking about making a decision for The Lord Jesus, we should do so then, as tomorrow, for us, may not come.

6

ASK

"Ask, and you shall receive; Seek, and you shall find;
Knock, and the door shall be opened to you."
(Matthew 7:7)

For many years, my wife and I, would take our annual week vacation by going to a special cabin and lake in eastern central Wisconsin. Nearby, is a small town with very few stores or shops. Our usual routine would be to go into town on Thursday afternoon, to get a milkshake at the local ice cream store. On one such occasion, when I went into this particular ice cream store, Elayne stayed behind to wait in the car. As I came into the little front enclosure, I could hear that the person behind the counter was scolding two small boys. The middle-aged woman, who apparently owned the store, was lashing out at the boys for some reason. As I listened, I determined that the two boys, who each had ordered a double dip cone, did not have enough money between them to pay for the cones. Of course, they were already licking the cones, and this woman was really angry. Without thinking, I asked the woman how much money they were short. She said eleven cents. I said that I could cover this, as I put eleven cents on the counter. She took the eleven cents as she continued to chew these boys out. The boys ran out of the store, got on their bicycles, and took off like they had just been set free from a sure prison sentence. I ordered two milkshakes. As she was preparing the milkshakes, I thought about how she reminded me of a Navy boot camp commander, or a grouchy schoolteacher. As she handed me the two milkshakes I had ordered, the thought came to mind to give her one of the ASK cards which I carried with me to give out as witness cards. Inside, I immediately said No, but since I had learned by then to follow such an urging, as It may be from The Lord, using this time to reach someone. So without too much courage, as she handed me the change from my payment, I handed her the ASK card, saying, "This is for you – the only GOOD news – have a good day!" She didn't respond in any way, and I was out of the store in a flash. As in many similar situations, I didn't give this incident another thought.

Almost a month later, when we were exchanging fishing stories with our son Chris, and his wife, Sheryl, Chris remarked that he had forgotten to tell me about an unusual happening when he was in Wisconsin during their fishing trip. That particular year, Chris, his wife and their children went to the same cabin to spend their vacation. In fact, they were there the week following our stay. Chris mentioned that on one particular day, they went into town to get some ice cream at the same store I had visited during our stay in the area. When he went into the store, he noticed that an ASK card had been taped to the inside of the store window. Facing out was the large print ASK, and of course, facing in, was the small print with other scripture verses as well as the salvation message. Could it be that the Lord had reached this woman through His Word? Chris told her that he sure liked the card she had in the window. She said that she did too. Chris asked her where she got the card. She answered, "Some fisherman was in here last week and gave it to me!"

Maybe at some point in her life she asked The Lord to come into her life, or maybe someone asked for her, in the form of an intercessory prayer. At any rate, she did get the message, and apparently accepted to make a decision for The Lord.

When I was in the store, the week before, I thought she would probably throw the card away. The Good Lord, however, knows His people, and His timing is always perfect. The secret is to ASK - following are the words on the ASK card:

(front)   Ask, and you will receive
           Seek, and you will find
           Knock, and the door will be opened to you.

(note: the first letters of Ask, Seek, And Knock, spell ASK!!)

(back)   For the one who asks, receives. The one who seeks finds. The one who knocks, enters. The Good Lord is a gentle and loving Person. He will not force anyone. He created sons and daughters, not slaves. He gave each of us a great gift, our free will. We must freely choose Him. To ASK IS THE SECRET. Dismas, the criminal crucified beside Jesus, asked "Lord, remember me when You get to Your kingdom." Dismas is in paradise, for Jesus said, *"This day you will be with Me in paradise."*

I ask Jesus to come into my heart for he said, *"And him that cometh to Me, I will no wise cast out!"* What must I do then to be saved? Admit that I am a Sinner, and ASK Jesus to save me, for He alone is The Way, Truth, and Life (John14-6).

"For if you confess with your lips that Jesus is Lord, and believe in your heart that GOD raised Him from the dead, you will be saved."

(Romans 10:9)

"Christ Jesus came into the world to save sinners."

(1Timothy 1:15)

Lord Jesus save me for I am a sinner.

ASK — SEEK – KNOCK

7

NEVER GIVE UP ON PRAYER

"Rejoice always. Pray without ceasing."
(1Thessalonians 5:16-17)

In the course of my business contacts, I developed a close friendship with a business owner in a small town about thirty-five miles from our office. In the year of 1969 I first met John. He always greeted me with a joyful word – usually he would say something like, "Well Lawrence J., what are you doing up here?" or, "How are you doing Lawrence J.?" We could tease each other easily because we each knew that we liked one another. Through the years, as we grew closer in our relationship, John would ask me to do personal work for him as well as business insurance projects. John helped to start his company from scratch until it rose to unusual stature in their field of endeavor, finally reaching the highest rating and reputation. John, of course, also grew in financial strength, but he didn't flaunt it. John gave freely to his church and other charities. Never did I see John in a suit. Plaid shirt, blue jeans, dungaree jacket, and a baseball cap, with a company logo; that's how John dressed. A very likable person who honestly liked people. He was a very emotional man with deep, strong feelings. One never had to wonder what John was thinking, for his honesty kept his personality out front for everyone to see. During the twenty-five years, from 1969, when we first met, to 1994, we would meet for lunch or breakfast, at least seven to ten times a year. Often, we talked on the phone. He frequently would visit our office in Bettendorf, Iowa. I was invited to his home, on a farm, to meet his wife and daughter.

In late 1993, John called me to ask if I would have lunch with him that same day. He didn't say why, but I could tell by his voice, that it was something important, so I changed my schedule to see him that very day. We met at a local restaurant. With tears in his eyes, he told me that he had been experiencing severe headaches, so he went to his regular doctor, who referred him to specialists. The tests showed that he most certainly had a brain tumor. He was obviously devastated by this news and asked me to pray for him. I started that very day. We kept in touch by phone. After a few weeks, he told me that he had been scheduled for brain surgery at a The Mayo Clinic of Rochester, Minnesota. After surgery, I talked with him by phone while he was in the hospital. John told me that the tumor was cancerous, and he was getting both chemotherapy and radiation for treatment of the cancer. When he returned home, we met for breakfast where he shared very personal things with me. Every Friday, he had to come to Moline, Illinois to take a blood test as part of his treatment. We made a commitment to meet for breakfast every Friday. If, for some reason, he couldn't make the breakfast meeting, either his wife or daughter would call me to let me know. During one of these breakfast meetings, he asked me a question about The Bible. Soon we started sharing openly about The Lord, while reviewing bible verses. During these weekly breakfasts, John asked many questions about The Lord, The Bible, sickness, suffering, the condition of the world, what is God's plan for us, and many other areas. Often, I would tell John of the many miracles The Lord had worked in the lives of our family.

One particular breakfast meeting, John asked me how a person could know if he were saved. I asked him if I could ask him two questions, not to hurt him, but to help him. He agreed. I told him I was pretty sure of his answers, and he would be surprised. First, I asked John, "Do you believe that the Man, Jesus Christ, Who walked this earth some two thousand years ago, Who was crucified pronounced physically dead, was truly God in the Flesh?" John said, "Yes, I can't say why I do, but I do." Then I asked him, "Do you believe that His Father raised Him from the dead, that He is alive now, others saw Him, and that He sits at the right hand of the Father, in Heaven?" John said, "Yes, I do." "John, you're saved," I said. "No one could convince you of that. If you confess with your lips, that Jesus is Lord, and believe in your heart, that His Father raised Him from the dead, you will be saved."

During the following weeks, John and I talked about many other scripture verses; John had a spiritual joy about him even in the midst of this strenuous medical ordeal. At one meeting, I gave him a small witness card that had a 'sinner's prayer" on it. I asked him to pray the prayer on his own, in a personal way, to ask Jesus to come into his heart. At a later meeting, he told me that he did. We continued to meet every Friday, until May of 1994, when John's condition had worsened. He accepted every medical direction recommended, with bravery. In July, of 1994, he was at home in a special hospital bed, with medication administered for the pain. A few days before John died, I stopped at his home to visit him. We held hands, talked, and shared our mutual love and admiration.

John was a good man. He loved his family. He did things for his family, which was very unselfish. He provided for them while living, as well as after his death. In August of that year, I was able to deliver a check for one million, two hundred thousand dollars to his wife and daughter, the proceeds of a life insurance policy John purchased from me seven years earlier. He proved his love by giving of himself.

When at the funeral home for the visitation service, I was waiting for the line of people to diminish, before I talked to his wife and daughter. While looking at a large board of photographs, celebrating precious times in John's life, I overheard two women talking about John. Normally, I do not speak out to people I do not know, but these two women were talking so open and personal about John, that I asked, "Are you friends of John?" "Well, I guess you could say that; "We are his sisters," one of them said. They seemed so cheerful, that one could almost forget that we were at a funeral service. "How do you know John?" one of the two sisters asked. I replied, "I've done some insurance work for John."

She asked, "Are you the insurance man?" Without knowing what would happen, I answered, "Yes!" She grabbed me by the arm to march me across the room, stopping behind a smaller man who was talking to a group of other people. She tapped the man on the shoulder, and as he turned around to face me, she said, "Rudy, *this* is the insurance man." With tears running down his face, he immediately hugged me. Finally, he composed himself, and said, "Thank you, thank you, thank you, for witnessing to my brother, John. For twenty-five years I prayed to God, that He would send someone to witness to my brother, John, and He chose you."

Rudy and I were instantly new friends. That's how The Lord works. John had told his brother Rudy about his position on the subject of The Lord Jesus before he died. Rudy is the spiritual hero. He faithfully prayed for twenty-five years. The Lord heard his prayer in 1969; it just took until 1994 for the circumstances to line up to accomplish His ends. The Lord can work through anyone, who is sensitive to other's needs, teachable, and available to do His work. Rudy didn't know that I had met his brother twenty-five years earlier. Neither did I, until I got back to the office to check the files. Sure enough, I met John in 1969, the year Rudy started to pray for his brother's salvation. The Lord had to groom me to be ready when the right time came. Can you see the power of persistent prayer? Pray without ceasing!

8

I SAW HIM

"Who do you say that I am?"
(Matthew 16:15)

Some years ago, in 1985, Mildred, an elderly woman from Wilton, Iowa called me to ask me to come talk to her about a complicated farm-estate problem. A friend of hers, another business client of our insurance company referred this woman to me. Bill told her that I would take the time to listen and possibly I could help her. With no idea of what I would run into, I went to meet with her.

There were two farms involved. An elderly couple who owned the farms, were friends of Mildred's. The couple resided in a nursing home in Muscatine, Iowa. As we discussed the situation, the woman handed me a large legal document, at least an inch thick, which had been prepared by attorneys who represented a University from another state. In reviewing the situation I found that it was the elderly couple's intention to leave the smaller of the two farms to the University after both of their deaths. The larger of the two farms would be left, by will, to their only living relatives—two nephews who were currently operating and managing the farms. The elderly couple had signed the papers, but

41

weren't sure that the document was correct in carrying out their intentions. Mildred gave me the document to review. I took it to my office, where over a period of a few days, I read the rather complex legal document for content. After review, I found that the University would own *both* farms at the couple's death, and their nephews would only receive *income* from the farms while they managed the properties. At the death of the elderly couple, the nephews would *not* receive ownership of the larger farm. It seems that the out-of-state attorneys were not looking out for the interest of the elderly couple, but rather, were dishonest in their actions, to possibly win favor with the University.

I told Mildred that I would need to meet with the elderly couple to describe the content of the document. She arranged a meeting at the nursing home in Muscatine. The final outcome was to help them obtain the services of a *local* attorney, whom I knew, and whose integrity was unquestioned. The local attorney understood the problem and as a legal representative of the courts, could handle the out-of-state work that had to be done. The attorney challenged the out-of-state firm and was able to get things reversed to the original intentions of the elderly couple. They appreciated my efforts and we became good friends. One of the problems in this situation was that Flavel, the elderly husband was ninety-seven, senile, and not able to make a decision or even comprehend the document, which he had signed. The wife, Olga, age ninety-nine, had very poor vision. In fact, she only had a small area of vision in the lower left area of her left eye. This made it very difficult for her to read, which is why she had asked Mildred, her friend to get someone to help.

When I first met Olga, she introduced me to her husband, who did little more than nod to acknowledge that I was present. Olga was sharp mentally, alert, and quick witted. Her health was good – she was able to get around freely. The first question Olga asked me was, "What church do you attend?" I told her that I was a Christian, and named the particular denomination church I attend. Then she asked, "Who do you pray to?" I answered, "Jesus." Olga said, "No, No, Larry. You pray directly to God. There is no need to pray through Anyone." I explained, "Jesus said, *"I am The Way, The truth, and The Life. No one can come to The Father except through Me!"*(John14:6) Then in John, Chapter 1, starting at verse 1, it is written, *"In the beginning was The Word, and The Word was with God, and The Word was God.... And The word became flesh!"* She held her ground by stating that Jesus is God's Son, but He is not God. We visited on this point every time we got together during the two months it took to accomplish the work for her. Olga would say that Jesus is mainly our example of how we are to live. Still, she would not budge in her position.

Olga never read the Bible on her own. She mainly followed what others had told her about The Lord. Olga was so honest and so frank; it was a joy to visit with her. We developed a good relationship. She would even call me in my office in Davenport, Iowa to talk over points she would be thinking about. On one occasion, I gave her a small plastic card that had a salvation message on one side, and a picture on the other side. The picture on the one side, was taken from an airplane at a high altitude, while flying over mountainous terrain in the country of China. The photographer who took the picture was an atheist, who was working as an aerial photographer taking pictures for mapping purposes. When he developed the film, he immediately noticed an image of a Man's face formed by the arrangement of snow on the ground below. The image startled the photographer so much that he started to search for any knowledge of The Lord. He obtained a Bible, read The Word, and eventually became a Christian. Without too much difficulty, one could make out The Man's face in the snow. When I explained this story to Olga, she looked at the card for quite a while. Finally, she looked up and said, "It's okay, Larry, if you feel you see a Man's face in the snow. If it makes you feel better that you see such a thing, that's fine." How well I remember praying for Olga, as I would drive back to Davenport after each visit. I prayed that she would be able to see the truth about Jesus, and that she could accept Jesus as her personal Lord and Savior. On the drive back to Davenport, I remember crying with sadness in my heart because Olga was not able to see the truth. I cried out to The Lord, that he would fill her with His grace, to let her see the truth, and understand the truth, so as to be able to make a free decision for The Lord, unencumbered by the enemy.

Early one morning, about 7:00 a.m., even before I left home for the office, I received a call from Olga. Olga said that something unbelievable had happened in the middle of the previous night. She was coming back to her bed, after using the bathroom and she stubbed her toe on the leg of her bed. She was angry and she had to balance herself against the dresser to keep from falling. On the dresser she had the plastic card I had given her resting against a tape dispenser. The nightlight in the room had the plastic card slightly illuminated. Olga exclaimed loudly, "I saw Him, Larry! I saw Him! Jesus' Face in the snow! You were right!" Olga was so excited. This simple experience persuaded her to the point that there was no confrontation in our future meetings. Our discussions about Jesus were open and heart-warming. When she was in the hospital and very sick, I visited her. I told her that Jesus really loved her. She nodded, as if to say, "I know." Then, I added, "Olga, when you see Jesus, tell Him you love Him!" Olga answered with a question; "What if you see Him first?" I replied, "Then I'll tell Him that I love Him and that you will be coming shortly." She laughed loudly, even though very sick.

With all my heart, I wish I could tell you with certainty, that Olga actually accepted Jesus in her heart as her personal

Lord and Savior, I can only hope The Lord was able to break through the religious training she had received; to reach down and lift her up. I hope The Lord was able to raise up the right person to touch her. Olga died at age 102. At the funeral, the person presiding over the service gave a talk about God and His Son, Jesus. How Jesus was born as our example of how we are to live. That Jesus and God are two separate Persons. That Jesus is God's Son but that He is not God. Nothing about Jesus dying on the cross for our sins. Nothing about Jesus as our personal Lord and Savior. Nothing about Jesus not sinning, even though He lived as a human being for thirty-three years; or His defeat of the enemy; or that it was foretold in the Old Testament that He would be born of a virgin – God is with us Emmanuel! I learned where Olga had received her earlier religious training.

On one occasion, Jesus asked the apostles, *"Whom do they say that I Am?"* The apostles answered that some say Jesus is John the Baptist, reborn; some say Elijah; or one of the prophets. (Matthew chap16:13-17) Jesus then asked them, *"But Whom do you say that I am?"* Simon Peter answered, "Thou art Christ, The Son of the living God." Jesus answered, *"Blessed are you Simon Barjona, for flesh and blood did not reveal this unto you, but My Father, which is in Heaven."*

This, then, is the most important question we face in life; *"Who do you Say that I am?"* Thomas, the apostle who was not present the first time Jesus appeared to the apostles after His resurrection, said, "Except I shall see His hands, and put my finger into the nail prints, and thrust my hand into His side I will not believe!" This shows a pretty firm position where a man was frustrated by a situation where he put faith in a Man and a cause, only to be let down. (John20:24-29) Again, after eight days, Thomas was with the apostles in the upper room. Then again came Jesus, with the doors being shut. And He stood in their midst and said, "Peace be unto you!" Then He said to Thomas, *"Reach hither your finger and behold My hands; and hither your hand and thrust it into My side and be not faithless, but believing."* Thomas answered and said unto Jesus, "My Lord and My God!" Jesus then said, *"Thomas, because you have seen Me you believe; blessed are they who have not seen and yet believe."*

That's me – that's you. We have not seen Jesus as the apostles have, but we are expected to believe in Him, to be called blessed. Olga said to me in a phone call, "I saw Him, Larry! I saw Him!" That is all I have to go on. Hopefully, Olga is in The Lord Jesus' presence to see Him Face to Face.

Jesus was killed because He claimed to be God. He was either 'right' or He was 'wrong.' If He was wrong, really not God, then he did so for one of two reasons. Either He was a liar, or He was mentally unstable, possibly insane to claim such a thing. It doesn't fit that He was a liar, for no one lies to be killed, especially by such a cruel method as crucifixion. A man may lie to save his life, but not to be killed. The second choice was that He was insane. If He was insane, would His mother stand by, below the cross, to watch such a cruel and inhuman death, or would she simply say to turn Him over to her, as He was not responsible for what He was saying. She could not say such a thing, for she knew Him as both her son, in the human sense, and as God in the spiritual sense. She knew Him as the fulfillment of The Old Testament, Emmanuel – God is with us!

The only other choice is to believe that He is Who he said He was. He is God. He said, *"My Father and I are One.*(John chap10:30) My only two choices are to accept Him, or to reject Him. If I accept Him, I will live in Heaven with Him for all eternity. If I reject Him, I will live out of His presence for all eternity. Whom do you say Jesus is?

9

OTHER THINGS
GIVEN TO YOU

"Seek ye first the kingdom of God, and His righteousness, and all these other things shall be added unto you."

(Matthew 6:33)

At age seven, I can remember going to church by myself, Sunday after Sunday, since my parents did not attend church. In the wintertime I would sit near the front of the church, so that after service I could walk down the center aisle, between the taller people, touching their soft coats. It felt good to touch such soft clothing. On one particular Sunday, I particularly remember this man's coat, because it was the softest material I had ever felt. It was tan in color. Even though I marveled at its softness, I never coveted owning such a coat, or even thought as one might expect, that when I was older, I would own a coat like this one. Later in life, as I saw other coats like the one I had seen as a young lad, I found out that this type of coat is called a 'cashmere' coat, made of special wool found in the Far East. This type of coat I learned, cost well above the average man's coat.

It would be safe to say that I never thought about this experience again until I was age forty-seven. During the year, when I was age forty-seven, I wrote a thirty-nine page letter to my eight brothers and sisters. The letter was a healing letter that covered some of our early family experiences. In the letter, I asked for each of us, brothers and sisters, to forgive our parents for faults and failures, at least in our eyes, as well as to forgive each other for any possible emotional injuries we may have caused one another during our growing years. The same letter was sent to each of my four brothers as well as my four sisters. In the letter, there was a call for each of us to accept Jesus as our personal Lord and Savior; to serve Him in this life; and to be with Him in the life hereafter.

Even though I did not want or expect a response from my brothers and sisters, I did receive a different response from each of them. Some a word, some a call, and some sent a letter to acknowledge their feelings.

To the day of this writing, in 2001, some twenty-four years after sending the letter, my brother Michael and I have never talked about the reason behind my receiving a large box from him a few months after I sent his copy of the letter to him. My guess is that Mike was using this way to show his love and appreciation for my taking the time to share my thoughts and testimony with him in the letter. The return address on the box was; "Temple Gates of Heaven," the name of the synagogue where Mike worked. The box contained clothing, which I was able to use, as Mike and I are about the same physical size. I reasoned that the clothing must have come from a rummage sale held at the synagogue, although I am not sure, because Mike and I have never discussed the box or it's contents. Each article of clothing was almost new and fit me perfectly.

You may have guessed what happened. When I opened the box, the first article on the top was a black 'cashmere' coat, like new. It fit me like it was tailored just for me. As I took it out of the box my mind flashed back, for the first time ever, to the time I felt a coat like this when I was a young lad in church. Immediately, inside, I said, "Thank you Lord, for I know this came from You, through my brother Mike." This gave me great joy. I didn't have to pay one cent for it. The label inside read "100% Cashmere." I didn't have to plot and scheme how I was to earn the money to purchase such an item. The thought of owning such a coat never even crossed my mind. I marveled at how the Lord works. Yes, I experienced the softness of such a coat some forty years earlier, but since The Lord knew this, and He also knew that I was not coveting such an item, He let me have it as a witness of His love, which He has for each of us, and His Word that says, "These others things will be added unto you." I was seeking, with all my heart the Kingdom of God and His righteousness, and He was adding other things unto me. Almost immediately, I saw the lesson He was teaching me by this surprise. If I seek after things, He most probably would not help me get them, because they would become my primary focus and I would miss the more important aim of my life, which was to have a personal relationship with The Lord. If I seek The Lord, He can give me what others spend a lifetime seeking, without hindering my relationship with Him. There are many other examples of this truth in my life, but I wanted to share this one with you, about the cashmere coat, so that you may look for similar experiences in your own life.

The cashmere coat gave me great service. It lasted almost seventeen years, before the lower seam in the back just plain wore out, from the many times in-and-out of the car, as I traveled to appointments, day after day, year after year, in the insurance business. Toward the end of the winter of 1998, Elayne, wanted me to have another coat, just like the one that provided me with so many years of service. This type of coat kept me so warm during the cold winter months.

One of the main things I noticed about this type of coat is that I could not feel the cold car seat, as I would get in the car on a frigid morning to go to the office. This was a true blessing. Such a coat would be very expensive. I just could not see spending the money on a new coat, so I did not look for a replacement. In fact, I forgot about the need for a new dress coat.

That Fall, our son-in-law, David, came to town with his wife Felicia, our daughter, and their children. They planned to stay with us, in our home for a few days. As soon as they brought their suitcases and other items into the house so that their car was unloaded, David brought in a coat, and insisted that I try it on. The coat was soft and black. The label inside read, "100% Cashmere." It too fit me perfectly. It was in better shape than the coat I received from my brother, Mike. David said that the coat belonged to his grandfather, Buss, who had died that same year. The coat didn't fit him, so he wanted me to have it. David didn't know my other coat had worn out, but The Lord did. Isn't He good? Up to the time of this writing, I have been kept warm by the second cashmere coat. Two cashmere coats in one lifetime! Both at the time of need, without having to seek after the items, The Good Lord provided, to keep the promises of His word. We seek after Him, His Kingdom, and His Righteousness, and He adds other things unto us. Blessed, be His Holy Name.

10

NO DOOR KNOB

*"Here I stand, knocking at the door. If anyone hears
Me calling, and opens the door, I will enter his house,
and have supper with him, and he with Me. "*
(Revelation 3:20)

For over thirty years I have been involved in Wednesday
night Christian teaching of young people in the seventh and eighth grades. The meetings are church sponsored,
taking place in the school classrooms. Class size is usually
from twelve to fourteen students, both boys and girls.

Young people present quite a challenge. They look for
and expect answers to questions on just about any subject.
How much I've learned from them, with their endless search
for truth. I've grown to love each group of students I am
associated with at the start of each new year. Once in a while
there is a tough student assigned to the class I moderate.
Usually, this type of person doesn't want to be there. It's a
case of the parents forcing this child to come. One particular
year, I had a student, Mike, who was just plain mean. He was
disruptive to the rest of the class, and he was disrespectful
to me. This young man was really trying my patience. The
stress of my regular workday, class preparation, scheduling,

51

and in addition, physical fatigue, was wearing me down. I was very seriously considering giving up the position to a younger person. One class, the young man was too much of a handful. Just before the class ended, I gave a little talk about how I was having some personal problems, which might make it necessary for me to consider resigning my position as class moderator. They, of course, knew that I was a volunteer. I asked them not to take it personally, if indeed, I did resign, and did not return the following Wednesday. Even though I had not made my mind up for sure, I wanted to let them know, just in case I did not come back. If, in fact, I did not return, I asked them to give the new person, whomever that would be, the attention necessary to get the spiritual guidance needed, to live life as a Christian. I told them to always look to The Lord Jesus for their answers.

When class was over, I was erasing the blackboard, when I heard the sound of someone clearing his throat. Turning around, I saw Rick, a quiet student, standing behind me, all alone. Everyone else had left. Somewhat tense, he started by saying, "Mr. Lyons, I'm having trouble with this class." "I'm not surprised," I answered, "Am I too old for this? Am I too preachy? Would it be better to have someone younger, who can relate to you better?" I was really trying to give him an easy out, as well as fortify my reasons for resigning. Rick then surprised me by his response. He said, "No, what I'm trying to say is that it is starting to make sense. You see, my dad died a few months ago, of a heart attack, and I've been trying to handle the hurt. When I get home each Wednesday night, after our class, I tell my mom everything we talk about in class. Like, when you said Jesus is knocking at the door of our heart, and He doesn't have a doorknob on His side of the door. So, we have to turn the knob to let him come in. It's starting to make sense." Then Rick started to cry. So, I hugged him, and I started crying too. How could I let this young man down? If only one person is reached by the Word and compassion of Jesus, It's worth it. So, I continued on, with renewed zeal, sharing with the young people, and telling them of the love Jesus has for them. At the time of this writing, eleven years have passed, since meeting with Rick that evening, which makes him twenty-five years old. Hopefully, Rick has continued in his walk with The Lord Jesus. We don't always know the outcome, we can only be faithful to our promise to "Let our light shine," and let The Lord do the rest.

Yes, Jesus loves each of us so much, that he gave each of us a doorknob on our side of the door. He doesn't want to force anyone. He wants each of us to freely choose Him. Notice, He didn't say 'I stood at your door, and knocked once,' but rather, He continues to knock. As long as we are breathing, Jesus is knocking. I can choose to accept Him, and let Him in, or I can reject Him, to keep Him out. Surely, this demonstrates the ultimate in true unconditional love from our Lord and Savior.

11

CHILD-LIKE FAITH

"Verily, I say unto you; except you be converted and become as little children, you shall not enter into the kingdom of heaven."

(Matthew 18:3)

About seven years ago, when I was at Sam's Discount Store, in Davenport, Iowa, to pick up a file cabinet for the office, an impressive young man helped me load the cabinet into our mini-van. When I offered the young man an ASK card (a witnessing card, with a salvation message), he said that I had given him one of these cards when I had him as a student in religious education, at St. Paul The Apostle School. He told me that his name was Klindt. Immediately, I remembered him, as he was an exceptional young man, with a deep love for the Lord. He told me that he was only working for Sam's for a week, as a fill-in, as he was in between school sessions. It just happened that I came when he was there.

Then after three years passed, my wife and I came to Sam's again to do some shopping. Today, I saw Klindt again. We were trying to decide which checkout line to use. There were quite a few people in each line. A young man, an employee of Sam's called to us from the far line at the other end of the store from where we were standing. He had just opened up a new checkout lane, so called to us to come down. Neither of us recognized each other at first, but when I saw his nametag, with the name, Klindt, on it, I greeted him by name. Klindt looked at me for a moment, and then said, "Mr. Lyons, so good to see you." As he was checking out our items through the register, he said, "I'm not trying to flatter you or anything like that, but I really learned a lot in CCD (Christian-education-class), from the real-life stories you would tell." I mentioned to Klindt that I would never forget him, in fact, I had planned on writing about him in one of my writings. He asked me, "Why?" I reminded him of the class where I introduced my Best Friend to the class, and how he had responded that night some thirteen years ago. Klindt said, "That's incredible! I do remember that evening!" Klindt was twenty-two by this time. We were in class together when he was only thirteen, and then I met him again, for a second time, when he's at Sam's on a temporary basis because he is between college class schedules. Is it a 'coincidence' that he called us to his checkout lane, during the only week he would work at the store? Or, did The Good Lord allow me to again witness the promise of His Word, as it works in the hearts of His people?

There were about ten to fourteen young boys and girls in that CCD class on that Wednesday evening, some thirteen years ago, when Klindt made such a lasting impression on me. We were discussing Jesus, and the fact that each of us had to make a personal decision as to our relationship with Him. Without any forethought, I held up a blank piece of white paper, telling them that this was a picture of a man whom we should all know. They all looked at me, each with a blank look on their face, and then they looked at each other, with a puzzled expression, as if to say, 'Has this man gone off the deep end?' I then explained, "This is a picture of Ronald Reagan; what can you tell me about him?" Wow, they gave me a lot of information about Ronald Reagan. He was our current president at the time, his wife's name was Nancy; he came from California; he had a horse farm; he liked jellybeans; and many other facts about the man. I then went over to the door of the upper-classroom, opened it up, and said, "Yes sir, please come in!" In make-believe, I ushered the invisible person to the head of the large table we were sitting around. I said, "I would like to introduce you to Ronald Reagan, do any of you know him?" Each of them looked at me with a blank stare, like I had lost it. Again, in make-believe I ushered the invisible Mr. Reagan back to the door, opened it, and thanked him for coming. Then I said to the class, "Oh, I see, you know a lot 'ABOUT' Mr. Reagan, but you don't 'KNOW' him!" Quickly, I went over to the door to open it again. "Yes Sir! Please come in! Class I would like to introduce you to my best Friend. His Name is Jesus." I paused, and each one stared at me with a blank look, for at least ten seconds, while I looked at them first, and then toward the invisible Jesus, I said was here in our midst. Then, I said, "OK, you can do a number of things: you can ignore Him – He won't press you; you can argue with Him – 'Like Who does He think he is!'; you can attack Him – He won't fight back; you can reject Him as no one of importance; or, you can accept Him. What would each of you do if He were here?"

To my utter surprise, Klindt, the quiet, soft-spoken, young man of just thirteen, with his voice cracking, as tears came down his cheeks, said, "I'd run to His feet, and hug Him, and tell Him that I love Him!" Across from Klindt sat Mike, the young man that had all the answers, and he turned white as if the blood had drained out of his head. Klindt was living the situation. Jesus was present to him, and he demonstrated his love for The Lord Jesus. I said, "Klindt, that's why you're saved. It's that simple. Hidden from the wise, but seen by meek. It's that simple. You meet Jesus, fall in love with Him, and accept Him as your personal Lord and Savior."

This class was one of the greatest sessions I have ever had with young people. The Lord taught us all a great lesson that evening; Unless we humble ourselves, we cannot even see Who He is. Plus, I got a chance to see Klindt, as a grown man; one whom any mother and father would be proud for their daughter to bring home as their choice for a husband. Klindt still has this same love for The Lord Jesus, and Jesus let me see it again today, along with the growth in his life. Praise, Honor, Glory, to You Lord Jesus, for helping Klindt, not to be 'CHILDISH' but 'CHILD-LIKE.'

12

WAIT ON THE LORD

"They that wait upon The Lord shall renew their strength: they shall mount up with wings as eagles: they shall run and not grow weary: and they shall walk and not faint."

(Isaiah 40:31)

Many times in my life, I have come up against a crisis, where it seems at first glance, that there was no way out. My prayer would usually be a prayer of rescue – get me out of this mess. The Good Lord most often has not taken me out of the situation, but rather, He has carried me through it. In going through it, I learn to trust Him.

In the midst of the trial, I will ask myself this question: "Has The Good Lord brought me to this point in my life to destroy me? Or rather, will the day come that I can look back on this particular situation to see that not only did He help me, but I have learned a beneficial lesson by going through the experience?" Often I have heard it said, "You must have faith!" This is good to hear, but the statement is incomplete, for we are not told to have faith in a specific thing or person. Do we have faith that everything will turn out all right? Do we have faith in ourselves? Do we have faith in a condition, or place, or thing? Faith is defined in scripture as, "*Faith is confident assurance concerning what we hope for, and conviction about things we do not see.*" (Hebrews 11:1) Also, verse 2 tells us, "*Because of faith, the men of old were approved by God.*"

So, if we look at scripture's definition, we must come to the conclusion that our faith must be in God in order to please Him. For, in Hebrews 11:6, it is written, "*Without faith it is impossible to please Him. Anyone who comes to God must believe that He exists, and that He rewards those who seek Him.*"

My faith was tested greatly in a recent encounter with a fairly common, but painful affliction. On Saturday, March 30, 1996, while at the lumber store picking up some lumber for some shelves in the basement of our newly purchased home, I developed severe pain in my groin area, which quickly spread to the lower left-side of my back. I was just barely able to load the lumber in the mini-van. When I reached home, my wife, Elayne, had to help me unload the lumber. The pain persisted until at 3:00 p.m. I started vomiting clear liquid. As a result of this Elayne became very alarmed, insisting that I be taken to the hospital. I did consent to go to an emergency outpatient clinic, so Elayne called our son-in-law, Nathan, who came over to drive us to the clinic. Through blood and urine tests, the doctor said that he suspected a kidney stone, but other exams would have to be done later at the hospital. An antibiotic was prescribed for the infection that was detected. On Monday, April 1st, I saw my regular physician, who referred me to St. Luke's Hospital for outpatient X-ray Dye tests, to see if a kidney stone was the cause of the extreme pain. Early Tuesday morning, I was at the hospital, stripped to a nightshirt, sitting in the hallway by myself, waiting for the staff to arrive in the X-ray department. I was cold, lonely, tired, apprehensive, frustrated, and in pain. Alone in the hallway, I began to reflect on a dream

I had just days earlier, while I'd been asleep, but right at the point of awakening. I heard an unfriendly voice say, "When you left Maryview Lane, you lost your cover." Maryview Lane was the name of the street where we lived for over forty years of our married life. We had just moved into our smaller home on East Garfield a month before. At Maryview Lane, we experienced a most unusual peace for all those years as we raised our ten children. Now, on this morning, as I sat in the hospital hallway, it felt as if the walls were coming in. We were having problems with our home we had just purchased. It was an older home and many repairs had to be made. Our daughter, Anna, had emergency surgery for ovarian cancer. There were many business problems as well as strained relationship problems within the family. Could it be true? Did we lose our 'cover' when we made this move to Garfield Street? In talking to The Lord about it, I said, out loud, but quietly, with no one around me, "Lord, I look to You for my 'cover'!" At that instant, from around the corner, came a nurse, and she placed upon my chest and arms, a white flannel blanket. I guess it had been just taken from a dryer, because it was so warm. She didn't say anything. As she walked away, I reached out for her arm and said, "Please, wait a minute!" Then I asked, "May I ask you a personal question?" "Sure," she answered. "Are you a Christian?" I asked. Quickly, she answered, "I sure am!" Then I told her what I had just said to The Lord Jesus the instant before she came around the corner. She was so moved that one could easily hear her joyful laughter at the end of the hallway. I thanked The Lord for the blanket and reflected at how good He is. The nurse was on the way with the blanket to cover me when I was saying that I looked to Him for my cover.

While waiting in the hallway, another patient, a young woman, was wheeled down the hallway in her hospital bed to the X-ray department. She said she needed special tests done as she had experienced erratic heartbeats. She seemed quite anxious. As we visited about our situations, I asked her if I could ask her a personal question. She said, "Yes!" "Do you love The Lord?" I asked. "I certainly do," she replied. "Then, there is nothing for either of us to be anxious about," I said, "For The Lord has written in His Word, that all things work together, for good, to those who love The Lord, who are called according to His purpose." (Romans 8:28) She agreed. I could see the change in her composure.

The x-ray technician, who performed the many x-rays of the dye sent through my system, was a most compassionate young woman. She seemed genuinely concerned about my condition. During the procedure, which lasted about an hour, we visited about many things. While sitting on the x-ray table, after the tests were over, I felt compelled to pray with her. I asked if we could pray, and she said yes. The prayer was: "Lord Jesus, bless Jenny in all ways, and be the guiding light throughout her life!" We were instant friends due to our common love for The Lord Jesus.

During the week, from Tuesday, April 2, to Tuesday, April 9, I was referred to a urologist. He said the x-ray report indicated a kidney stone about the size of a 'BB' or about three to four millimeters in size. It was lodged in the left urethra tube, between the kidney and the bladder. The doctor said to drink plenty of water, as there would be a 75% chance of flushing the stone out, without the need of surgery. For the intense pain, a special prescription was prescribed. Since the medication made me nauseated, I did not use it except for a few times. Also, they gave me a strainer to screen all urine in hopes that I would pass the stone. I was told to look for something the size of a grain of sand. If I found it, bring it in to be analyzed. On Monday, April 8th, the pain was so intense, that I had to call the doctor. An appointment was set up to see him on Tuesday morning, April 9th. More x-rays were taken. He told me that he would have to 'go in' and get the stone. Also, he would rather do the surgery in the urology hospital, rather than the regular hospital, as he felt the equipment was better, and he felt more comfortable there. So, I would have to hold off till Friday, April 12th, as there were no openings till then. When I arrived home on Tuesday morning, after the doctor's visit, the pain had increased to a very high level. I was trying to remember scripture verses of importance to me. I wanted to keep my mind on The Lord, and not on the problem. There was a verse I was trying to recall, but I could not find it as I searched in The Bible. On the floor behind the recliner I was sitting in, was a 'Concordance' which could help me find the verse, but I couldn't get up to get it because of the pain. Elayne was in the basement, unpacking, as we were hardly started with our endless task of emptying the many boxes. At about 1:00 p.m. on that day, I asked The Lord to help me find that verse. All I could remember about the verse is that it had the words 'sound mind' in it. I knew it was very important to me at that particular time. Almost instantly, after I asked The Lord, Elayne came up from the basement to hand me a small booklet she had found in a box in the basement. She was taking books out of the box to put on the wall shelves in the basement sitting room. The front cover has the title, "God's Promises For Your Health." Elayne said, "This is for you!" I asked her where she got the booklet, and she told me that she found it between two books as she was emptying a box. Upon opening the book, I noted on the inside cover, the note I had written, "Received from Bill Bisbey – 10-28-1982." Bill is a friend of mine, who is now with The Lord. For fifteen years, the booklet sat in the box, waiting for this special occasion. At the front of the booklet, there was a personal witness by the writer, followed by fourteen pages of scripture verses, containing ninety-one verses about health and healing. The writer started out by stating, "The main purpose for this booklet is to give you scripture verses to meditate on so that you will know God's will for your healing." My heart jumped with joy! As you might have guessed, on page seventeen, was the verse I was looking for; the very verse I had just asked The Lord to help me find. The verse leaped into my spirit as I read it. I claimed the verse for my life. I hung onto the verse and that day, committed it to memory. The verse is: 2 Timothy 1:7 *"For God has not given us the spirit of fear, but of power, and love, and a sound mind."* How good The Lord Jesus is.

(Note: As a help to you who may be reading this, I am adding, for your review, the ninety-one verses referenced in the little booklet given to me. They are at the end of this section.)

The pain persisted throughout the day, and into the evening. At about 11:30 p.m., I was in the recliner, by myself, since Elayne had fallen asleep. She was worn out from trying to help me in any way she could. Elayne would pray over me. She would anoint me with oil every evening before she would go to bed. Due to the pain, I had to sleep in the recliner. That particular night, the pain was so intense, that I could not lie down, I couldn't eat or sleep.

That evening I cried out to The Lord Jesus. "Lord Jesus, I need Your help. Where else can I turn to Lord? People can't help me! Doctors have done all they can. Lord, you made the doctors, me, and all that is around me. If You don't help me, who can?" I quoted scripture verses which I had committed to memory, and put my name in where it was appropriate, in order to claim the verse for my life. Some of the verses were: (Isaiah20:40) *"They that wait upon The Lord, shall renew their strength; they shall mount up with wings, as eagles; they shall run and not grow weary; and they shall walk and not faint."* (Proverb3:5-6) *"Trust in The Lord with all your heart, and lean not upon your own understanding; acknowledge Him in all your ways, and trust in Him to direct your paths."* In this particular verse, I made it personal by saying, "I, Larry Lyons, will trust in The Lord with all my heart...

etc." Of course, I prayed my newly memorized verse: (2Timothy1:7) *"For The Lord has not given us the spirit of fear, but of power, and love, and a sound mind."* (Philippians 4:13) *"I can do all things through Christ, who strengthens me."* (Matthew 7:7-8) *"Ask, and you will receive, seek, and you will find, knock, and the door will be opened for you. For the one who asks, receives. The one who seeks, finds. The one who knocks, enters."* (1John 4:4) *"Greater is He that is in you, than he (Satan) who is in the world."* (Roman's 8:28) *"We know that all things work together for good, to those who love The Lord, who have been called according to His purpose."* (1Corinthians 10:13) *"No test has been sent to you that does not come to all men; but God, is faithful, who will not allow you to be tested beyond what you are able; but with the test, also make a way to escape, that you may be able to bear it."* Through this verse, I reasoned that my escape was Jesus; I must lean on Him since in my strength, I could do nothing. With my hand on my left kidney, I said, "Lord Jesus, if this is from You, to teach me something, or to allow witnessing for Your purpose, I will accept, it. If it's from the enemy, I will not accept it!" Spiritually, I saw it as an enemy attack, with The Lord allowing it for His purposes. I'm sure the enemy wanted me to curse God, or at least call out "Why me? Why are You doing this to me?" Instead, The Spirit Of The Lord urged me to call out to The Lord for help. "Where else can I turn Lord? Only to You. You are my Helper. You are my Provider, my Saviour. In You only, will I trust." Soon, my heart turned to others, whom I knew to be very ill. With great compassion, I prayed for The Lord's mercy and forgiveness, for His ministering angels to be sent to care for Elizabeth, Karen, and Jeanette, who were members of our prayer group. I prayed for Elayne, for each of our ten children, their spouses, and for their children. I prayed for specific needs as they came to mind. The pain subsided. Restful sleep came shortly thereafter. It was a most wonderful spiritual experience to feel the presence of The Lord. To know that He cares. To sense the love that He has for each of us.

For the rest of the week, up to Friday, the day set for the surgery, the pain was not as intense. In fact, I considered not going through with the surgery, but I also felt The Lord was allowing this too, for a humbling and teaching experience. I had to trust Him in all things. The word had spread of my condition. There were many who prayed for me. I observed that those who did call me by phone to check on my condition, were also those who had been hurt deeply in some way, and felt free to try to comfort me. It seems to me, that if we are hurt deeply in some way, we more easily can reach out to another in the time of need. One such person, named Dick, who has his own business, called me. I mentioned to Dick that when the attack comes, it's hard to pray. I told him that if I didn't have the scripture verses committed to memory, I most probably would not have tried to look them up. I ended my conversation with him, by saying, "About the only thing that pulls you through something like this, is the prayers of others." Dick said, "Larry, as you said that, I had a vision of you being pinned down by the enemy, so that you could not even get a look at him, but I'm in a position where I have a clear shot at him – by praying." When Dick said that, I got goose bumps. This was a revelation to me, as to why we need to pray for one another, as a name comes to mind. The Lord says in His Word, to pray unceasingly; (1Thessalonians 5:17) *"Pray without ceasing!"* When we pray for someone, this releases The Lord's power in that person's life. Not that we are good, or that our prayers are powerful, but that HE IS GOOD, and HE IS POWERFUL. The enemy confronts The Lord about our sinfulness, and that He should not show apparent favoritism, but Dick and others were praying for me, so The Lord could act. How beautiful is The Lord. How righteousness is His Name; the Name above all names, The Name Of Jesus.

Well, I did have the surgery on Friday afternoon, April 12, 1996. After visiting with the anesthesiologist for about twenty minutes or more, while waiting for the doctor, I was urged to ask him a question. I asked him if I could ask him a personal question, and he said, 'Yes.' So, in a sincere way, I asked, "Do you love The Lord?" He grimaced, with a puzzled look, to finally answer, "I'm an agnostic!" "I'm sorry you have been hurt so badly in the past," I said. He continued, "My mother was killed by a robber, in her home. I see so many good people suffer, that I am not sure there is a God, or even if there is, if He cares." I have been praying for him, but as yet, have not been able to see him in person. He agreed to meet me for lunch, but he didn't return my calls.

Just before the anesthesiologist put me under, I said, "Lord, into Your hands, I commend my spirit." I didn't know if The Lord would call me home to be with Him, or if this would come later. The next thing I remember was the voice of a very kind person saying, "Larry, are you going to keep sleeping, or are you going to get up." I opened my eyes and saw the nurse's name tag, with the name, 'Nancy.' "Are you telling me it's over?" I said. "Yes," she answered. I asked, "Was I a good patient?" and she said, "You were just wonderful." Nancy, was the 'recovery nurse.' Though she was in the operating room, I had never seen her before. She was so kind, and so caring. I asked if I could ask her a personal question. She agreed, so I asked, "Do you love The Lord?" Immediately, she answered, "Yes, I sure do." I said, "Isn't it amazing that two strangers have so much in common and are immediate friends by our common love for the Lord Jesus!" Nancy, of course, agreed. Then, I said, "Nancy, Tuesday, April 9th, was my worst day of pain. It was a significant day for me!" She said, "Why, is that the date of your baptism?" I said, "That is incredible, why would you ask such a thing?" "Well, is it?" she replied. "Yes," I said, "And do you know what? On that date, the enemy tried to steal my spiritual rebirth, by attacking me on that important date." I was baptized at age three, and can remember that baptism very vividly. Until that moment, speaking to Nancy, It did not occur to me that the attack came on such an important day. The Good Lord truly had given to me a sound mind, as I had claimed in the verse, when praying on that previous Tuesday. *"For The Lord has not given us the spirit of fear, but of power, and of love, and a sound mind."* My mind was so clear. My sight was so clear. There was no nausea. I had such a strong love for the people around me. After about an hour of recovery, I dressed, and walked to the car, as our daughter Anita, had come to drive Elayne and I home.

At the time of this writing, five years after the surgery, I still enjoy good health. The fourteen pounds lost, are still gone, and that is probably good for the body in which I am living. My body is also being surprised, as it sees much more water than I was giving it before. In reflection now, I can say that what I gained mainly from the experience, is that I learned where my heart is. Scripture says, *"Where your treasure is, there will be your heart also."* (Matthew 6:21) The Lord Jesus is my treasure, and that is where my heart is. When the attack comes in life, where do I turn? Do I turn first to people? Do I turn to The Lord? And, if I do turn to The Lord, do I ask "Why me?" Or, am I angry with The Lord because He is allowing this particular thing in my life? As I had done so many other times in my life, when problems came up, I asked The Lord Jesus for help. He did indeed help, in the past, and again in this severe problem. I praise Him for being The Lord of my life. I pray that I will always serve Him. Never do I want to be a poor witness for Him, nor do anything in my weakness, to grieve Him, but at the same time, I know that in His love and compassion, that He does forgive me when I do fall and confess this to Him. In waiting on The Lord, I can run and not grow weary; I can walk and not faint!

As a further tribute to The Lord, I would like to relate to you what happened on our annual fishing trip, which we took in June of 1996. Even though weak, we still kept our reservation at a Minnesota cabin, to go fishing the first week of June. On the last day of the week of fishing, Friday, the 7th of June, while my head was on the pillow, early in the morning, I heard a friendly voice. It was at the point where I was either asleep, or awake. The voice said, "There were good times in the past, there'll be better times ahead; but, the BEST is yet to come!" This had to come from The Lord, in stark contrast to the earlier word from the enemy of 'losing cover.' As I reflect on these words, I notice that "time" is mentioned in the past, and ahead, but when "the best" is mentioned, there is no 'time.' This is the "Eternal Existence," with The Lord Jesus; in His Place, which He calls "Heaven." Jesus wants each of us to "BE THERE."

ADDENDUM SECTION #12
(Bible Verses)

Note: In Section 12, "Wait On The Lord," Ninety-one verses relating to health and healing were referenced. For the interested reader, these may be read in scripture. 2Tim1-7 is the verse I hung on to in my struggle with the kidney stone. The other verses are as follows:

Exodus chap 15 : 26
Exodus chap 23 : 25-26
Deuteronomy chap 7:15
Deuteronomy chap 32 :39
Psalms chap 41 : 3
Psalms chap 103 : 2-3
Psalms chap 107 : 20
Proverbs chap 3 : 7-8
Proverbs chap 4 : 20-22
Proverbs chap 12 : 18
Proverbs chap 12 : 21
Proverbs chap 13 :12
Proverbs chap 13 : 17
Proverbs chap 16 :24
Proverbs chap 17 :22
Proverbs chap 18 :21
Isaiah chap 53 : 4-5
Isaiah chap 57:19
Jeremiah chap 30:17
Ezekiel chap 34:16
Hosea chap 11:3
Malachi chap 4: 2
Matthew chap 4 :23
Matthew chap 6 : 33
Matthew chap 7:1
Matthew chap 8 : 16-17

Matthew chap 9 : 22
Matthew chap 9 : 35
Matthew chap 10 : 1
Matthew chap 12 : 15
Matthew chap 13 : 58
Matthew chap 14 : 14
Matthew chap 15 : 30
Matthew chap 16 : 19
Matthew chap 19 : 2
Matthew chap 21 : 14
Mark chap 1 : 34
Mark chap 3 : 10-11
Mark chap 5 : 28-29
Mark chap 5 :34
Mark chap 6 :13
Mark chap 6 :56
Mark chap 10 :52
Mark chap 11 :23
Mark chap 16 :16
Mark chap 16 :17-18
Luke chap 4 : 30
Luke chap 5 : 15
Luke chap 6 : 19
Luke chap 9 : 1-2
Luke chap 9 : 6
Luke chap 10 : 8-9

Luke chap 13 : 12-13
John chap 10 : 10
John chap 14 : 12-13
John chap 14 : 27
John chap 15 : 7-8
Acts chap 4 : 9-10
Acts chap 5 : 16
Acts chap 10 : 38
Acts chap 19 : 12
Acts chap 28 : 8
Romans chap 4 :20
Romans chap 8 : 6
Romans chap 8 :16-17
Romans chap 8 : 37
2 Corinthians chap 3 : 5-6
2 Corinthians chap 9 : 8
Galatians chap 3 : 13
Galatians chap 3 : 29
Ephesians chap 6 :10-12
Philippians chap 4 :19
Colossians chap 1 : 13
2 Timothy chap 1 : 7
Hebrews chap 2 : 14
Hebrews chap 10 : 35
Hebrews chap 11 : 6
Hebrews chap 13 : 8
James chap 4 :7-8
James chap 5 : 15-16
1 Peter chap 2 : 24
2 Peter chap 1 : 3,4
1 John chap 3 : 8
1 John chap 4 : 4
1 John chap 4 : 17
3 John chap 1 : 2
Revelations 1:18

13

FLEECE OF WOOL

*"And God did so that night; for it was dry upon the
fleece only, and there was dew on all the ground."*
(Judges 6:40)

For the first thirteen years in the insurance business, even
though an independent, I shared an office with a life
insurance agency. The first ten years were spent in downtown Davenport, Iowa, and the next three years were in central Bettendorf, Iowa. There was always an inner desire to
have a separate office of my own, as I wanted to service all
of the insurance needs of the individuals and businesses who
came to me for insurance. The agency I was with specialized
in life insurance only. Clients who came to me had needs for
service in auto, homeowner, and business insurance areas.
Many wanted me to get into those areas of insurance as they
had developed a trust in me and wanted to get all their insurance from one person. As the gap in our approach to serving
client-needs widened, I knew that I would have to make a
move, to leave the agency.

There were, of course, the natural concerns of: no capital;
added expenses associated with my own office; insecurity on
my own; and the necessity to provide for the financial needs

of our family of ten children. Most everyone discouraged me. The failure rate of agents on their own was and is quite high. But the urging kept on. There was an accountant friend who wanted me to share office space with him in a new location. He was going off on his own also, and by sharing space, we could help reduce the office expenses. There were many directions in which I could go. In fact, Elayne, had offered to work part time with me in the office in order to help out. This really appealed to me as she does so well on bookwork. Also, she has such a good way with people. She is so giving. In talking this through with my Elayne, the best idea we could come up with was to move the office home, where she could help me with the paper work, as well as answer the phone when I would be out on appointments. Not only did Elayne agree with this idea, but she urged me go ahead to bring the business home, until I could find a desirable location. This would be the easiest way to accomplish having my own office, within our financial means.

When I called the local phone company service center, to discuss my phone needs, I was helped by a very special young woman, who showed real interest in my situation. Trying to explain my ideas to her over the phone was very difficult, so she suggested that I come downtown to the main office, where we could cover the phone possibilities in more detail. On the way down to her office, I asked the Lord to help me with this most difficult decision. I prayed, "Lord Jesus, if You want me to leave the insurance business, I will; if You want me to move the business home, I will; if You want me to move to a separate office location, I will; but, I need a sign that I am in Your will. Lord, if I can get an easy phone number, I'll know You want me to move the business home; if not, I'll move to another location."

After much discussion with the young woman, she said I could have a phone number at another location, but the phone number pre-fix would have to be the same as our home phone pre-fix, if I wanted the phone to ring at both locations, home and office. Our home phone pre-fix is '355.' So, I asked her if she assigned numbers at random, or does someone pick the next open number available. Or, did they have a special system for assigning new phone number listings? She explained that another girl did that in another department. Then, I asked her if I could get an easy phone number. "Like what." she responded. "Well," I said, "If I must have the pre-fix '355' in order for the phone to ring at home as well as at an office location away from home, then how about all 5's – like 355-5555." She called the person in charge of number assignment, and said, "We have a Mr. Lyons here in the office, and he wants to have an easy phone number. Will you see what you have available?" After a bit, she wrote down (2112)-(0110), and two other numbers which I do not remember. She said, "What about one of these?" I told her that I was trying to make a difficult decision, and the phone number I would get was very important. I asked her if she could call the person back to see if an easier phone number was available. "Me again." she said as she got the same person back on the phone. "Mr. Lyons is a very persistent person, but he's a nice guy. He wants an easy phone number. Will you see what you can do?" The other person must have asked what she meant by 'easy' for she replied, "Well, he wants all the same digits, like all 7's." After a long wait, she wrote down the number '355-5555.' I was shocked! I asked her if that number was available. She said that the number just became available a few days before, "But, who would want that number?" she asked. I quickly said, "I do!!"

The phone number was ours. We still have the number today, some twenty-two years later. Now, we have the business located in our own building, in downtown Bettendorf, Iowa. After twelve years at home, The Good Lord provided us with a small building, in which to house our insurance business. At the time of this writing, we have two sons, Chris and Paul, a daughter, Anita, Chris's wife, Sheryl, in the business. I prayed! The Good Lord Jesus answered! Our business phone number is what I asked for – 355-5555.

In sincerity, I asked The Good Lord Jesus for help with this business decision. I would have to say that I was inspired to ask for a certain number – 355-5555 -, which The Lord had just made available a few days prior. The move home was supposed to be temporary, but lasted twelve years. I was able to get to know our children better. What a most wonderful experience. As the business grew, more of our family asked to come into the business. The Good Lord provided the necessary income to allow them to work in the business, with adequate income. The Good Lord has richly blessed us with a business, in which, we can help so many people.

Some years after asking for the special phone number, I was telling the story to someone, when he said, "What you did, Larry, was to 'Set out a fleece!'" I asked the person to explain what he meant, so he related to me the story of Gideon, in the Old Testament. Gideon was told to go into a certain battle, which involved a high degree of risk. His entire army could be demolished. To be sure that the message came from The Lord, he asked The Lord to give him a sign. He would set outside of the tent, a woolen fleece. The next morning, if he found the fleece was completely dry, while the ground around was saturated with heavy dew, then he would know that the message was from The Lord. Of course, the next morning, he found the fleece completely dry, while the ground was super wet with dew. In order to absolutely be sure, he asked The Lord to make the fleece saturated with dew the next morning, while the ground would be dry. The next morning, the ground was dry, and the fleece was wet. Gideon, and his men, went into battle, and defeated the enemy.

In my case, it was not that I doubted The Lord's presence, or strength, but I wanted to be sure that I was in His will. The Lord is so good! He is concerned about relatively unimportant details, like phone numbers. If we ask Him, He will respond, because He is God! He is Good, and He cares about even the smallest details.

14

FIRST CLASS

"Give, and it shall be given to you. Good measure, pressed down, shaken together, running over, will they pour into the fold of your garment. For the measure you measure will be measured back to you."

(Luke 6:38)

In the year of 1966, we purchased a new Volkswagen Bus to carry our ten children to and from school, but also, we would be able to take the children with us on family vacations. One year we were able to take the children to California so that we could visit my six brothers and sisters, who lived in Southern California. In the following year, we took all the children to the state of New York, in order to visit my sister and brother, who lived in Schenectady, New York. As we traveled on these trips, we would camp at evening time, in a large tent. We have many happy memories of these trips. Even today, when we get together, the children all laugh and talk about those good times.

Eventually, the VW Bus wore out. We were in need of another vehicle to allow Elayne to drive the children back and forth to school. The children were frankly embarrassed by the rusty old VW Bus. I really didn't know what to do!

So, in March of 1978, while I was driving along Kimberly Road, in Davenport, Iowa, I prayed to The Good Lord for help in this tough decision. My prayer was, "Lord, when You do something for someone, You do it First Class! That's the way You are! I'm real concerned about what to do for a vehicle. I don't want to put the family in debt by buying a new car, as our finances are strained now. Help me Lord to do the right thing, within Your will. I don't know whether to get another van, or what! In Jesus Name, I pray!"

In September of that same year, I took Elayne out for her 49th birthday. I asked her during our visiting over the meal, what her preference would be if she had a free choice for another vehicle. Of course, being the person she is, Elayne said, "You know we can't afford another car!" I replied, "I'm not talking about 'afford,' I just want to know if you had your choice, what would you choose." "Well, I don't want another van! It's too hard to climb up into a van. I would like a smaller car, with a seat that sits high so I could see out above the hood of the car; one that turns easy, and one where I can carry things in the back, like the VW Bus – like Maria's (our daughter) Mercury Bobcat, but not exactly, as it rides a little too hard. I don't know what I want. I would have to look around to see what is available." This answer really surprised me as I was considering looking around for another VW Bus, which would have been completely wrong.

In October, a month later, I had to go to San Diego, California to attend the CLU Commencement, as I had graduated from The American College, in Bryn Mawr, Pennsylvania, with an insurance degree. I was to receive my diploma in San Diego. That year was also our 26th wedding anniversary, so Elayne agreed to come with me. After the graduation ceremony, we went to the Los Angeles area of California, as I wanted to see my brothers and sisters, who lived there. Also, I expected to be able to see my sister Julie, who lived nearby, in Hesperia, California. Julie's health was not good, so above all, I wanted to see her, to offer comfort in some way. As soon as we arrived at the home of my brother Bob, and sister-in-law Sheila, where we would be staying, I called Julie to see what would be a good time to go out to Hesperia, so that we could visit. Julie asked me almost immediately after saying 'Hello,' where I was. I told her that we were at Bob's and then she asked how we got out to California. I told her that we went by airplane. She then asked if we had a one-way ticket, or if it was round-trip. I told her, of course, that we had a round-trip ticket, as we got a better price that way. Julie then inquired if we could get a refund if we didn't fly back. This so surprised me that I asked her what she meant by this question. Julie then stated a situation that to me, was off the wall. She said she had two cars and wanted us to have one of them. I was caught off guard, so I said that I would check with Bob on airline schedules, and call her back. Since Hesperia is about 200 miles East of Los Angeles, I would have to get some sort of transportation out there if we were to leave Julie's to drive back to our home in Davenport, Iowa. No one could help me with what Julie was talking about. They didn't know of any details or what the car situation was with Julie or what her plans were. After much discussion, checking with transportation schedules, and the like, I finally remembered that I had to be back in Davenport by a specific date, as I had a random Internal Revenue audit, which I had to make. So, we would not be able to drive back. When I called Julie to tell her of this situation, she would not bend in her plans. If we could not come out to get the car to drive back, then we could not come out at all. She said she had decided to give us the car in March, and since then, her whole life had turned around, so she would not change her mind. My head was reeling! I called her several times during our two day stay at my brother Bob's home, but she would not change her mind. We were not able to see Julie on the trip. It hurt me as I wanted so desperately to comfort her. But, she did say over the phone that her health had improved. We flew back to Davenport. As I thought about the whole situation, I remembered that she had said she had decided to give us the car in March. This is the same time I prayed to The Lord for help in deciding what type of vehicle to get. For some reason, it had always been hard for me to 'receive' from someone. It is always easier for me to 'give.' In fact, we had given many vehicles away, up to that time, to people in need. If I refused Julie by not accepting the car, I could hurt her. Giving could help her. So, finally, I called her and agreed to come out to California over Christmas school break, as our son, Daniel, would be home from college, and he could help me on the two thousand mile trip back home. We flew out to California on December 15th of the same year, without even knowing what year or type of car we were going to see. To our surprise, when we got to Julie's, we found a 1977 Ford Pinto Hatchback. It was in perfect shape, with low mileage. The color was blue – a first color choice for Elayne. Julie wouldn't take a cent. "It makes me feel so good to know you will get good use out of it," she said. After a wonderful visit with Julie, we headed out. It was wintertime. We went through mountains, snowstorms, severe ice conditions, and real tough weather difficulties, but arrived two days later, back safely in Davenport, Iowa. It was on a cold, dark, Wednesday evening that we pulled into our garage at home, just a few days before Christmas. It was suppertime, so all the family was together to see what we had brought home. I kissed Elayne, then turned the garage light on so all could see the new car. As they were all Ooo'ing and Aaahhh'ing, I went into the house to call Julie, as I had promised her that I would do. I told Julie that we arrived home OK. The first thing she asked was, "How did you like the car?" I told her that I was really surprised; that the car handled beautifully. Then, Julie said something that really touched my spirit. She said, "You know, Larry, that Pinto is the Top-Of-The-Line! There is nothing available for that car, that isn't on it! It has a special seat that climbs up on a special track because I'm so small, and need to see out. (Elayne, also, is small, and this was part of her request for her 'first choice'). It is The-Top-Of-The-Line!" It hit me hard, what she said, almost to the point of tears. But, tears of joy! I had said, back in March, 'Lord, when You do something for someone, You do it First Class' and now, Julie says, 'Top-Of-The-line.' Truly, the Pinto, through Julie, was a gift from the Lord. How good The Lord is!

We drove the Pinto everywhere for many years. It was Elayne's car. She did so enjoy the ease of handling. It was spunky, so Elayne had fun driving it around. The Pinto took all the children to and from their many activities; it carried the groceries home often; it carried building materials when we would add onto the house. Finally, when the Pinto served us well for many years, we gave the car to a nephew in need. He, and his family, drove the Pinto for many years of additional service. Incidentally, we also gave the VW Bus away to a needy family when we got the Pinto. The Lord is Good? He always gives back 'Running over!'

15

THE DOVE

"He shall be Peace." (Micah 5:40)

A
ll the world is asking for Peace. Is it a place, a thing, a possession, a condition, or a state of mind? Or, is Peace a Person? In Micah, it is written, "HE shall be Peace!" Peace is a Person. Peace is Jesus! To know Jesus is to know Peace. If there is no Jesus, there is no Peace.

NO Jesus = NO PEACE
KNOW Jesus = KNOW PEACE

One of my friends, a pharmacist named John, is now with The Lord. He died of leukemia at a young age – in his thirties. He left his wife and four children. When he was in town visiting, we would go out to lunch. Most of the time, he was gone to Bethesda, Maryland, where he served as a volunteer in the research and treatment of cancer and leukemia. As a pallbearer at his funeral, I met a friend of his who told me that John held the hand of over two hundred people, who died of leukemia, while he was at the Bethesda center. John lived for over four years with the disease.

At one of our lunches, we went to Bishop's Cafeteria in Bettendorf, Iowa. He had his usual favorite – baked beans and Italian Beef, Aus Jus. He was so thin. The leukemia had taken its toll on John. I remarked to John that he was a tremendous witness to many people, as he did not come across as a bitter man, nor did he lash out or complain. He shared with me a prayer, which he said every day, and this prayer helped to carry him through, one day at a time. He gave me a printed copy of the prayer, and I made a copy of it before returning it to him. After memorizing the prayer, I, too, have been saying it at the start of each day. The prayer is as follows:

Vs-1   I got up early one morning
And rushed right into the day.
I had so much to accomplish,
I didn't take time to pray.
Problems just tumbled about me,
And heavier came each task.
I wondered why God didn't help me,
He answered, "You didn't ASK!"

VS-2   I wanted to see joy and beauty,
But the day toiled on, gray and bleak.
I wondered why God didn't show me,
He said, "You didn't SEEK!"

Vs-3   I tried to come into God's presence,
I used all my keys at the lock.
God, lovingly, and gently, chided,
My child, "You didn't KNOCK!"

After each verse, I would add my own personal response. For example: after verse one, I would say, "Lord, I do ask for Your help with the problems of the day. Lord Jesus, please help me to know the Father's will for me this day. Holy Spirit, please help me to do The Father's will. After verse two, I say, "Lord, You know joy and beauty are all around me. I am the one who does not see. I pray that I would see just a glimpse of Your Joy and Beauty, today, so that I Know that I am in Your service." After verse three, I say, "Lord, I do knock to come into Your presence, (while tapping my heart five times), please open the door, and let me into Your presence."

One morning, after several years of saying this prayer every morning, I was tying my tie, getting ready for work, and was looking out the sliding door of our second story bedroom, toward the back yard of our residence. At the time of this writing, this would be about twenty years ago. Our bedroom overlooked a small second story deck attached to the back of our home. I was praying the above prayer. When I got to the second verse, and said, "Lord, Your Joy and Beauty is all around me – I am the one who cannot see – I pray that today I could just see a glimpse so that I would know that I am in Your service." Then, at that instant, a morning dove came down over the rain gutter, from the roof above, and landed on the deck railing. It was only four feet from me. He started bobbing his head up and down, looking at me through the glass door. Only a second or two passed, when its mate came and it too landed on the railing beside the other. Then the two of the them bobbed their heads up and down as they looked at me through the glass door. After a few minutes, they left together, in formation, as they flew over the hill in the back yard. It was truly awesome, as The Lord had just shown me a glimpse of His Joy and Beauty. Living, as part of His creation! Very peaceful! Later that day, when I arrived home from the office, Elayne, said something very unusual had happened that day. When I asked what had happened, she related that a pair of doves had moved into the pine tree in our front yard. Soon, young ones were born. The following year, a pair made a nest in a little roof extension, under the garage roof overhangs. Each year, a pair of doves has come to that extension to raise their little ones.

On one particular day in December, when we had our insurance office at home, my wife, Elayne, hollered loudly, to get my attention. "Come quickly," she said, in a loud voice! I came from office at a run because I thought she had fallen and needed help. Instead, when I got to the dining room, I saw her looking out the large dining room window with binoculars to her eyes. "Look," she said, "Count the doves!" As I looked through the binoculars at the telephone wires behind our home, I counted seventy-two doves lined up on the wires. Apparently, they used our backyard as a meeting place to gather for their winter trip south. It truly was awesome! It was so inspirational to see. The Good Lord has given such a physical sign of His Love and Peace, even if only through His doves.

Even now, at the time of this writing, as we live in a much smaller home, we have doves living on our property. We have their song of peace every morning. In fact, the day after moving into our present home, about one mile form our home of forty years, as I walked out of the front of the garage to go into the backyard, a pair of doves flew from the garage roof to the backyard, over my head. "Thank You, Lord," I said. I took it as a sign of the love and concern The Lord has for His people. Elayne and I know that Peace is not a place or a condition. We know that Peace is a Person! We know that "He shall be Peace!" Jesus is Peace!

16

THE GREAT PROVIDER

"If God clothes in such splendor the grass of the field, which grows today and tomorrow is thrown into the fire, how much more will He provide for you, oh weak in faith."

(Luke 12:28)

Have you ever faced bills to pay with no money to pay them! Have you ever had too much month at the end of the money? Well, my good wife Elayne and I have had this happen in the past, especially when we had to satisfy the needs of ten children, while struggling to build an insurance business. Almost every day in downtown Davenport, Iowa, where I had an office for ten years, I would stop in a little church to talk to The Lord. Simply, I would ask Him to help me earn enough income to pay the bills and raise the children. If we had more income than what was provided, we very likely could have spoiled the children. As it was, we had enough money to supply their needs, and even at times, their wants.

One of my clients, who has become a good friend, said to me one day, "Do you know why I respect you and your wife Elayne?" I tried to dodge the subject, but he persisted, until finally, he said," I'll tell you why! Because your kids get excited about nothing!" When I asked him to explain, he told the story of what happens when he takes his children to a restaurant for a meal. They complain about the food, argue on the way home, and do not even thank him when they get home. On the other hand, he related, "You take your kids to Whitey's Ice Cream Store in the VW Bus, for a simple ice cream cone, and to them, that's a big deal!" This story, from my friend, does show how our children did gain a healthy attitude about values, since we were not able to lavish things upon them.

If we had a need when raising the children, or even now, with the children gone, if we have a need, we would pray about it, to ask The Lord for His help. I can't remember a time He did not come through, with usually a better, more abundant answer than what we asked for. One such occasion, in our insurance business, about 1988, we had our children, Chris, Paul, and Anita, in the business with us and the cash flow was at the bottom. It was Friday morning, with payroll due, with three families counting on a paycheck to meet specific needs. There was little or no money in the business checkbook. I went into my office, shut the door, and tried to figure out what to do. I didn't want to borrow any money at the bank, as this would only solve the present problem, but could cause more serious money crunches down the road. To get alone with The Lord, I left the office to go to the post office and pick up the mail at our Post Office Box. On the way, I visited with The Lord about the situation, about how I did not like to borrow money, and that he could provide the answer.

Earnestly, I asked The Lord for His help. "But in all things, Lord, Your will be done!" I added. When I got the mail at the Post Office, there was only one piece of mail that could possibly be a commission check, and this check was from Travelers Insurance Company. Usually, this check was for about only a hunderd to one hundred and twenty dollars, which wouldn't solve our problems. I didn't even bother to open this piece of mail. When I got back to the office, I gave the mail to Anita to handle, and went into my office to again seek The Lord about the problem. The only thing I could come up with was that I would have to go to the bank and borrow at least enough money to cover the others in the office, so that they could get a paycheck. Elayne, and I would have to wait. I couldn't ask them to wait; this would not be good stewardship. In a way, I felt like a complete failure.

A short time before I was to leave to the bank, Anita came into my office to put a check in front of me from Travelers Insurance Company. The amount of the check was $4,250. Immediately, I got angry with them, saying that Travelers was causing us further problems. Once before, they had given us a large commission check in error, and it was such a hassle to get it straightened out. In my mind, which I also told Anita, they had been paying us commissions each month on a group health case for some three to four years, and now, in error, they came up with a single payment of duplicate commissions. I told Anita that we would have to return it to Travelers, hoping that we could get it straightened out before they sent Internal Revenue Service a 1099 Income Tax form, in error. I asked Anita to take the two previous calendar year income files, and I would take the current income file. I told her that I was sure that when we took the individual monthly checks for all the months involved, we would get a total equaling the $4,250 they had sent us in error. As I started through the current income file, my heart started to pound. I wasn't finding any commission check stubs from Travelers for the group health case in question. I started to wonder; is it possible; could Travelers have forgotten to pay us? Could we have missed this account? Soon, Anita, came back into my office and said, "Dad, there aren't any check stubs in either year's income file!" Both of us almost went limp. We checked with Travelers – the money was ours! We could make payroll, with much to spare. I was so joyful! I praised The Good Lord Jesus and thanked Him for His Goodness and Mercy. I was so elated, that I took Elayne for lunch at our favorite Chinese restaurant. It was great to bathe in the Goodness of The Lord.

While at lunch, I saw two women at another table, which we knew from many years previous, but had not seen in a long time. Usually, I am somewhat reserved, so I would not have thought to impose on their time together, but on this day, I was so joyful that I wanted to go over to tell them the good news. Elayne was somewhat reluctant, but as we were leaving, I went by their table and told them the good news that had come to us. They seemed genuinely excited for us. About five years later, I met one of the women at a church healing service, when in a group of people; she started to tell the story to them. She related that she had taken her friend to lunch, as this other woman was at the bottom with nowhere to turn. She said that when I told the story of the unexpected money to them at the restaurant table, the story really lifted the troubled woman in spirit. The woman is now back on track and even closer to The Lord. She thanked me for having the concern to tell them of our good news.

Isn't The Lord Good? All along, He knew that the commission on that group health case was not being paid. All along He knew the money crunch was coming, In fact, He knew it was in the mail slot at the Post Office when I prayed! In time of need, when we pray, The Lord can bring about circumstances to help us, far beyond our wildest wishes. He is in control. The Good Lord arranges circumstances to bring about His will. He teaches us, through faith how, when, and what to pray for, according to His will. The Lord is The Great Provider! He guides and directs those who love Him – to supply all their needs.

17

THE BALL BEARING

"Dismiss all anxiety form your minds. Present you needs to God in every form of prayer and in petitions full of gratitude."

(Phillipian's 4:6)

The Good Lord is concerned about every detail of our lives. Not even a single sparrow falls from the sky without His knowledge (Matthew 10:29). The Lord wants a personal relationship with each of us so that we can come to Him with every detail of our lives, expecting Him to be concerned, responding to our desire, always ready to help.

On one of my business trips to California, when the children were little, I saw in the front window of a retail store, a small laminated card with a catching phrase printed in it. It read, 'Lord, help me to remember, that nothing can happen today, that You an I can't get through together.' I was so inspired by this writing, that I bought ten of the cards, so that each of our ten children could have one of their own. Regularly, I would see the card displayed in their rooms, or even on their note-boards when I would visit them in college. That message has always meant a lot to me, and I notice it also has had an impression on the children.

Some years ago, there was situation that came up where I sure needed the help of The Lord, even though, to most, it would not have been considered important or critical. Most people would say this type of problem is one where you should work it out on your own. Certainly not a case to pray about and bring The Lord in on. Surely, He has more important things to be concerned about!

In a previous section of these writings (#14, entitled 'First Class'), I mentioned the story of my sister Julie, giving us a 1977 Ford Pinto. Julie lived in California, and she of course did not know that I had prayed to The Lord for an answer as to what to do about getting another vehicle for the family. She gave us the Pinto at the perfect time of need, and it served us well for many years. It did, however, have a peculiar problem, which caused us some headaches. The Pinto had a very complicated carburetor, which was designed to meet the rigid requirements for emission in California, where she lived. The carburetor was called a 'Variable Venturi' carburetor. The calibration of this carburetor was very critical for good performance. If not done correctly, the engine would shut down for no apparent reason, which it did many times, most often in heavy traffic, causing much stress, especially for Elayne. Something had to be done. Eventually, I decided to take the carburetor apart, as I had some experience repairing cars for many years. My Goal was to dismantle the carburetor, clean the parts, and install a new kit so that there would be new gaskets and seals.

I purchased a carburetor repair-kit, and dismantled the carburetor. After cleaning and reassembling, the condition did not improve. After questioning many mechanics, I learned that a special vacuum gauge was necessary to calibrate the various settings. The gauge needed a mercury column in order to accomplish the very sensitive adjustments. Apparently, there was only one repair garage where there was an auto-specialist who had such a gauge. I made an appointment to have him check and adjust the carburetor. The appointment was set for a particular Monday. He would need the car for the full day, so I was to drop it off early in the morning. On the Saturday before the appointment, I was mentioning the problem to the members of our family. One of our children had a friend, who was present, and he was studying auto-mechanics at a local Community College, named Scott Community College. He said that he had a text-book, which he noticed covered that type of carburetor in some detail. He felt it might help, so he brought it over for me to use, to see if it would give me any suggestions. Upon reviewing the material in the book for some time, I realized that it only gave instructions on how to dismantle and reassemble the carburetor; nothing about the theory or adjustment of such a unit.

In looking over the drawings in the book, something caught my eye that was most unusual. One diagram showed a small ball bearing, about the size of a regular 'BB' which was suspended above a small hole in the top of the carburetor. After the top section of the carburetor was installed, the small metal ball would be held in place, to pop up and down, as needed. This surprised me as I did not recall seeing such a small ball bearing when I reassembled the carburetor. Could this be the problem, I thought. I was sure there was no small ball bearing, so the manufacturer must have neglected to install such a ball during assembly. This must be why we were having intermittent engine shutdown. Should I try to get a small ball bearing to put in the hole, I thought! Should I tell the mechanic about this to help in trouble-shooting the problem. It would be important for him to know this before he started calibrating the carburetor settings. Late that Saturday night, I took the top off of the carburetor to verify that, as suspected, the ball bearing was missing. So, I decided to tell the mechanic on the following Monday, so that he could use this knowledge in his checkout of the unit under operation.

On the way home from church on Sunday morning, when I was thinking about the problem, the unexpected thought came to me that maybe the carburetor had the bearing in it originally, but maybe I poured it out when I emptied the residual gas out of the carburetor bowl. Now, I had a dilemma! Was it there, and had it fallen out, or was it left out during manufacture? After we pulled into the garage, my wife, Elayne, and our children went into the house. I stayed behind, still pondering the problem. There, in the garage, I prayed, or talked to The Lord about the problem, in my spirit. I said something like, "Lord, only You know what happened! I need Your help. I need to know if that ball bearing was in the carburetor, and it fell out when I tipped the carburetor body over to pour out gas, or, was it left out? If the ball-bearing is here somewhere, Lord, would You help me find it, so that I can be correct when I talk to the mechanic on Monday morning?"

'Where did I pour that gas out,' I thought! Soon, I remembered that I had emptied the gas under the willow tree in the backyard. I went over to look under the willow tree. The season was fall, so the ground was covered with leaves. There were literally thousands of small dried willow leaves under the tree. The situation looked hopeless! There were so many leaves, I couldn't even see the ground. Since I had an overcoat on, I tucked the coat tails under the back of my legs, and bent down to the ground. Looking around, seeing all those leaves, made me so frustrated, that I stood back up and started back into the house. As I started into the back door of the garage, I remember saying to myself, "Larry, here you ask The Lord for help, and then you don't exercise enough faith to even look!" I went back out under the willow tree. Standing in the middle of about a six-foot circle, where I thought I might have poured the gas the week before, I bent down again to look at the leaves covering the ground. For about a minute I looked at the leaves, almost mesmerized by their number and similarity. Finally, I reached down to pick up a leaf that was sitting on another leaf, covering it up. The leaf was sitting cup-down. The leaf underneath was sitting cup-up. In the cup of the leaf underneath, was a brightly shining ball bearing. Inside, in my spirit, I said, "Thank You Lord! Thank You Lord!" I picked the ball bearing up and headed for the house. Approaching the house, I could see Elayne and all the children looking out the dining-room window, with puzzled looks on their faces. They all had the look like, 'Are you okay? What in the world are you doing?' When I showed them the ball bearing, and told them what I had done, we all rejoiced. Naturally, I put the bearing back in the carburetor before our Monday morning appointment with the mechanic. Eventually, we got the Pinto to perform without stalling. What a relief!

So, you see, The Good Lord is concerned about us in all ways. He is ever ready to help us. All we need do, is ask, then, step out in faith. I don't always do it, but when I do, I marvel at His compassion, His power, and yes, His concern about even the small details. To this day, I do not know if the Lord led me to the bearing I had poured out a week earlier, or if He made a new bearing because He knew it was important to me, and I had asked Him for help. All I do know is that I witnessed a small miracle that day. Once again, I was reassured of the concern and goodness of the Lord Jesus, Who is Lord of all!

18

DESIRE OF OUR HEARTS

"Take delight in The Lord and He will grant you your heart's requests."

(Psalm 37:4)

At age eighteen, I entered the United States Navy. After fourteen weeks of indoctrination training, called boot camp, at Great Lakes Naval Training Station, north of Chicago, Illinois, I was stationed aboard the naval ship, U.S.S. Hambleton, DMS-20. This ship had a crew of two hundred sixty-seven men. The U.S.S. Hambleton was a minesweeper, which meant our duty was to scan the ocean floor in search of mines. The most common method of such detection was to sweep the entire ocean floor with a large net dragged behind the ship. The net was equipped with special cutters which cut the cable anchoring the mine to the ocean floor, or, at least, trip the mechanism so that the mine would surface. When surfaced, we would destroy the mine with either high-powered rifles or depth charges. The object was to rid the harbor or other water area from mines so that the other ships in the convoy could proceed into the area without fear of being destroyed by mine blast.

On one particular cruise, we were off the coast of New Foundland, in the North Atlantic. We had not seen land for over thirty days, which of course made each of us very lonely. It was winter time and the ocean was very rough with large waves and strong winds. The word went out from the Ship Commander that we were to receive mail the next day, so naturally, I was excited as I did so want to hear from someone from home. Hopefully, I might even get a letter from my girlfriend. The next day the sea was very rough, but in spite of the bad weather, a helicopter, carrying our mail, landed on the deck of The Midway aircraft carrier, a sister ship in our convoy. The carrier was right next to us in the ship placement. When we were underway at sea, our ship was plane guard for The Midway. That meant that if a plane went into the sea, by accident, on either take-off or landing, our job was to search for any survivors. In the inclement weather, getting the mail was quite a task. First, from our ship, a small line was shot, by rifle, over the Carrier. Then, we tied a heavier line to the small line. The large Carrier stayed somewhat stable in even heavy waves due to its size. Our ship being very small, in comparison, rolled and tossed with the waves. Therefore, men on our ship would have to run up and down the deck, holding onto the rope, to keep the line tight and keep the line from dipping into the water. A pulley was placed on the heavy line at the Carrier end, and the 'mailbag' was placed on the pulley. As the heavy line was kept taught, the pulley was pulled over to our ship, until the mailbag was safely on our ship. On this particular day the sea was so rough that the mailbag was dunked in the water. The mail was not lost, but it sure got water-soaked.

It was a joyful day, for not only had I received a letter from my family at home, but also one from my girlfriend. Immediately, I ran to the electronics shack, where I worked, to dry out the letters. The letter from home was good news! The letter from my girl friend was earthshaking. I was devastated. There was no one on the ship with whom I could talk about something so personal and hurtful. How could I be so misunderstood? My girlfriend said that since I had not shown her any affection, she could not picture being married to me, so it would be better to end our relationship now, rather then let it presumably go on till I was able to go home on leave. Anyway, she said that she had met a real nice young man, who was a fireman, and they were going steady. To say that I was crushed or hurt would be a gross understatement. First, I thought of writing my feelings down, or at least trying to explain myself to her in a letter. I had then and still have today, such respect for women. I had decided as a young man that I would never touch a woman until and if I should marry. My girlfriend had apparently misread my actions.

After a long evening of heartache and loneliness, I finally decided to do nothing. I asked The Good Lord to help me through this period, to help me do the right thing. I realized that this must be the Lord's will for her and I should not attempt to hurt or confuse her with my input. The next day, I wrote her a short letter of encouragement. I told her basically that I understood and wished her the best in life.

The Lord taught me a great lesson during that lonely time out at sea, He taught me that He is The Only One I could turn to with my hurts, needs and desires. The day I wrote my girlfriend a letter, I also told The Good Lord that it was my feeling that I should marry, but only if it was His will for my life. In my heart I really wanted the responsibility of taking care of a wife and providing for a family. So, on that day, I started praying a simple prayer, which I'm sure The Lord inspired me to pray. Every day for almost two years, until I met my Elayne, I prayed this prayer; "Lord Jesus, please send me, someone who needs me, like I need her. Let us each be the person with whom we could happily share the rest of our lives together." I never went looking. Neither did I date, except for one double date with a friend, as far as I can remember. The personal loving relationship of a lifelong commitment with another person was really attractive to me. I really wanted the job of looking out for and protecting another person in the holy state of marriage.

When I was discharged from the Navy at age twenty, I returned to Davenport, Iowa, where I grew up as a young boy. I stayed with my parents and obtained full time employment at Industrial Engineering Company, in the repair of electric motors. In the evenings I would go roller-skating, or ice skating, for both fun and exercise. Usually, I would go by myself, but sometimes a male friend would come along.

One evening, in the month of November, during the year I turned age twenty-one, I went rollerskating by myself, as I had done many times before. I would skate on the 'all skates,' while sitting down on the sidelines during the couple skates. Skating lasted from 7:30 p.m. until about 10:00 p.m. Usually, I was the last one on the floor. That particular night, the manager had to come out on the floor to tell me to get going as it was after 10:00 p.m. As I was taking my skates off, I noticed that other people were just putting their skates on. When I asked the manager what was happening, he told me that there was a private skating party that would last until midnight. After much pleading, he finally agreed to let me stay, but he said that I had to stay out of their way, and only skate on the all-skates. This was no problem for me as this was what I did anyway. At about 11:00 p.m., there was a couple's skate, and in addition, it was a "ladies choice." I sat all by myself, clear back at the rear of the skating rink to wait for the couples skate to end. In the middle of the ceiling, there was a multi-faced mirror turning around, with little light rays dancing on the walls as it turned. Out of the crowd of skaters emerged this little young lady, dressed in a tan skirt suit. She headed for me, pointing her finger at me as she stopped in front of where I was seated. I raised my shoulders, as if to question her, when she then nodded, as if

97

to say yes, while she motioned with her hand, that I should get up to skate with her. Let me tell you, she looked like ten million dollars. We skated the ladies-choice skate and every couple skate the remainder of the evening. The manager had asked me to stay out of their way, which I did, but this young lady initiated the action, and I really liked her. All I learned about her that night, was that her name was Elayne Werthmann. Also, I learned that the skating party was organized by a church youth group. During the following week, I called every Werthmann listed in the phone book, until finally, I found her. In fact, I found out later, that some of the 'Werthmanns' called Mabel Werthmann, Elayne's mother, to see 'if that young man had found Elayne yet.' Yes, I found her and I saw a lot of her during the remainder of November, and the month of December. I really liked her. Sweet, innocent, and cute; someone whom I could really enjoy taking care of. Sometime later, I learned that Elayne had not been out on a date for two years, as she had given up on men. She said she couldn't find a man she could trust! Her younger brother, Roger, had just been discharged from the Army, and he taunted her that she was going to be an 'old maid.' The taunting worked, because she did go roller-skating with him to the church youth gathering, which is when we met. Elayne said to me later, that she asked me to skate to see if I was really that shy, or just conceited.

When out to dinner one evening with Elayne, nearing Christmas time, Elayne mentioned to me that a previous boyfriend of hers was coming home for Christmas leave. He wanted to see her. In fact, she said he wanted to marry her, and asked me what I thought about it. First of all, it really hurt me inside, but immediately, I turned to The Lord for help. Inside, I said, 'If this is what The Lord had planned for her, I can't stand in the way." So, I said, that since she brought it up, it was something she had to resolve in her own mind, or it wouldn't be fair to her. She asked, 'What about you?' and I said that she would have to make a free decision, and then we would have to go on from there. I remember how it hurt! Here, I put my heart on the table, only to have it almost torn in two. As I remember, Christmas came and went. Sometime near the end of January, the next month, I called her to ask her if we could see each other. She did agree to see me, but she did not sound joyful or encouraging on the phone. I remember driving out to her farm home, where she lived with her parents, and how confused I was. 'Why am I going through this added hurt?' I thought. She was only seeing me so that she could let me down easily, I was sure. Well, we did go out to dinner, and eventually, I asked her if she had seen the young man at Christmas time. She simply said, "Yes." Then I asked her, reluctantly of course, what had happened. She told me that he did come out to the farm to pick her up and as they were driving into town, she knew it was wrong, so she told him to take her back home, so he did. I could hardly believe what I was hearing! I said, "You mean you are not going to see him again?" Again, she said, "Yes." Naturally, I asked, "What about us?" and she answered, "That's up to you." Well, as you can imagine, I was ecstatic. Elayne, and her well being meant so much to me. In fact, The Good Lord had taught me a valuable lesson in this early relationship with Elayne. He taught me that if I was willing to give something up, I could have it. The Lord wants to be first in our lives. It's the only way it can work. If we do not have Him first, then someone else, or something else, is first, and we are doomed for failure. I was willing to give Elayne up, even though I loved her so deeply, and The Good Lord saw fit to bless our relationship. Believe me, I saw a lot of Elayne after that evening. On a Tuesday evening in February, I asked to see her. When she left home, her mother told her that she was sure that 'Larry was going to ask you to marry him.' Mabel, Elayne's mother, said she was sure because I was acting out of character, as on Tuesday evenings I was usually at my Naval Reserve meeting. It would have to be something special to miss one of my mandatory reserve meetings. Mabel was right! When Elayne got home that evening, she was able to tell her mother that once again, mother's intuition won out. We decided on a marriage date, October 4, 1952. On theTuesday evening I asked Elayne to marry me, I drove her to the church where she attended, and where we would be married, and parked in front. It was a solemn question, with sincerity of purpose, so I felt the best place to ask her would be in front of the very church in which we would exchange vows—if she said 'Yes.' Again, I was scared to death, but at this writing, a few months before our 48th wedding anniversary, I can tell you that The Good Lord has honored our commitment to Him, and to each other. Yes, we do love each other, but as well, we like each other. Elayne is my best human-friend. I do so enjoy being with her. I still enjoy taking care of her, just watching her grow in stature and love of The Lord. The greatest protection Elayne has from me not hurting her, is that The Lord Jesus is first in my life. The greatest protection I have in Elayne not hurting me, is that Elayne has The Lord first in her life. We were married at age twenty-two for me, and just turned twenty-three, for Elayne. We are more in love now than when we first started on our journey. Most find it hard to believe, but we have never had a fight. Not because we are good, but because The Good Lord is so good. We have included Him in our lives, allowing His Grace to help us in our relationship. For a marriage to work, it takes three; The husband, the wife, and The Lord. At the time of this writing, Elayne, and I, have been blessed with ten children; four sons and six daughters; twenty-seven grandchildren, and five great-grandchild. How could two people be more blessed than this?

The Lord is so Good! He gives each of us the desires of our heart; that is, if we delight in Him, and in His Word, and have a personal relationship with His Son, Jesus. I can still recall the night on board ship when I got the letter from my girlfriend. How lonely and hurt I felt. The Lord knew best! He had a plan for Elayne and me. He had to condition each of us until the timing was right to meet. I know He arranged our meeting, just as He directs our footsteps today. Also, He is even concerned about every detail. Just to illustrate this fact, let me tell about a healing that took place which I am sure He, again, arranged. Some years ago, as I was coming out of church, well after service, as I was an usher and had to straighten out the materials in the pews, I noticed a woman in the vestibule of the church. She was staring at me. As I approached Elayne, who was standing near her waiting for me, the woman called me by name, and said, "You don't remember me, do you?" Surely, it was The Lord who helped me recognize her. I introduced Elayne to the girl, now a married woman, who had written me the letter when I was in the Navy, some forty-five years earlier. She was in town for her mother's funeral. We had a good visit. I wished her the best, and she knows in her heart that there is forgiveness in my heart for any hurt she may have caused me. She looked tremendously relieved that we had this chance to meet to experience this healing. Isn't The Lord Good? Isn't He a Great Father! He doesn't always give us what we ask for, but He always gives us what we need, because He knows best. He teaches us to ask according to His plan for our lives so that joy will abound. He gives each of His children the desires of his or her heart!

On the subject of marriage, there is one verse in scripture which I think of often. The verse is in Ecclesiastes, Chapter 4:12. It is written: "Where a lone man can be overcome, two together can resist. A triple-ply cord is not easily broken." When a husband and wife include The Lord in their marriage, a triple-ply cord is formed, and the 'Power and Grace' of The Good Lord holds the marriage together.

19

EYES TO SEE

"Humble yourselves therefore under the mighty hand of God, that He may exalt you in due time. Casting all your care upon Him: for He careth for you."
(1Peter 5:6-7)

Our first two children, Chris, our firstborn son, and Maria, our firstborn daughter, were born with eye problems. Chris had one of his eyes with underdeveloped rods and cones at the back of the eye, which allowed poor vision in that eye. Due to the poor vision, this eye turned inward rather than pointing straight forward. Maria's eyes would wander so that when looking forward, the eye not focusing on some object, would roam up or down or to the right or left. Either eye could roam depending upon which eye she was using to focus. Both children were very beautiful in appearance, but in each case, the eye problem was a definite distraction. Children at school could be very cruel. Many times they came home from school saddened by the comments of other insensitive school children. For Elayne, my wife, and I, this caused much concern. Our hearts went out to them as they faced an unloving, uncaring world, in which any handicap, no matter how slight, is considered inferior.

Every day, following the birth of both Chris and Maria, I would go to The Good Lord in prayer. My prayer was a simple request; "Lord, please let Chris's and Maria's eyes straighten out so that they will not be handicapped by this defect through life!" I felt in my heart that The Good Lord did not cause this problem, but rather, did allow it for His reasons. Whether or not they would be healed physically, I would trust The Lord, for there was no One else Whom we could turn to for help. The doctors did all they could. We followed every suggestion and treatment recommended by the doctors we visited. When Chris was three or four years old, we put a black patch over his eye with the normal vision to force him to use the weakened eye, in hope that it would strengthen the vision. This was done at the recommendation of an eye specialist. The patch was on every day for over a year without any improvement.

For years, I continued to pray every day, seeking a healing from the Lord. Finally, within a few months period of time, we received a positive direction to proceed for both Chris and Maria. A doctor in Davenport, Iowa, suggested a surgical procedure for Chris. On the weakened eye, a portion of the longer horizontal muscle was removed and stitched into the shorter horizontal muscle. This evened the two muscles out in length. Almost miraculously, Chris' eye was straightened out by surgery. His vision in the weakened eye did improve somewhat, but also, the taunting from other children completely stopped.

The same doctor, who performed the surgery on Chris, referred us to an eye specialist at The University Of Iowa Hospital, in Iowa City, Iowa. A consultation appointment was set with this doctor at his Iowa City hospital office. The doctor, by the name of Doctor Burian, was on sabbatical from his homeland, Poland. He was world renowned for his eye research. At the University of Iowa Hospital, he was doing research and teaching in the Eye Section of the hospital. Our local physician wrote him regarding Maria's condition. After reviewing the medical records forwarded to him, Dr. Burian contacted us by mail, suggesting a preliminary meeting to look at Maria's eyes. After several visits, over a period of three weeks, Dr. Burian suggested surgery, even though as he said, the procedure to be used was very unusual. Others told us in the Eye Department at the hospital, that there was probably no other physician in the country who would have even attempted surgery in such a case, as the possibility of success was very slim. Dr. Burian charged us only $200 for his entire services. A regular hospital bill would have been between $4,000 to $5,000. This was really a blessing, since at the time, we did not have health insurance, so we couldn't have easily handled a large medical expense.

The date for the surgery on the first of Maria's eyes was scheduled. Since Elayne was expecting our daughter Felicia at the time, and needed to care for our other six children at home, she could not come with us to Iowa City for the scheduled surgery. When Maria and I arrived on the day before the surgery, Maria's head was placed in a special machine, and the doctor put a large pair of eyeglasses on Maria's eyes. She was asked to track with her eyes, a spot on a projector screen, as it rotated in a clockwise direction. One eye would track the spot, while the other eye would wander randomly. When the spot on the screen would rotate in the opposite direction, Maria's other eye would track the spot, while the eye not tracking the spot, would wander at random. With Dr. Burian, there were eight student doctors in the room, when these tests were done. Dr. Burian asked each of the student doctors for their opinion as to which eye muscles they would recommend for surgery, and in addition, he asked for a length, in millimeters that they would suggest taking from the long muscle, to put into the shorter muscle. Each student gave a different muscle configuration and length as a rec-ommendation. After long discussions, with explicit reasons for each one's recommendation, Dr Burian interrupted the conversation very abruptly. "No! No! No!" he said. "Dis is vut ve vill do!" he said, speaking with his foreign accent. Dr. Burian's decision was totally different from any of the other doctors. So he gave a detailed analysis as to why he had come to his conclusions. The student doctors were amazed at his findings, but of course, since they did not have his expe-rience, they agreed with him. They also seemed amazed, as they understood what he was telling them, and why he had come to these conclusions.

Surgery was scheduled for the following day, so I stayed over night with Maria at the hospital. The staff put a bed in Maria's room so I could be near her. On the day of the sur-gery, Dr. Burian hit me with an unexpected decision to make. Dr. Burian said that he really liked Maria, but he feared that if he only did one eye, we might have trouble getting her back for the second eye surgery. Her full cooperation would be needed for the surgery. He wanted to do the surgery on both eyes at the same time. There was no guarantee that the surgery would be successful. I didn't know what to do! I called Elayne for her input. While talking to Elayne over the phone, she reminded me that Dr. Burian was the only physician who was even willing to look at her, much less try to do anything to help her, so maybe we should accept his recommendation. I asked The good Lord for help with this most difficult decision. "Both eyes at one time!" I thought. What if the operation was not successful? Would she be in even worse condition? Could it negatively affect her vision permanently? As I prayed and reflected, it came to mind that I had been praying for almost ten years for a healing. Maybe, this was The Lord's answer! I would have to trust 'The Mighty Hand Of God!'

On that day, a special surgical procedure was performed on both eyes. Both horizontal and vertical muscles were involved in the surgery. This was a very unusual procedure, never performed it the hospital before. Again, since Maria was very emotional about the whole situation, I stayed over night with her at the hospital. On the day after the surgery, the doctor took the bandages off that were covering her eyes. Immediately, I saw the stitches, some bleeding, and dark discoloration. I remember thinking to myself, "What have I allowed them to do?" Dr. Burian said that he was satisfied with the surgery, but he would have to see how it comes along. He scheduled a follow-up visit after a two-week healing period. Maria and I rode home on the sixty mile trip to Davenport. Along the way, I talked to The Lord, asking Him to help Maria with the trauma, and to give us peace about what had just happened. Surprisingly, the eye muscles healed very quickly. We saw some improvement in the positioning of Maria's eyes. When we returned for the follow-up visit, Maria was back to her cheerful self and very friendly with Dr. Burian. Again, Dr. Burian put Maria in the special machine. When the spot was rotated clockwise, both of Maria's eyes tracked the spot. When the spot was rotated in a counter-clockwise direction, both of Maria's eyes tracked the spot. What a blessing! Dr. Burian was overjoyed! He told us that in all his experience, he would only see such a condition once every five years or so. Naturally, none of the student doctors at the hospital had ever seen such a case. For a full year, we went to the University of Iowa Hospital for follow-up checks. On one such appointment, Dr, Burian said he was so pleased with the results that we did not have to come up to Iowa City anymore. Also, he wanted to say 'Goodbye,' since he was returning to his home in Poland because his research work was done.

Maria's eyes are fine, even to this day in 2001, at the age of forty-seven. She needs glasses in order to read, but her vision, with glasses, is excellent. A miracle has happened! It took ten years of prayer for The Lord to arrange schedules so that Dr. Burian could come to The University Of Iowa Hospital, to take care of Maria. We cast our cares on Him, for He cares for us! Dr. Burian was probably the only physician in the country, if not the world, who could have done this surgery. The Good Lord tells us to 'Pray, without ceasing.' He tells us to humble ourselves under 'His Mighty Hand.' Elayne and I, thank the Lord for answer to our prayers in this request, as He has with so many requests during our lives. I'm sure as time goes on, there will be other times when we will need His help, and we trust in His Faithfulness; for He cares for us.

20

GUARDIAN ANGEL

"The Angel of The Lord encamps around those who fear Him and delivers them."

(Psalms 34:8)

In March of 1950, I was stationed on base at the Naval Shipyard in Charleston, South Carolina, awaiting my discharge from the Navy. My regular enlistment time had come up for renewal and I had decided not to re-enlist. The ship I was serving on prior to being put on shore at Charleston was going over to the Tokyo, Japan area, and there was no provision to discharge naval personnel in Japan, so they had to put me on shore at the Charleston Naval Base. Also, since my time was actually up when I would be in the Japan area, they decided it was easier to put me on shore, rather than take me to Japan and try to figure out a way to get me back to the United States to be discharged. While waiting for discharge time, I stayed in a somewhat deserted barracks in Charleston. Also, since they were rather upset with me for not re-enlisting, they gave me duty referred to in the Navy as 'dirty duty,' which you can imagine was less than favorable clean-up details. This duty lasted about a month.

The ship I was serving on was a destroyer-mine-sweeper, named the U.S.S. Hambleton-DMS-20. This type of ship would be one of the first ships to go into a water area where it was suspected that mines were present. The enemy mines would be cleared out so that the regular ships could enter without encounter. A couple of years after my eventual discharge, I heard from another sailor, while on a two week naval reserve cruise, that the U.S.S. Hambleton had hit an enemy mine while on duty in Tokyo Bay while mine-sweeping, and was sunk. The man told me that according to the story he heard, there were no survivors. Prior to this writing I contacted The Directory OF American Fighting Ships Historical Center in Washington, D.C. The department head, with whom I talked, said that as far as records went into 1996, he could not give me an answer for certain of the ship's outcome. The record was unclear in that notes on its disposition indicated possible use as a target ship, or scrapping, after damage. When I asked him about the possibility of it being sunk as reported to while on a Naval Reserve cruise, he indicated that it was possible, as records were not accurate in all cases. If indeed, it was sunk, as I heard, The Lord surely protected me, by allowing me to be put ashore, or I too would have been lost with the rest of my fellow sailors, in a sunken ship.

After about two weeks of duty at the Charleston naval Base, I was called into the Master At Arms office. This man was in command of the barracks in which I was staying. He asked me if I had any idea what had happened in the barracks the evening before. Basically, I told him that I had finished my work assignment, went to the mess hall for supper, wrote some letters, and then turned in to bed at about 9:00 p.m. He asked me again if I was aware of any commotion in the barracks during the night, and I assured him I was not aware of anything unusual. There were eight sailors on the second floor of a large barracks, where I slept. We spread out, so that each of us had a bunk quite separate from one another. During World War II, this barracks housed over two hundred men. The base was a training base during the war; so many recruits were there. When I was awaiting my discharge, there was no training going on. The barracks was used for 'transients,' as we were called, while we were awaiting final discharge papers.

The Master At Arms then proceeded to unfold for me a story that was both scary and uplifting. Scary, because it involved me and the unusual danger I was in, without knowing. It was uplifting because I could see how The Good Lord, once again, had protected me; stationing His Guardian Angel over me to protect me in time of danger. The officer told me that they had a prisoner escape the prior evening. The prisoner was a former Philippine cook, who had become emotionally disturbed, while out to sea, and had to be locked up in 'solitary' in the base prison. He had apparently caused physical injury to other naval personnel, so he was put ashore, under guard, until they could determine where he could get the help he needed. During the previous night, the crazed man had broken out of prison. He had somehow obtained a butcher knife, and was being chased around the base by military guards. At about 3:00 a.m., he entered the building in which I was sleeping. He made his way to the second floor with the guards in pursuit. At the entrance to the large room, in which the other sailors and I were sleeping, the guards stopped, as they were afraid they would alarm him too greatly. The guards watched, as he ran to the bunk where I was sleeping. I slept on the bottom of a double bunk. With the knife held in hand, over my chest, he leaned down to apparently listen to my breathing. In the dark it was difficult for the guards to see exactly what he was doing. They were about to turn on all the lights, when for some reason; the man withdrew the knife from over my chest, and moved quietly to the doorway at the entrance. As he started to go down the stairway, the guards were able to tackle him. Finally, they subdued him as they reached the ground floor. The man was returned to maximum security.

Naturally, when The Master At Arms told me the story, I was surprised and very thankful. At that time in my life, when this story unfolded, I was a very light sleeper. For some reason, that night I did not move, so I am still here to write about it. Maybe, an Angel Of The Lord stopped me from breathing for a bit, or maybe the same Angel caused the man to become confused. Whatever happened, I know The Good Lord was involved. My spirit tells me that an Angel Of The Lord was involved also; for The Lord assures us in His Word, that if we fear The Lord, and love Him, His angels will protect us, no matter what. In His Word, He has written, "An Angel Of The Lord encamps around those who fear Him, and delivers them." First, we must fear The Lord, because He must punish evil, as a just God. In Proverbs, 9:2, it is written, "The beginning of wisdom, is fear of The Lord; and knowledge of The Holy One is understanding." The fear of the Lord grows to reverence, then to understanding, and finally, to honor, where The Good Lord becomes 'Our Father.' Eventually, after forming a true personal relationship with Jesus, we can call Our Father,"ABBA." In the verse at the front of this writing, the word "encamp" is used. The word means; 'to set up a tent and prepare for battle.' The Lord's 'Guardian Angels are always moving about wherever The Lord's people go, to set up camp. They await any possible enemy attack, to deliver The Lord's people. I know on that day, some sixty-one years ago, a young sailor was delivered from the enemy and I am so thankful to You, Lord, for Your undeserved Love and Grace.

21

SING JOYFULLY UNTO THE LORD

"Sing to The Lord a new song, for He has done won-drous deeds… Sing praise to The Lord, all you lands; break into songs; sing Praise."
(Psalms 98:1 & 4)

In 1963, I joined the barbershop chorus in Davenport, Iowa at the encouragement of our neighbor, Cecil. Almost immediately, I was a member of a quartet called, "The Opening Knights." After some years, the quartet broke up. A second was formed, called "The Wacky Keys." This quartet was together for about a year and a half. Soon after, another quartet was formed, called "The Chord Hawks." This quartet, off and on, was together for about 3 years. In "The Opening Knights," I sang baritone first, then bass. In "The Wacky Keys," I sang lead. In "The Chord Hawks," I sang lead. Then, in 1969, a new quartet was formed, called "The Four Bits Of Fun." In "The Four Bits Of Fun" quartet, I sang tenor. This quartet was together for about eleven years. The quartet sang for entertainment at office parties and con-ventions in seven different states. Being a comedy quartet, we were in demand throughout the region. We appeared in Barbershop Shows, as well as at many meetings as the main entertainment. The quartet charged a fee, so we were able to obtain uniforms and props used in comedy songs. Often times, we would take the wives out to dinner with the proceeds. For over eleven years, "The Four Bits Of Fun" entertained audiences all over the Midwest, with good clean comedy, which was always well received.

Our baritone, who was extremely talented, did all the musical arrangements. In all, there were about seventy-five songs we could perform, so material was not a problem for us. After about ten years into the quartet relationship, someone gave us a song, which was very suggestive; it was definitely not in good taste. Our baritone arranged the song to barbershop style, and we learned to perform the song. About this same time, I had purchased my very own Bible, and The Good Lord had given me a strong desire to read The Word. Also, The Holy Spirit was teaching me the truth of scripture. Since the quartet was very important to me, I did not have the courage to take a stand about us learning this song. We learned the song, and we performed it in public. Soon, wherever we went, people requested to hear the song. Every time we performed the song, I would come under strong conviction, it would take several days for me to crawl out of the hole I would fall into. Finally, even though I knew in my heart, it would cause dissension; I knew I would have to take a stand. At one quartet rehearsal, at the home of our bass, I stopped the singing as we practiced that particular song. I told the quartet members that I was not being fair with them by withholding my feelings. I shared with them how the song affected me when we performed the song, and that I would prefer not to sing the song anymore. We had some seventy-four other songs, which were good clean entertainment. Predictably, one of the quartet members 'blew up.' He lashed out at me for taking such a stand. One of the other quartet members stood up for my position, only making it worse. Immediately, I knew we were in big trouble. After a minute of silence, the one who was really hot stormed out of the room, onto the porch. After about five minutes, he came back into the room, gathered up his musical materials and left. I knew it was over! We had five musical engagements, which we had committed to do, which we honored. Our last performance was as the 'Headliner Quartet ' on the Central States District Comedy Show, in Davenport, Iowa. The performance was the best we had ever done. It was over! For eleven years, I had sung tenor in this quartet. There was a terrible void, even though, in my heart I knew I had done the right thing.

About a year later, as my wife and I, were driving back from Chicago, following a family reunion at my brother's home, Elayne asked me a question 'from out of the blue.' She asked me, "What are you going to do about your singing?" Almost without thinking, I blurted out, "I think I'm going to get into a gospel quartet, and I don't even know what that means!" Elayne must have recognized that there was a change in me after the break-up of our quartet.

A short time after Elayne asked me this question, I had a most unusual dream. In the dream, I was entering a large room that had many doors into the room. There was a low-hanging light positioned above a large, round, oak-grained table. While I was admiring the heavy grain in the top of the table, two men came up to the table from the left, while one man came from the right. Due to dark background, I could not see the faces of the three men. I could only make out their silhouettes. While I was straining to see, one of the men asked, "Larry, would you like to sing a song?" "Boy, would I!" was my immediate reply. One of the men blew his pitch pipe to tell us the key, and away we went. I was singing tenor. It was the most beautiful harmony I had ever heard. The song was brand new to me. I had never heard it before, so I couldn't believe that I was singing it. While I was singing the song, with great joy in my heart, I said to myself, "Larry, you've got to remember this song when you wake up!" In my spirit, I knew that I was sleeping. Soon, I woke up. From the dresser, I grabbed a pencil and piece of paper, and ran into the small bathroom. Elayne came running into the bathroom to see if I was sick or needed help. After assuring her I was OK, I proceeded to make musical lines, writing down words and musical notes, in hopes of retaining the melody. Since I have had no formal musical training, I had to do the best I could. The song was a gospel song, with such powerful words, that I was greatly moved. While singing the song to myself the next morning, I had a certain joy in my heart. Upon entering the Bettendorf, Iowa, Post Office, I was met by a former quartet member, named Dick, who asked me why I had such an apparent glow on my face. Dick, who is now deceased, was one of the most talented musicians I have ever met. I told him that I had heard a song in a dream. Of course, out of curiosity, he wanted to hear the song. As I sang what I could remember of the song, Dick lit up like a Christmas tree. Then Dick said, "Larry, don't lie to me! Where did you get that song? It's a perfect arrangement. It has verses, bridges, introduction, and it even has a closing that is most unusual." Even though I persisted with my story, I do not believe he ever felt that I told him the truth. I know, in my heart, I heard the song in a dream; but, since he said it was a perfect arrangement, I also knew in my heart, it came from The Lord.

As time passed by, I was only able to retain two of the verses of the song I heard in the dream. To this day, no one has been able to arrange this song to barbershop style. This is as it is supposed to be, I guess; because the song is apparently a gift from The Lord. In my spirit, I heard the joy and splendor of the singing that will be sung in the presence of The Good Lord. Two of the verses I did retain are as follows;

May The SON shine over on this lowly life,
May The SON shine over on this world of strife.
May The SON Shine over on the things you do,
May The SON Shine over on you.

Though He came and no one cared to know His Name!
Yes, He came to free us from this world of shame.
Came to show us how to do the Father's will,
And He carried His cross to the hill.

I have never written a song. I am not able to read music, but I have been gifted to sing whatever part is missing in a vocal quartet. In the quartet, singing the song above, I sang tenor, higher than I am able to actually sing. Please trust me, the sound I heard, was simply indescribable.

Following this dream, I knew I wanted to sing in a gospel quartet, singing spiritual songs in barbershop style. So, I sent a letter to the other three members of "The Four Bits Of Fun" quartet, telling them of my desire. I asked each of them to contact me if they were interested in this type of quartet. The member, who was so disgruntled, was the only one who responded. I gave the former quartet members a period of time to respond to me. On the last day, of this time period, this member came over to our home to tell me that he was not interested in being a member of such a gospel quartet, but, if I was able to put in together, he would be interested in coaching the gospel quartet.

Several weeks later, on an early morning, I was coming out of a restaurant, following a breakfast appointment. A former barber shopper, named Tom Kerkhoven, met me on the way out. Tom asked me to join him over a cup of coffee. During our meeting, Tom asked me how the quartet was coming along. I, of course, told him how "The Four Bits Of Fun" quartet had broken up. When he asked me what I was going to do, I told him that I would like to be in a gospel quartet. He said, if I was able to get something going, I could count him in. I have always liked Tom, so it was a great encouragement that he was interested. Tom sings bass, beautifully. A few months later, Elayne and I, were at an all-night prayer vigil at St. Paul's Church, in Davenport, Iowa. During a break in the service, I was in the church basement, having a cup of tea. At about 3:30 a.m., Jim Oliger, a former barber shopper, came down for coffee. Jim asked me about "The Four Bits Of Fun" quartet. As with Tom, I told him that the quartet had broken up. He asked me when it happened and what I had planned to do. When I mentioned the gospel quartet, he said he would be interested in this type of singing. Jim was a natural tenor. In my mind, I could see the quartet developing; Tom at bass, Jim at tenor, and I could sing lead. After a bit, we got together to discuss who could be a possible baritone. We finally came up with Dick Rode, who was in the Davenport "Chordbuster" chorus. Dick also had exceptional musical talent, so he would be a real asset to the quartet, in the musical arrangement of songs. Several weeks after we asked Dick if he was interested, he called to say it sounded like a real challenge, and count him in. So, "The Good News In Harmony" quartet was formed but after a few rehearsals, Dick said that he would not be able to continue as baritone, because the voice range was too tough. He suggested we look for another baritone. We reviewed every possible combination, to see if we could come up with any way that we could stay together with the same members. We really liked each other, and got along so well. The critical starting point was that realistically, Dick could only sing bass, as this was his true voice range, and singing baritone was causing him to strain his voice. Tom agreed to move from bass to tenor. Jim would move from tenor to lead, and I moved from lead to baritone. With this arrangement, the quartet flourished for sixteen years. We sang at hospitals, nursing homes, and for shut-ins. Old time gospel songs, like

"Just A Closer Walk With Thee," "How Great Thou Art," "In The Garden," etc. We would sing in patients' rooms at the area hospitals, witnessing many miracles before our eyes. The Good Lord blessed the quartet. Our commitment was honored; there was never a singing engagement missed due to any illness or voice problem.

About six years ago, in 1995, our bass singer, Dick Rode, began to experience voice problems. He finally decided to step aside in the quartet, rather than jeopardize the sound we made as a quartet. We thought at first that we were done, but our lead, Jim Oliger, thought of an ex-barber shopper, with whom he sang in a quartet some years ago. When Jim Oliger asked George Pitcher if he would like to sing with us, he was quick to say 'yes.' Jim stayed at the lead, I stayed at the baritone, Tom switched from tenor to bass, his natural range, and George came in to sing at tenor. This gave the quartet an entirely new sound. The sound created was just beautiful. It seemed that people did so enjoy our singing. The Lord has been able to minister His love to his people through our singing. It has been very gratifying. As of 1996, we had been together for eighteen years. In singing groups, of any kind, this is highly unusual. Even more unusual, is the fact that we sing without any musical accompaniment.

The Good Lord has continued to honor our commitment. People in nursing homes do not get much live entertainment. It is with much sadness that I must tell you of a great loss to our quartet in July of 1998. Our lead, Jim Oliger, contracted cancer late in 1997; his health deteriorated to such a point that we sang our last "singout" on February 13,1998. It was at The CrossTown Nursing Center, in Silvis, Illinois. After the sing-out, we took our wives out to supper. It was one of the best performances we have ever done. Then, on July 21, 1998, our lead, Jim Oliger, died. Jim is now with The Good Lord, singing harmony with others, in pure worship of The Lord. Oh, how I miss this man. He was full of joy. Jim was always humming, or singing, it seemed. When the quartet rehearsal was at our home, I could hear Jim coming up to the house, as he left his car to walk up the sidewalk. I'm sure I will get a chance to sing with him again, in pure worship of The Good Lord, without any human restrictions.

When I think back to 1963, and all the years I sang in secular quartets, for the world, it makes me so thankful for The Good Lord to allow me to sing, for Him, in such a quartet as 'The Good News In Harmony.' At the time I sang for the world, it was unthinkable for me to quit such a quartet as "The Four Bits Of Fun." When The Good Lord touched my heart, I took the risk of taking a stand for Him. It cost me the "Four Bits Of Fun" quartet but even though devastating, I was still at peace with my decision. The Good Lord honored my move by letting me have the privilege of singing in a gospel quartet for over eighteen years. I have been able to sing barbershop style, which I do so enjoy, while at the same time bring The Good News to His people. On top of this, I have had the joy of being with four other men whom I have grown to love as my own family. Who could ask for more? How good The Lord is! Singing in the gospel quartet has been a true joy; levels above my experience in singing for the world. For all these years, I have been able to sing with three other men; to "Sing To The Lord – A New Song! For He Has Done Wondrous Deeds."

At age seventy-one, in 2001, at the time of this writing, I do not know where I will go with my interest in singing. I do trust in The Lord! I anxiously await what He has in store for me next. This much I know: once, though only in a dream, I heard the sound that will be made on the 'other side'; and it is my hope that He will allow me to participate, in His presence, in pure harmony and song, for all eternity. For, my heart longs to honor Him by breaking into songs and singing praise.

22

ALL THINGS WORK
FOR GOOD

"And we know that all things work together for
the good of those who love Him; who are called
according to His purpose."
                                    (Romans 8:28)

W hile in my office, on a Friday afternoon, In July of
1992, I received a telephone call from our daughter-in-law, Sue, from St. Luke's Hospital in Davenport, Iowa.
Sue told me that her husband, our son Peter, was in the emergency room, as he had been injured in a very serious fall at
work. All the way home I prayed for Peter and the situation.
I pleaded the Blood of Jesus as protection for him. I asked
The Lord for His intervention. After picking up Elayne at
home, we both prayed for Peter on the way to the hospital.

When we came into the emergency room, Sue met us
and told us that Peter, a carpenter, had fallen eighteen feet
from a scaffold to a marble floor below and landed on his
head. The doctors had informed Sue that both of Peter's
wrists were broken, some teeth were broken, and his forehead was shattered. His vital signs were okay, but appeared

that there was a tear in the main aorta to his heart. The doctors were performing a chest X-Ray at the time we were first talking to Sue. Sue left us almost as soon as we got there, to go back into the emergency room. Because of the hectic pace in the emergency room, they would not let us, as parents, go in. Within a few minutes Sue came back to the waiting room. We could not at first communicate with her as she was sobbing uncontrollably. A chaplain, who was at the hospital as an intern, from Dubuque, Iowa, came into the emergency room at this same time. The chaplain, Gaylor Nelson, was able to calm Sue down. Sue then relayed to us, through tears, that Peter had a seizure while on the operating table in the operating room. She had seen his eyes rolled back into his head. Still, we kept praying. Many thoughts raced through my mind. Peter is such a good person. He is always smiling. He is always helping others. Peter is so loved by everyone. He is a craftsman in his work; so well respected by all the workers in every building trade, as well as the homeowners whose homes he built with such care and quality. When I saw that the chaplain had calmed Sue, I left the emergency room waiting room to go out into the hallway, to talk to The Lord. "Give us strength Lord to handle whatever happens!" In my heart I felt it was an enemy attack. The Lord had not caused this to happen; it was an enemy attack, only allowed by The Lord. For His purpose. As I was walking and praying, in the hallway, the chaplain came running up to me from behind. He laid his hand on my shoulder, to comfort me. I learned later that he was only at the hospital for the summer, as he was interning as a Presbyterian minister, and this was part of his training. Gaylor was a kind man and I liked him. As his hand was on my shoulder, he asked me a question, more or less to get me talking. In order to minister to my immediate needs, he was trying to find out where I was feeling. I believe he asked me something like; "Well, what do you make of all this?" I replied, "I know this! The enemy had planned to kill

Peter, but Peter is still alive. Even if The Good Lord would allow Peter to be with Him, I will still trust Him; for, 'I know that all things work together for good to those who love The Lord, who are called according to His purpose.' Good will come from this! I don't know how, but good will come from this!" Gaylor stood there staring at me, almost white. Finally, he said; "I can only add a four letter word to that! Amen! Where did you get such faith?" I answered, "Gaylor, you're a good man, and I like you. You belong in this work. You're doing a good job. But, you can't help me. My wife, you met her; she is a most wonderful person; but, she can't help me. There is only One Person Who can help me in this situation, and that's Jesus; I came out here in the hall to talk to Him about what is going on in there (the emergency room)." At this point we were back at the emergency room. A doctor and a nurse were going into the waiting room, so we went to join the other family members. By this time, Peter's brothers and sisters had arrived at the hospital, and they were also in the waiting room.

The doctor's name was Dr. Joe Lohmuller. Coincidentally, he had just finished surgery, when Peter was rushed into the emergency. When Sue was asked if this particular doctor could check Peter out, she of course, agreed. They did not have a regular doctor at the time, and Peter needed immediate attention. The Good Lord is ahead in everything. Dr. Lohmuller was one of the top physicians and surgeons in the area. He had recently moved there from Rochester, Minnesota, where he had interned as a surgeon in the Trauma-Unit of the renowned Mayo Clinic. His training was in emergency care where surgery would be needed, due to accidents. Any physician not so trained, could have immediately requested surgery on the visible wounds. But, Dr. Lohmuller went to the vital signs first. He went on to explain to us that, at first, he found the possibility of a tear in the main aorta to the heart. Rather than operate, he requested a chest X-Ray. This showed that the tear was possibly on the inside of the aorta. Then he did an internal examination of the inside of the main aorta, using a small scope. This proved to him that it was only a severe bruise to the aorta, and no surgery would be needed. Another doctor, might have gone a different direction, using normal and acceptable procedures, and Peter would not be with us today. I believe, in my heart, that The Good Lord healed the damage to Peter's heart, and let the doctor find it. He told us that Peter's condition was serious; but, he would do all he could to help him. We all kept praying.

It was a couple of days before we got to see Peter. If I hadn't known this was our son, I would not have recognized him when I came into the intensive care room. His upper body was bruised, his eyes were deeply sunk into his forehead, while his forehead protruded forward, very swollen. I remember my first thoughts when I saw Peter—"This must be how Jesus looked when they beat His face, scourged Him, and finally crucified Him. In Isaiah 52:14-15, and in chapter 53:2-8, it is written:

"Even as many were amazed at Him – so marred was His look, beyond that of man, and His appearance beyond that of mortals.....There was in Him no stately bearing to make us look at Him. He was spurned and avoided by man, a man of suffering, accustomed to infirmity. One of those from whom men hide their faces, spurned, and yet we held in no esteem. Yet, it was our infirmities that He bore; our sufferings that He endured. While we thought of Him as stricken, as one smitten by God, and afflicted. But, He was pierced for our offenses; crushed for our sins. Upon Him was the chastisement that makes us whole; by His stripes, we were healed. We had all gone astray like sheep; each following his own way. But The Lord laid upon Him the guilt of us all. Though He was harshly treated, He submitted and opened not His Mouth. Oppressed and condemned, He was taken away, and who would have thought any more of His destiny? When He was cut off from the land of the living, and smitten for the sin of His people."

Jesus was a carpenter. Peter was a carpenter. Peter, at the time of his accident, was age thirty-six. I have often wondered what it would have been like to be present at the crucifixion of Jesus. The Lord let me see this by looking at Peter. As I looked at Peter, in bed in the intensive care unit, my heart pounded. Still, I had to trust The Lord, to be with Peter to see him through this enemy attack. Later that same day, Sue asked me to accompany her as she and her sister were going in to see him. While holding hands, we touched Peter, and I anointed him on the forehead, making the sign of the cross, while praying; "Peter, we anoint you in The Name Of The Father, and of The Son, and of The Holy Spirit; and we claim healing, in the Name Of Jesus, of Nazareth!"

Sue stayed with Peter the entire time he was in the hospital. She either slept in a chair in his room, or slept in a chair in the general hospital waiting room. The doctors could not operate on Peter's forehead to repair the damage, as his forehead was shattered into tiny bone fragments. He had to lie on his back for thirteen days, because if he raised up over about a thirty degree angle, his brain fluid would come out his nose. Miracle of miracles; Peter is still with us.

Finally, the medical equipment was disconnected from Peter. He could then tell us what actually happened. He was working, by himself, in a new home that was under construction. Peter was finishing up the trim in the atrium above the entrance archway. He had a stepladder positioned on top of a scaffold, in order to reach the trim work at the highest point, which was about twenty feet up in the air. With his carpenter apron on, filled with all his many tools, Peter was holding a trim board in place with one hand, while holding the air gun in the other hand, to shoot the trim nails in place, and fasten the board. As he pressed against the board, the ladder tipped backward, causing Peter to fall, headfirst, to the floor below. Peter said that as he was falling, he said to himself, "Peter, you better stay awake on this one!" He doesn't think that he was knocked out. On the way down, he hit his shoulder on the ladder, finally, breaking his fall with both outstretched arms which is how he broke both wrists. When his arms gave way, under the weight of his body, he hit his head on the marble floor. Peter said he immediately got to his feet, knowing he was in deep trouble. There was no telephone in the house because it was a new home under construction. He knew that he would have to walk to a neighbor's house to get help. So, he took off his apron to lighten his load. I asked Peter if this didn't hurt due to the two broken wrists. He said, "Yes, but not like my head was hurting!" Later, as the details started to filter in from other workers, we found that Peter, being the wonderful person he is, even tried to clean the area up before leaving. They found rags in the area where he had fallen. The rags were covered with blood; Peter had tried to wipe up the blood on the floor and off of the ladder and trim. Peter, after leaving the accident area, walked to the nearest home, about a distance of fifteen hundred feet. He found no one at home at the first home. Then, he went to another home nearby. He found a woman at home who was a nurse. She called an ambulance. Peter was determined to stay awake, rather than give in to the pain. This determination probably saved his life. What a miracle! The Good Lord was there to see him through. When Peter took off his heavy carpenter's apron at the job-site, he must have partially set his wrists, so no surgery was needed on his arms. Eventually, Peter was able to walk away from the hospital, to recuperate at home for six to seven months. Today, Peter is back to work. But, instead of working for his former employer, who laid him off when he returned to work, he has his own business and is doing well. People love Peter. The word is spreading about his quality work. Peter is very busy with many people waiting for him to get free to do their work. He has been restored to reasonably good health. He still has headaches and suffers some loss of taste and smell. We believe this qualifies as a miracle.

Once, while visiting Peter in the hospital, Dr. Lohmuller said, "Peter, there is no reason you should be here!" Peter thought he meant he could go home. That time did come, but what the doctor meant was that, in his opinion, having interned in the Trauma Center at Mayo's Clinic, Peter should have been killed by the injuries received in the fall.

The verse I claimed in the hospital hallway was that "All things work together for good..." What good could have come from all this? Now, in retrospect, after nine years, I can see areas of good. A lot of people were moved by what Peter went through. All the neighbors in the area in which he was working, sent him cards showing their appreciation for Peter as a 'person' as well as Peter the 'carpenter.' They sent checks to show their appreciation, totaling over seven hundred dollars. Everyone who knows Peter or came to know him through this ordeal, knows that they have witnessed a miracle. If Peter, and Sue, his devoted wife, could handle a problem of this magnitude, certainly, any of us could handle the relatively simple day-to-day problems we encounter. Peter and his wife Sue have been a witness to everyone of their love and unconditional commitment to each other.

Also, Elayne and I have noticed closeness between Peter's other brothers and sisters, which could not have happened without going through such a family trying experience. In my heart I hurt, when I think of what Peter had to go through; and what Sue, his wife, had to endure; as well as Joe and Luke, their two children, having to live through such a traumatic experience. Their family is strong! When I think of Peter, I also think of Sue, as they are one. When I think of Peter and Sue, I also think of Joe and Luke, as they are one as a family. Through this nightmare experience, Peter's family is a witness of unity to all who know them. This apparent tragedy has actually brought our other nine children closer together. When the accident happened, we called all the children. Four, at the time, lived in the Davenport area, while the other five lived out of state. All were praying for Peter. All communicated with each other about the situation, becoming closer in family bonding. Even now, when a situation comes up, needing prayer, we get calls from our children asking us to pray. The children call each other asking for prayer. We see our children going to each other's homes for get-togethers. Our children go out of town to stay at their brother's and sister's homes. As parents, we couldn't be happier to see our children close to each other as well as close to The Lord. We have what could be called a 'family prayer chain.' When a problem comes up, a call is made; then others are called to join in the prayer circle. When victory is received, which has been the case in all the situations we have prayed for, then, we call each other back to celebrate the victory in The Lord. Isn't The Lord Good!

Isn't it the truth – "ALL THINGS" work together for good for those who love The Lord, who are called according to His purpose?

23

LOVE ONE ANOTHER

"Beloved, if God so loved us, we ought to love one another."

(John4:11)

"There is no greater love than this: to lay down one's life for one's friends."

(John 15:13)

"The command I give you is this, that you love one another."

(John15:17)

In the fall of 1995, Elayne and I were talking about the possibility of going to the southwest part of the United States to visit our brothers and sisters living there. Elayne has a brother and I have a sister living in Tucson, Arizona. Also, I have two sisters and three brothers living in the Los Angeles, California area. We decided we would try to go out in the spring of 1996. But, in the spring of 1996 we sold our larger home to move into a smaller home, since all of the children were married and on their own. Also, in April of 1996, I had a kidney stone attack, followed by surgery, so we could not make the trip as planned. As the year progressed, our schedule got more and more complex, so a trip did not look even possible.

In checking with my sister, Marianne, in Tucson, Arizona, I learned that she had moved into a retirement home where full-time care was available, as her health was failing. Also, I learned that my oldest brother, Bill, who lived in Hesperia, California, had developed heart trouble. The condition prevented him from even driving an automobile. Since he really liked to drive, I knew this must be a hardship for him. He was a traveling salesman for many years; so driving was a way of life for him. In many ways, it seemed we should cancel even thinking about a trip, but I did so want to see my brothers and sisters, especially Marianne and Bill, as they were hurting.

Elayne and I checked into airfares for such a trip. Since there would be so many different cities in the travel schedule, the aspect of an air trip was very expensive. With the many miles for such a trip, we didn't know if our Taurus would make it back home. Then our children were concerned about parents at ages 67 and 66 making such a trip by auto. On the spur of the moment, we decided to go ahead and drive there the last week of August 1996.

Before we left the garage at our home in Davenport, Iowa, we asked The Lord to protect us on the trip, both going and coming. On the first leg of our trip, en route to Tucson, Arizona, we experienced rain most of the way. The terrain through New Mexico was desolate that time of year, especially with the low hanging clouds and rainy conditions. We had a beautiful time in the car, without distraction, to visit about a lot of things; our ten children, our twenty-four grandchildren, our new-old home we had just found, the Good Lord's help, and how good The Lord had been to us through these forty-four years of marriage. Our plan was to take tapes along to listen to, but we forgot the tapes, so instead we had three and one-half wonderful days to visit. How swiftly the time passed as we drove and talked!

On the third night out, we decided to try to make it to Alamogordo, New Mexico. As we approached a small town named Tula Rosa, on the outskirts of Alamogordo, we witnessed a most unusual sight, which turned out to be the single most visual highlight of the trip. Off in the distance, with a small mountain range as backdrop, with the sun going down, we saw the tail end of the most spectacular rainbow. When the rain diminished to a slight drizzle, the rainbow appeared suddenly. The colors were distinctly separated with the full color spectrum in vivid glow. We could see the mountain in the background through the rainbow. It was about 7:05 p.m. in the evening. As we continued driving toward the city of Tula Rosa, we could see the ground lit up in a golden hue, caused by the end of the rainbow touching the ground. The height of the rainbow appeared to be several blocks long. It wasn't a complete rainbow, but only the right hand end standing almost vertical, tilted to the left. It was almost breathtaking! Both Elayne and I said it was spectacular. As we felt the presence of The Lord, we shared the scripture verse in Genesis 9:12 -15, where it is written,

"This is the sign that I am giving for all ages to come, of the covenant between Me and you and every living creature with you. I set My bow in the clouds to serve as a sign of a covenant between Me and the earth. When I bring clouds over the earth, and the bow appears in the clouds, I will recall the covenant I have made between Me and you and all living beings, so that the waters shall never again become a flood to destroy all mortal beings."

This covenant the Good Lord spoke to Noah after the flood. No rainbow had ever appeared before that time on earth. Now, here in 1996, it was a sign for Elayne and me that The Good Lord was with us on the trip.

As we were sharing our thoughts together, we approached still closer to the vertical rainbow shaft. Then, all of a sudden, another rainbow appeared, coming from the other direction. It was just a short portion of a second rainbow, about a third as long as the first one. It crossed the vertical-slanted rainbow about a third of the way down from the top, forming an almost perfectly proportioned rainbow-cross. We were simply speechless. We talked about Jesus carrying His cross on a slant, but how that was in the past. That He rose from the dead and now sits at his Father's right hand in heaven, in all His glory and splendor. Here, now, the Cross was empty, in all splendor and glory. The spectacular display lasted for almost a full half hour. Finally, as we rounded the bend of the mountain range, just before entering Almagordo, with the rainbow display on our left, the clouds shifted, the mist stopped, and almost like with a light switch, the rainbow turned off. Both Elayne and I felt such a closeness to The Lord. We were so glad that we had made the trip. We knew He would be with us the rest of the way. On Sunday morning, we did find a little Spanish church in Almagordo. The people were so friendly that they even introduced us to the congregation as the visitors from the farthest distance.

We first visited Elayne's brother, Bernard, and his wife, Noreen, in Tucson. They were both so gracious to us in their hospitality, as we stayed with them for four nights before heading to California. While in Tucson, we were able to see my sister Marianne, for a full day on the first visit. On the second visit, we were able to have supper with her in her retirement home. During our stay with Marianne, she shared with us her concern over a growth on her liver found during her last medical check up. We prayed with Marianne before leaving. When we arrived back home, we received a postcard from Marianne, thanking us for the visit. Her last sentence on the postcard read as follows: "Oh! – A Miracle! The last CAT Scan shows everything NORMAL! Thank God. Love you and Elayne. Marianne," Isn't The Lord Good! If this were the only reason for the trip, it would have been worth it.

From Tucson, we headed northwest to Hesperia, California, where we were able to see my sister, Julie, and my brother, Bill and his wife, Shirley. We had quality time with each of them, but with Bill's health failing, I was not able to spend time with Bill alone as I wanted to. Bill was under heavy medication, so he was sleeping in his chair most of the time. I looked up to Bill as my older brother, who fought in the Second World War. Often, I would remember how the Germans captured him as a prisoner. When I was a boy of only age twelve, we received a telegram from the government saying that Bill was "missing in action, presumed dead." He was heavily decorated as a soldier. A parade was held for him when he arrived back in Davenport. I can remember seeing him riding in the car along with my other brothers Lambert and Bob, who also served in the military. Bill received the Purple Heart for his wounds. He also received a special award for endangering his own life to save the lives of many other fellow soldiers. While a prisoner-of-war for over a year, he was marched across Europe, from city to city, as the German army was retreating. At night, he would sneak out of the prison camp to go into the nearest city to get food and bring it back to his starving comrades. He would risk his own life, time after time, to help others. How I loved my brother Bill. It hurt me to see him suffering now. Even though I couldn't communicate with him, I was so glad that I had told him some years earlier, over the phone, that "I love you, Bill, cause you're Bill, no other reason."

Some years earlier, when I was visiting my brother Bill in California, my sister Angie was there at the same time. She had come down from Portland, Oregon, where she was living. After I had left for home, Bill and Angie were seated at the table eating a meal that Bill had prepared. Bill said to Angie that he had a question that he would like to ask her. He caught her by surprise, as they were not talking about anything important. Bill asked, "What kind of God would send His Son here, and then sit there and watch us kill Him?" Angie, shared with me later, that she didn't even have time to prepare for such a question, but immediately answered, "Would you accept for a moment that He came here Himself?" The question was a deep one, which shows Bill was seeking the truth, and it shows how loving and caring Bill really was. The answer was perfect. Jesus said, "The Father and I are One." Jesus is Immanuel, which means; "God is with us."

How I wanted to talk with Bill when I was in Hesperia, but it was not possible. It hurt to leave Bill, but we had to continue on to see my other two brothers and sister in the Los Angeles area.

My brother, Lambert, who had come out to Hesperia with his girlfriend Joyce, led us across the desert into the Los Angeles area. First we stopped at Lambert's company in Sylmar, California. We stayed at a small hotel near his company. From this central point, we were able to go out on short trips to spend some quality time with my brother, Bob, my sister Katherine, and my other brother Lambert. As we stopped at each person's home, we took pictures of each brother or sister with Elayne and me. Each day was packed with travel and visiting. It was so good to see each of them. What a wonderful family to be a part of! Here we were, over two thousand miles away from home, in the heart of Los Angeles, with all the heavy freeway traffic, and we felt the protection of The Good Lord. Even though leaving each of them was so hard, it was worth all the stress of the trip to see them.

When we finally arrived back home in Davenport, Iowa, we were both thrilled for having taken the trip, even though we were exhausted from the general ordeal of auto travel and motels. It was so good to have seen every one of the brothers and sisters we had planned to see. One of the first things I did when we arrived back was to have eight extra sets of pictures made so that I could send a set to each of my four sisters and of my four brothers. In addition to those in Tucson and California, I sent a set to my sister Angie, in Portland as well as my brother Mike, in Schenectady, New York, as neither of them was able to come to California at the time we made the trip. With the pictures, I sent a letter to each brother or sister telling them how much I loved him or her, and how proud I am to be in the same family with them. My sister, Angie, called me from Oregon to tell me how moved she was when she saw the pictures of brother Bill, as he had lost so much weight that his outward appearance had so changed. Angie said that she knew she would have to make a special trip to Hesperia, California to see him. So, within a week, Angie was in the Southern California area to spend quality time with our brothers and sisters. Angie was able to communicate with Bill while she was at his home. Shirley was going to show Lambert something, and left the room. Angie said to Bill, "You know, Bill, I want to see you on the other side, and we can't get there except through Jesus and what He did for us on the cross—- to take our place, so that we might have a way." Bill replied, "You mean I get an exemption?" Angie said, "Yes, yes, Bill – do you believe what we have been talking about?" At that point Angie said that Shirley and Lambert came back into the room. Bill didn't speak, but nodded his head as if he was saying, "Yes."

About a week and a half after Angie's visit to California, I received a phone call from Lambert. Bill had died at home, during the night. Neither Angie nor I was able to make it to the funeral. I'm so glad we were able to see him while alive and to show our love for him. How I will miss my brother, Bill! Elayne and I are happy that we made the trip! Little did we know that this would be the last time to see Bill alive. In my letter to Bill, which I sent along with the Pictures, I said that my hope and prayer was that he would be with The Lord in heaven and that we will be able to share all eternity together. My hope is that Bill would not only be my physical brother, but also my brother in Christ. Sometime after Bill's funeral, Angie shared with me that she was in her church at a regular service when she was hurting about the uncertainty of not knowing if Bill had truly accepted Jesus as his personal Savior. While the Pastor was preaching, Angie opened her Bible and her eyes fell on the verse that Jesus said when He walked this earth. He said, "If you truly loved Me, you would rejoice to have Me go to The Father..." (John 14:28). This verse spoke to Angie. Did that mean that Bill is with his Father in Heaven?" Shortly after Angie read this verse, she called Bill's wife, Shirley. Shirley remarked that this was the verse that was used at Bill's funeral. It was confirmation to Angie and Shirley. They were both crying and rejoicing long distance!

When Elayne and I arrived back in Davenport, we held hands in the car, even before we got out. While parked in the garage, we thanked The Lord Jesus for His protection and help on the trip. I said, "Mission accomplished!" Elayne nodded, smiled and said, "Amen." And we don't even know what that mission was. But this I know: how much I truly love my brothers and sisters, with His love and my own.

24

ANGEL GEORGE

"Be not forgetful to entertain strangers; for thereby some have entertained angels, unaware."
(Hebrews 13:2)

E arly one morning, we received a telephone call, which awakened us with a start. It was about 3:30 a.m., so it was with some apprehension that I answered the phone. The woman speaking on the phone asked if this was "Lawrence J. Lyons speaking?" When I said, "Yes!" she stated that she was calling from the emergency room of Moline Public Hospital in Moline, Illinois. She said that our son, Daniel, was injured in an automobile accident. She also said that Dan had asked her to call me to ask me to come to the hospital. I asked if Dan was conscious. She said he was, but she did not give me any other details.

The season of the year was full winter, so I quickly took a look out the window, to be greeted by a raging blizzard in progress. In talking the situation over with Elayne I decided it was not practical for her to come with me to the hospital, since the weather was so inclement, and because we had other young children at home. One parent would have to stay behind. Elayne, was concerned about me driving alone in such a storm, since I had to cross the Mississippi River into Moline. Illinois, en route to the hospital. The snow was deep and usually this meant that the bridge would be difficult to navigate. Elayne asked our youngest daughter, Anita, to come with me. At the time we had a 1977 Ford Pinto, which was not the most dependable type of vehicle to put up against this type of storm.

Of course, as soon as I got the call, Elayne and I started to pray for Dan's protection. Elayne and I, each pray for the Lord to protect our children every day as a routine. It was not an easy trip to the hospital. The wind was blowing with great force. The snow was coming down so heavily; it was almost a complete white out. How badly was Dan injured? Would he be permanently injured or handicapped? Where did it happen? What would I say to him when I arrived at his side? Was he by himself in the car at the time of the accident? Were others injured?

Anita and I pulled into a snowdrift at the emergency entrance to the Moline Public Hospital. When Anita and I rushed unto the emergency room, it was so good to see Dan, awake, lying on a medical table, apparently in one piece. Immediately, Dan said, "I'm OK!" Dan said he was waiting for the results of some X-rays and other tests. It was so good to see that Dan was able to talk with us. Inside, I thanked The Good Lord for his protection. As Dan was speaking, a doctor came into the room. He said that Dan had to be admitted until they had a chance to review all the tests. Anita and I followed Dan as they wheeled him down the hallway to a private room.

Once inside the room Dan immediately started telling what had happened. He said that he and his fiancé, Sandy, had been watching a late television movie in her home, when they both fell asleep. When Dan awoke, he knew he would have to get going, so that he could get to his work place in the morning. Sandy lived in East Moline, near the

Moline Airport, so Dan would have to travel on the Interstate almost all the way home. Dan was living with us at the time, awaiting his marriage date. Dan was driving his 1973 red and black Ford LTD. The car was a four-door type, so it was heavy and durable. As Dan was traveling North on Interstate 74 in Illinois, he approached an entrance ramp, which allowed Interstate 280 traffic to enter onto Interstate 74. When he got even with the entrance ramp, he moved over into the left lane, to allow a semi-trailer tractor to enter onto Interstate 74. When the semi got even with Dan, the wind pressure from the semi caused Dan to lose control of the car. Dan's car started to slide, and finally slid into the snow covered grass median in the middle of the highway. Dan didn't remember how many complete 360 degree turns his car made, but he knew there was one and maybe more; things happened too fast. The car was turning around rapidly, when it crashed into the end of a heavy metal guardrail. The guardrail crashed into the rear right side door of the car, and the car came to rest with the metal guardrail inside the car, just inches from the gas tank. There are, of course, many 'ifs' in this story, but one 'if' is that 'if' the car wasn't so heavy and sturdy, Dan might not be with us today.

Dan said that he was knocked out, but he doesn't have any idea how long. When he came to, he was on the passenger side of the front seat. The car was upright. The engine was still running and the headlights were still on. When he reached over to turn off the ignition, he noticed he could not use his right arm, so he pulled on his right arm to sort of test its strength. Then he sat in the driver's seat, turned off the engine, and tried to figure out what to do. At this point he heard a knock on the driver's window. When he rolled the window down, a friendly man greeted him saying not to worry, that he would be okay. The man said for Dan to sit still, because he had a very deep cut in the top of his head. Dan said at the time, he was not even aware of the cut. Dan said the man reached through the window with a clean white linen cloth. The man twisted the cloth to form a lump or knot in the middle. Then he put the lumped part of the cloth on Dan's head and tied the two ends under Dan's chin to keep the cloth in position. Then the man asked Dan to get out of his car; he said it would be warmer in his truck. The man helped Dan out of his car, up the ravine, into his white pickup truck. The man said the ambulance would be coming along soon, so not to worry. When Dan asked the man his name, he simply responded, "George!" Soon, Dan said, the ambulance came to take him to the hospital.

At this point, as Dan was telling us his story, the doctor came into the room. He said that all the tests were excellent. There were no injuries requiring surgery. Dan had a bone broken in his right arm, just below the shoulder. The bone did not have to be set. Apparently, when Dan pulled on his right arm when in the front seat of the car, he must have set the bone. The doctor said that X-rays showed that the two pieces were so closely aligned, that he was going to let it heal by itself in the broken position. The doctor also said that whoever dressed the head wound at the accident scene knew what he was doing, as the wound had already started to heal. Stitches were not necessary to close the head wound.

Anita and I stayed with Dan until we had received word back on all the tests. Dan did not have to stay over night. We were able to take Dan home late in the afternoon, that same day. Dan is aware that he is very fortunate. He lived through a miracle. There are still many unanswered questions concerning the accident and surrounding details. One of the main questions is; at 3:00 a.m., on a snowy, cold, winter morning, where did a white pickup come from? How did the man, 'George,' know that Dan's head was cut so deeply? Why did he have a clean white cloth with him when he came up to Dan's car? How did he know what to do to dress the wound in the dark? How did he know that the ambulance was coming? Who called the ambulance? Dan couldn't remember seeing the pickup truck drive off. The man 'George' was not there when the ambulance attendants took Dan into the emergency vehicle.

Dan's 1973 Ford LTD was damaged beyond repair, but Dan's life was spared. Dan and Sandy are now married, and as of this writing, they have three wonderful children; Kristina, Timothy, and Andrew. I have reminded Dan a few times since the accident, that one day he will meet his 'Guardian Angel.' I would not be surprised if his guardian angel's name was, "George!" Naturally, we think of angels coming to us in shining light, with wings, but The Bible tells us that sometimes we have angels in our presence, yet we are unaware.

25

THE PHYSICIAN

"And Jesus went forth, and saw a great multitude, and was moved with compassion toward them, and He healed their sick."

(Matthew 14:14)

"But when Jesus knew it, He withdrew Himself from thence, and great multitudes followed Him, and He healed them all."

(Matthew 12:15)

O n Sunday, December 1, 1996, my wife and I were coming home from church, when Elayne mentioned to me that she had talked personally with The Lord Jesus. She said that she prayed in church; "I know Lord Jesus that You healed me, and the enemy is trying to steal that healing from me; but, I'm going to trust in You, that my healing is complete – I won't complain!" Almost instantly, Elayne said, her back pain was gone. I'm so happy for her that her faith in Jesus is that strong, for she is a witness to me and all who know her.

The reason it is so fitting to write about this incident, at this date, is that when I arose on that morning, December 1,

1996, to get ready for church, I found Elayne in the bathroom, holding onto the wall to balance herself. She said she could not put any weight on her right foot, because the pain in her lower back and right hip joint, was too severe. On that morning, we found her cane, which she had used in an earlier fall, and with the use of the cane, she was able to hobble around a little bit. I told her that she would have to stay home from church, but that I would go. It had snowed during the night, so I did not want her to go out in the snow, with the possibility of slipping. While I was shaving, Elayne came into the bathroom to tell me that she was coming with me, as she was feeling much better. I tried to convince her that she could not go, but, at the same time, I did not want to discourage her, if indeed, she was feeling better. I did not want to rob her of her healing, or admit that there was a problem, if The Good Lord was acting in her behalf. Apparently, as we were seated in the pew, at the church service, that morning, the pain had come back. Elayne prayed to The Lord Jesus, and that's when the pain left.

The start of this special encounter with The Good Lord, in a personal way, happened some five years earlier, on May 11, 1991. During the evening that day, Elayne, and I went to the Moline Southpark Shopping Mall, with Madonna, her sister, and Don, her brother-in-law. We went together to look for a pair of walking shoes for Madonna. Since it was early evening, we stopped at the Mall Food Fair for a fast-food meal. This food area is a circular array of small restaurants, with a variety of foods, ranging from Mexican, to Italian, to Chinese, along with special dessert stores, such as "Whitey's Ice Cream." Each of us seemed to order something different to eat. After we each found our special choice to eat, we gathered together at a table on a half-circle pedestal-like platform. On the half-round edge of the platform, a person could step off of the platform, onto a gradually sloping walking ramp. Usually, Elayne, and I, would always walk together, holding hands, but on that particular evening, Madonna and Don finished eating their food well before either Elayne or me. They started ahead of us, to walk off the platform, onto the ramp. Elayne started to follow them, with me walking fast behind, trying to catch up, so that I could hold her hand. I was about twelve feet behind Elayne, trying to catch up, as she stepped off the platform onto the ramp. Elayne's right foot went onto the ramp first, followed by her left. Since the ramp sloped downward, from right to left, her left foot traveled farther than her right foot, so she lost her balance. This would be similar to when one steps off a ladder, thinking they were on the last step, and then the foot goes farther than anticipated, causing a loss of balance. In losing her balance, Elayne started to fall forward, so she instinctively started to run to keep from falling. She ran across the diagonal ramp, onto the flat floor of another eating area. She ran from twenty to thirty feet, faster, and faster, trying to catch her balance, and, all the while, she was falling at a steeper and steeper angle. Finally, Elayne, crashed headlong into an empty table, which was part of the equipment furnishing the eating area. I saw her fall, as she hit the table with her head, arching her back. Then she fell, face down, under the table, hitting her face on the metal table legs. Elayne was lying, face down, on the floor, under the table, as I came running up to where she was. There was a pool of blood under her face, so I was both scared as to what had happened, and angry, that this could have happened to such a wonderful person. I saw it happen, and I was helpless to do anything about it. I couldn't do a thing to prevent it. I was angry that I was not holding her hand, because, if I were, it would not have happened. I knelt down over her back, and asked if she could hear me. Elayne replied, 'Yes." I asked her if I could roll her over, and again, she said "Okay." Carefully, I rolled her over, and sat her up under the table. Her face was covered with blood, which I started to wipe off with my handkerchief.

After removing some of the blood, I noticed a deep punc-ture wound on her right temple, which is where the large quantity of blood was coming from. Almost immediately, a man dressed in tan pants and a short sleeve white shirt, was kneeling just to my left, under the table with us. He had a clean white flannel cloth, and a bowl of ice cubes. He put a large quantity of ice cubes in the cloth, and applied the ice-pack, which he formed, to Elayne's right arm, just under the shoulder. I remember thinking at the time; Why is he doing that? – Elayne is bleeding from her temple! I took one of the ice cubes, wrapped it in my handkerchief, and applied it to the deep puncture wound on her temple. I remember the man saying to Elayne; "Now, don't worry! You're going to be fine! Just relax now!" He was so comforting. As the man and I knelt next to Elayne, under the table, our eyes met, only a foot apart, or so. He was such a nice man. There was so much compassion in his eyes. I asked him, "Are you a doctor?" He smiled, and simply answered, "No."

Just as quickly as he appeared, he was gone. Elayne continued to hold the icepack on her arm, where the man had placed it, while I held the ice cube on her temple. The bleeding stopped. By this time quite a crowd had gathered. Elayne said she was so embarrassed; she felt so foolish to have been so clumsy. Soon, the security people were there, along with an emergency vehicle, and the fire department. They started to take her to the emergency room at the local hospital. I interrupted the procedure, and asked Elayne what *she* wanted to do; whatever Elayne wanted to do, is what we would do. Not what they were telling us had to be done. Elayne said she wanted to go to Express-Care in Davenport, Iowa, because this is where her doctor had his office. Madonna and Don had been standing off to the side with the crowd where the fire personnel and the security officer were waiting for me. They made me 'sign-off' a form that said they were not responsible for anything that happened after we left since they felt the best treatment was for Elayne to go to the local hospital for treatment. I signed the release forms. Elayne would *have* done, what she *wanted* done. Elayne told me later that as she was running down the ramp, all she could think about was The Three Stooges. Also, she did not want to have anyone see her in a stretcher, so this is why she wanted to go to Express-Care in Davenport.

As we were traveling across the Mississippi River, en route to Express-Care, I asked Madonna, and Don, if they had seen Elayne fall. They said that upon hearing the commotion, they turned around just in time to see Elayne hit the table. They were in shock at what happened, so they stood off to the side as I was tending to Elayne. I asked them if they could tell me where the man with the white cloth and ice cubes had come from. They said that they did not see him come, but only saw him under the table with us. I asked them if they could remember seeing the man leave or where he went. Again, they could only recall that all of a sudden, he was no longer there. Madonna and Don also wondered why the man put an icepack on Elayne's right arm.

We arrived at Express-Care at about 8:00 p.m. Coincidentally, or was it a 'God-Instance,' Elayne's doctor, Dr. John F. Collins, was on duty. This doctor is a very compassionate man, so Elayne was further calmed by his presence. First of all, he looked at the right temple wound, and said we had done the right thing with the ice cube. The bleeding had completely stopped. After cleaning the wound area, he applied a small bandage. No stitches were necessary. Then, he took the icepack away from Elayne's right arm. To our surprise, he said, "That is the deepest bone bruise I have ever seen. If the ice had not been applied immediately, a serious blood clot could have formed, which might have taken your life." So, that was why the icepack was applied to Elayne's arm! When it had been applied by the man at the accident scene, there wasn't any discoloration in that area of the arm, but, by the time we got to the doctor's office, heavy bruising had started to show. Elayne's arm, at the area of the bruise, turned deep blue-black shortly after the doctor's visit, and remained that way for almost a year. Even today, in December of 1998, some seven years after the accident, a slight shadow, and lump can be seen in the bruise area. During that first doctor visit, Elayne told the doctor that her right hand was hurt badly. X-Rays showed that there were two broken bones; one in the area of the right ring finger between the wrist and the finger; and the other break was in the right ring finger bone, below the first knuckle. Elayne's hand was put in a cast, and her finger in a splint.

About a year and a half after the fall, Elayne's back started to give her problems. On her own, she took over-the-counter medicine, with no relief for the pain. Eventually, Elayne went to her doctor for stronger prescription medication to relieve the pain. No relief came. She had regularly gone to her own chiropractor for routine maintenance adjustments, but at the suggestion of one of our sons, we scheduled an appointment with a chiropractor-specialist, skilled in severe back injuries. The chiropractor doctor took full spine X-Rays, as part of his examination. Adjustments were given, along with physical therapy, every day for about two weeks. Elayne's lower back was not getting any better. In fact, the pain was getting worse. On one of the last visits to the specialist, he called me into the counseling room, to show me the X-Rays. On the X-Rays, he showed me that the right hip joint was bone-on-bone, while the left hip joint had very little cartilage in between the bones. He was very concerned. I asked him if he could help Elayne. "I will try my best," he answered. Then, I asked him what the X-Rays meant to him, and he indicated that Elayne was heading toward hip-replacement surgery. Hearing this just made me feel sick. This chiropractic treatment was in the summer of 1994. Since the chiropractic treatment was not helping, Elayne scheduled an appointment at her regular doctor, Dr. John Collins. Just before seeing Dr. Collins, Elayne, and I, attended a healing service at Sacred Heart Church, in Davenport, Iowa. Elayne went forward at the service to be prayed for. She was anointed with oil and prayed over by the pastor of the church. The pain persisted, so we went ahead with the appointment with Dr. Collins. Dr. Collins ordered a set of X-Rays taken of Elayne's hip areas. When he got them back from the laboratory, he said he did not see any noticeable problem, that would cause the pain Elayne was having. He wanted to immediately schedule an appointment with Dr. Krueter, an orthopedic surgeon, but Elayne said to put if off for a month or so, as we had planned a fishing trip to Minnesota. As soon as we got back from our fishing vacation, we went in to see Dr. Krueter. We had the X-Rays with us that were taken at the laboratory, under the direction of Dr. Collins. While Elayne was in seeing Dr. Krueter, I was in the waiting room, praying to The Lord for her and for the doctor, that he would have compassion as well as skill in his interpretation of the X-Rays. While I was sitting in the waiting room, I thought Elayne was in the room consulting with the doctor, but instead, a nurse came out and asked me to come in to be with Elayne. The doctor had not seen Elayne yet. He was with other patients. When Dr. Krueter came in, I could see from his manner, that he truly was a doctor of compassion. The doctor questioned Elayne for the usual symptoms, problems, treatment, and any results, good or bad. She told him about all the treatment, including the chiropractic care. She told him that she still had the pain. Dr. Krueter went over to the viewing panel to study the X-rays for a few minutes. This was the first time he had seen the X-rays. He said, to our surprise, that he saw no problem that would cause the pain. Elayne and I both looked at each other, puzzled. Elayne asked him what he meant by that, so he called us over to the viewing panel to look at the X-rays. He said Elayne's bones were in excellent shape for a woman her age. When I looked at the X-rays, I couldn't believe what I saw! There was about a1/8 inch to 3/16-inch gap between each hipbone and leg bone. It was nothing like what I had seen before at the chiropractor's office. In my view, Elayne had been healed! The doctor did prescribe a medication to relax the inflamed muscles in the lower back area. When she asked him how long it would be before she would experience any relief, in a humorous tone, he said, "Hey, you gave the chiropractor a chance—now give me a chance." The first prescription lasted eight to ten days. The pain diminished substantially during the first prescription. By the time we got the second prescription filled, the pain was gone. She didn't need the second prescription. The pain had disappeared.

Since then, Elayne had been able to work around the house, help me on repair and building projects, take fishing trips, travel to California and back by car, and do all the other things anyone age 69 would want to do. That is why it is so fitting at this time to write about this encounter with The Lord Jesus. The pain came back for a short time in December of 1996, when she went into church to talk to The Lord Jesus about it; now in December of 1998, two years later, I realize that the pain has not again returned. Always, the enemy will try to steal back what The Good Lord Jesus has done for us. Our Lord allowed this to happen, to remind us that Elayne was truly healed, and that we need to have our trust in Him only, 'The Great Physician.'

I reflect back some ten years ago to May 11, 1991, when I was under the table at Moline Southpark Mall with Elayne, and with the kind man who comforted her. I asked the man if he was a doctor, and he simply replied, "No." I have always wondered; what if I had asked him if he was 'The Physician?' In my heart, I'm sure he would have said "Yes." Having seen the man, I believe He was The Lord Jesus, The Great Physician, Who put the ice pack on Elayne's arm, when nothing showed an injury at that spot. Scripture tells us,"...And He saw a great multitude, and was moved with compassion toward them, and He healed their sick." This same Great Physician healed Elayne at the healing service at Sacred Heart Church

Also, I reflect on the passage in scripture where Jesus is talking to the two disciples on the road to Emmaeus. They didn't recognize Him, until the breaking of the bread. Jesus can do what He wants, when He wants. Praise be to the Name of Jesus!

26

FAMILY REFLECTION

"Happy are you who fear The Lord, who walk in His ways. For you shall eat the fruit of your handiwork; happy shall you be and favored. Your wife shall be like a fruitful vine in the recesses of your home; your children like olive plants around your table. Behold, thus is the man blessed who fears The Lord."
(Psalms 127:1-4)

When Elayne and I, look back over the last fifty-eight years of our married life together, we can see how good The Lord has been to us in so many ways. We see The Hand of The Lord in everything we have done, and in everything that has happened to us. In retrospect, we can see good coming from both the good times, as well as the hard times. If you see the good in what has been done or in what has happened to us, we give The Good Lord Jesus all the credit, Who lives in our hearts, through The Holy Spirit, to the degree that we have given Him control of our lives.

The scripture chosen for this reflection has the preface, "Happy are those who fear The Lord." How can one be happy who fears The Lord, and even deeper, why should one fear The Lord? Fear The Lord is mentioned many times in scripture. Also, in scripture it is written, "God is love!" God is all Good and loving, and if so, why should He be feared? This question is to be answered by each of us, in our own hearts. We do find it in The Lord's Word, that He is going to punish evil; for it is written, "Vengeance is Mine, says The Lord! I will repay" Because Satan has turned against The Lord, his end is to spend all eternity in Hell, separated from The Lord. Also, all who have followed Satan, by rejecting a relationship with The Lord Jesus, have thereby chosen the same ending. So, first of all, we must fear The Lord in order to understand any of His other teachings. Scripture tells us, "The beginning of wisdom is fear of The Lord" (Proverbs 9:10). Fear grows into respect, then into reverence, then to honor and worship; and then to a personal relationship where we can call Him 'ABBA, Father.'

When Elayne and I were married on October 4, 1952, we did not have a personal relationship with The Lord. We knew a lot about Him but we did not know Him personally. We did know His commandments and we wanted to serve Him. To do His will was and is our goal. We prayed for His help and guidance. We married with a lifelong commitment, without even the slightest thought of what to do if it didn't work out. The Lord protected us from that type of conditional thinking. We both knew 'marriage' was very serious, so we did not take it lightly. We only had hope in The Lord, and in each other. Gradually our relationship with The Lord grew to one of trust. He would answer our prayers. We could sense His concern and His presence. We looked to The Lord as our Helper. As we grew spiritually, we learned to trust Him more and more, until in our forties, each of us made a personal commitment to The Lord Jesus by asking Him into our hearts as our Lord and Savior. We have learned two of His great promises and have applied these to our lives: First, that He is always with us, since He lives in our hearts, and second, that He will never allow us to be tested beyond our ability to resist. He will always provide the escape, so that we may be able to endure the test (I Corinthians 10:13). Usually, we find that Jesus is the escape.

In one respect we wanted to share some of the events and personalities in our lives, but we hesitated to do it, for fear of injuring anyone. Even though someone may feel that the Lord hasn't been watching over them at this time, scripture tells us that He loves each of us with a unique love, and pours out His love to each of us, in Christ Jesus. Please accept our reflections as a tribute to The Good Lord. Our intention is simply to praise Him for His Goodness. We believe Him in His Word, for He has written; "Without faith, it is impossible to please Him. Anyone who comes to God must believe that He exists, and He rewards those who seek Him" (Hebrews 11:6). Elayne and I do believe with all our hearts that He exists; that Jesus is God and that He died on the cross for our sins; rose from the dead; is in Heaven seated at His Father's right Hand; lives in our hearts through The Holy Spirit and will return one day soon to gather His people who have accepted Him. By testifying to His goodness, it is not to say that everything in our lives has gone perfectly, or according to *our* plans or expectations. We do believe though that "All things work together for good to those who love The Lord, who are called according to His purpose" (Romans 8:28). We thank Him for the good as well as the not so good as we grow in His Grace. We pray that you will see His Goodness, His Love, His Majesty, and will ask Him into your life, if you have not already done so, to share in His Mercy and Love.

Our first child, Christopher, came to us after nine months and four days of marriage. Chris was one month early, weighing in at four pounds and twelve ounces. Elayne had developed toxemia during pregnancy, with much sickness and complications. Labor was long and childbirth was diffi-cult. Elayne's parents were called to the hospital by hospital staff because they were concerned that she was not going to make it. Throughout this time, I prayed for her protection. Even though Chris' first glimpse of daylight was not easy, he was very healthy. Elayne made it with The Good Lord's help. When she was assigned a room, I was by her side when she awoke from the anesthesia. Her first words to me were, "Larry, no more." I understood, with complete compassion. Our doctor, Dr. George Morrissey, was a wonderful man. He warned us that we should not have anymore children because Elayne's condition during pregnancy was risky. We understood what he was telling us but we felt we could only trust The Lord. We loved each other and we loved The Lord. Maria, our first daughter was born one year later, in October. Then came Carla, Peter, Daniel, and Laura; with a miscarriage after Laura, and then Anna, Felecia, Paul, and Anita. We had ten children in thirteen years. We welcomed each new child, while cherishing the early years with them as we grew up together. Not one of our children was a mistake; nor were any unwanted. When Elayne would tell me that she was expecting, I would pray every day for her. My prayer was simple; "Lord please protect Elayne while carrying this baby, and during childbirth." Elayne never complained about any pregnancy, nor did she look to me with disdain or guilt. Elayne worked hard, and with joy, as a wife, mother, and friend, with a radiance that all who knew her could see. It seemed almost amazing that Elayne could deal with all the details that come with a home, an acre of ground, ten children, and a husband. Elayne made her own wedding dress and after we were married, she made drapes as well as diapers for each of our children, which she washed out by hand. Amazing! Often, the world criticized me to the point of ridicule, for having so many children. Elayne was always supportive, being the wife to me that is told of in Proverbs 31, 'The Ideal Wife.'

Years after our last child was born, Elayne was talking to some of the family members at a family gathering. I heard her relate that while carrying any of the babies she never worried about being hospitalized or anything negative happening. She went on to say in that discussion that she now realizes that many things could have happened, but she was not concerned at the time. She just went along, in blind faith, trusting that everything would turn out all right. When I heard her say that, I thought of how good The Lord is. As her husband, I prayed for her every day of her pregnancies, and The Lord answered, by shielding her from the worry and fear of childbirth. Children are important to The Lord. In fact, He says in His Word, that they "...Are like olive plants around your table." Children will inhabit The Lord's Kingdom in Heaven. From this world, there are only two things that will last into the Heavenly Kingdom; The Lord's Word, and His children. All else, in "the present heavens and earth are reserved by God's Word, for fire" (2 Peter 3:7). Yet today, I still pray for each of our children or their spouse when I hear of a pregnancy. In 2004, Kellie, Paul's wife gave birth to a son, Jacob. In 1999, Anita gave birth to a son, John, making our grandchildren a total at twenty-seven and a little girl, Abigail, is our first great-grandchild. During Anita's pregnancy, as with every other family pregnancy, I prayed every day, "Lord, please protect Anita while carrying her baby and during childbirth." When each of our grandchildren were in their mother's womb, I prayed, "Lord please protect Sheryl, Maria, or Carla, or Sue, Sandy, Anna, Felicia, Kellie, or Anita while carrying her baby and during childbirth." As of this date, Elayne and I have been blessed with eleven children; ten are living and one is with The Lord. We named our eleventh child "Christian," since we do not know whether this child is boy or girl because we lost this child to a miscarriage. We have twenty-seven grandchildren; twenty-six are living and one, Jonathan, went to be with

The Lord as a newborn baby. Babies are as important to The Lord, as they are to Elayne and me. Written in Psalms:139, "...And You created my inmost being; You knit me together in my mother's womb. I praise You because I am fearfully and wonderfully made; Your works are wonderful, I know that full well. My frame was not hidden from You; when I was made in a secret place. When I was woven together in the depth of the earth, Your eyes saw my unformed body. All the days ordained for me were written in Your book before one of them came to be."

When Elayne and I think about the family we are part of, we feel so blessed; for we know in our hearts that it was The Lord Who has blessed us with our children. It is impossible for either of us to even think of life, without one of our children. Who could we leave out? Not one! Do we love one more than another? Yes, I guess we do; we love the one who is sick more, till he or she gets well, and we love the one who is gone more, till he or she returns. As I think of Elayne's and my individual lives as well as the lives of each member of our family, I reflect upon what I learned in first grade. The answer to the age-old question of 'Why did God make me?' The answer still holds true today; 'God made me to know Him, to love Him, and to serve Him, in this life, to be with Him forever in the life hereafter.'

The Good Lord has blessed us in so many miraculous ways that most certainly, there is not room to recount them all in this writing but I would like to mention a few general areas of blessing. We were given the skills and resources to build our own home. Our home, where we raised the children, was built in four different construction stages, so that we ended with a five-bedroom home, with three full baths, on an acre and a quarter of excellent property, in a good section of the city. We lived in our home for forty years. Many who came to our home for a visit, told us that they felt a special 'peace' in our home. The family who bought our home, said they felt that 'peace' when they got within a block of the property. Eight of our children stayed with us until they were married. One entered an apartment with two girl friends before marriage. One entered The United States Air Force before marriage. Each of our ten children is married, and each is still married to their original spouse. Today, this is most unusual. As a family, we have always had good performance from whatever automobile we had at the time. Most all of our vehicles, through the years, provided us with over 100,000 miles of transportation. When an auto problem did occur, we were able to do our own repair. When a major auto breakdown did happen, it was in the garage, in the driveway, or at least very near home, so we would have no problem getting the repair work done. We took vacation trips to both the East Coast and the West Coast, with ten children, in a Volkswagen Van without any mechanical trouble. When we traveled on vacation, we camped out at night in a tent. Our children still talk about these times when they get together; they consider these family times as 'highlight' times. We always took the children with us on vacation. These were fun times. We were always provided with sufficient income to raise the children and pay the bills, even though I changed occupations from engineering to insurance sales. We struggled financially when starting out in the insurance business, but even during this time, we were provided with income when we needed it, in just the amount needed. At one period in our child rearing years, we went without health insurance for seven years, without health problems; and this is while having ten children. When it was time to sell our large family home, in 1996, we were able to sell it on our own. With all the children gone, we needed a smaller home, with less work to keep up. The ranch home we now live in, we found when it was not even for sale. (See Story #53) We are at peace in our smaller home, as we were in the other larger, family one.

We praise You Lord for all Your help through all these years. We thank You Lord for each of the children You have given us to love and cherish. We thank You Lord for their families. Now, we understand a little bit better what You meant when You said in Your Word, "Your children (will be) like olive plants around your table. Behold, thus is the man blessed who fears The Lord." (Psalm 127:4).

27

I KNOW YOU DO

"His commandment is this: we are to believe in the Name of His Son, Jesus Christ, and we are to love one another,as He commanded us."
(1John 3:23)

"Would you please call Roma and see if you can see her, because she is really in need of some help with her Medicare claims?" This is what Katie asked me to do one summer day. Katie and Bob owned the apartment building where Roma was living. They had become good friends since the only relative that Roma had was a distant, younger nephew, living in Arizona with no one locally to look after her. Katie and Bob were insurance clients in our agency, and they felt that with our more extensive insurance knowledge, we would be able to help Roma resolve the myriad amount of paperwork that goes along with medical health care claims. Roma's health was very poor. Because of her age and general health, she had to use a bottle of oxygen to aid her breathing and wasn't able to get around easily.

When I first came into her apartment, I saw piles of paper all over her living room floor. She had accumulated many bills and health statements for her extensive health care treatment concerning her numerous health problems. Included in these papers were statements from the physicians who provided care, itemized statements from the hospital for both in-patient and out-patient care, as well as Explanation of Benefit forms from Medicare to tell how individual health-care bills were processed. The information showed what was paid to whom and what Roma owed as balances to all her health care providers. The material was quite complex, and Roma had no idea of how to proceed. She said, "This is quite a mess – kind of like foreign territory!" After looking at the material for a while, and realizing that I could not get a handle on it during one visit, I asked for her permission to take all the material with me for review. I told her that I would try to put it in some sort of order, to show what, if anything, she owed on the medical bills.

In order to get an idea of what happened chronologically, I had to visit with her, in her apartment, several times. On one of these visits, when I came to her apartment door, I noticed that the door was partially open. Since she knew I was coming, she left the door unlocked. I knocked lightly on the door, and Roma said, "Come on in, the door's open!" Roma was sitting on a stool in the kitchen, talking on the phone. "Go on in the other room and look around," she said. She was on the phone for quite awhile, so I did just as I was told, I looked around. Roma was a woman of few words. Katie and Bob warned me that she spoke forcefully but I liked that quality. My guess, from the medical data, was that Roma was in her late seventies. Her apartment was well kept. As I glanced around the room, my eyes finally settled on a painting hanging on the living room wall, which I admired greatly. It was an original painting depicting an outdoor scene where a number of trees were shown bordering a beautiful mountain stream. The scene was spectacular. Looking closer, I saw that the painter's name was "Roma." What an unexpected surprise! As I looked on other walls, I found many beautiful paintings done by "Roma." I reasoned that Roma was just trying to let me into her life, gradually, by letting me see who she was and what her talents were. The paintings were beautiful, but I liked the one of the stream best because I could visualize where I would throw in my fishing line, if I were to ever fish there. When Roma came into the room, I complimented her on the paintings. Being a very humble person, Roma didn't spend any time on the paintings or my comments. I'm sure that she just wanted me to see that she did the work. And, the work was great! To me, Roma was a 'sleeper.' Not one to boast, but probably a woman of many talents. I felt blessed by The Lord that He allowed me to meet such wonderful people while servicing insurance needs. In most cases, as with Roma, we were led to people who needed our help and with The Lord's help, we were able to actually be of service. After much review, we resolved some of the bills by showing her how much to pay and to whom to make out the checks.

Roma's health deteriorated very rapidly. Soon after I met her, she was hospitalized once more with severe breathing difficulties. Since I had not completed the service work for her, I needed to go to the hospital for review of the claims. She was able to follow very clearly what I had to cover with her. Certain bills had to be paid, so after I explained this to her, she asked me to get her purse off the dresser. She took out her checkbook and asked me to make out the checks so that she could sign them. Roma knew that I was trying to help her, so she let me in to her life, ever so gradually. It was so humbling to prepare the checks, and then see her sign them in complete trust. I was at peace doing this for her, for I knew in my heart that it was the right thing to do. We did not charge her anything for the service performed.

Elayne and I, had to be out of town for about a week, but upon returning, I learned that Roma was still in the hospital. That evening, a Saturday, while working on one of the family cars, the thought came to mind that I should get up to the hospital, to see how Roma was getting along. First, I thought I would go up on the following Monday. Then, I thought I would go the next day, on Sunday. Finally, I felt compelled to go up that very evening. Quickly, I showered, changed clothes, and hastened to the hospital to visit Roma. When I arrived at the hospital, it was a little after 8:00p.m. in the evening. Her room was dark and Roma was asleep. I sat in the chair opposite her bed for about twenty minutes until she awakened. Roma acknowledged my greeting, but I could tell that she was really hurting and in no mood to talk. I tried to be kind to her in any way that I could. She listened to me, as I talked about things I thought would be of interest to her. After a short pause in my talking, I said, "The Lord loves you Roma!" She made a grumbled sound, which I did not understand. Again, after a time of silence, as I prayed in The Spirit for her, I said," You know, Roma, The Lord really loves you." Roma said, "It sounds like you're trying to convince yourself!" I smiled, and said, "You're right, I am, but I know He does!" Then surprisingly, she asked me to help her sit on the edge of the bed. She asked me to get her slippers from under the bed and to put them on her feet. I simply did as she asked. Then she asked me to get her shawl and put it over her shoulders, which I did. "Get my purse on the dresser," she said. Out of her purse she took a comb and handed it to me. She told me to comb her hair. Again, I did as I was told. She looked in her hand held mirror, and said, "You haven't combed it yet!" So, again I combed her gray silk hair. While I was combing her hair, I said, "Roma, I really do love you!" Now, how do you suppose she handled this, and what do you think she said to me? To my surprise, she answered, "I know you do." Roma had let me in. The warmth of that moment cannot be expressed in words. Roma again looked at her hair in the hand held mirror and said, "Terrific!" I helped her back in bed, sat with her for a while until she dozed off to sleep again. I left her room a very happy man.

Roma only lived a few more days. At her funeral, there were only four people present; the funeral director Bob, Katie, and myself. Katie was the Executor of Roma's estate, so I worked with her in the closing out of all the paper work I had been doing for Roma. Before her death, when I was visiting in her apartment, I complimented Roma on her 2-door 1973 Ford LTD automobile. It was always parked in the parking lot of the apartment building. Roma was very fond of that car. After her death, Katie said that Roma wanted Elayne and I to have the LTD, so she asked me to go around to get appraisals. We went to three dealerships, and the appraisals were very close, so we purchased the LTD from Roma's estate at a very reasonable price. Our children helped us do the much-needed bodywork on the car. We gave it a new paint job, This car, was Elayne's favorite ever for space and comfort. We drove all over the country in that car. The mileage was at 55,000 when we purchased it and it just turned 100,000 when our oldest son, Chris, took it over. He drove it another 60,000 miles and then gave it to a friend as a basic "short distance" car. The engine never had to be taken apart. Isn't The Lord good!

On my last trip over to Roma's apartment, to finalize my service work, Katie walked me to my car. She asked me to open the trunk. I did, but I didn't know why. Katie handed me a package and told me to take it because "Roma would want you to have this!" When I got home and opened the package, I found a real surprise. As you might have already guessed, it was a painting. But, not just any painting. It was a painting by 'Roma'—the painting of 'The Trout Stream.' I have this painting in our home to always remind me of Roma. To this day, I do not know if Roma told Katie to give me the painting, or if The Lord inspired Roma or Katie to do so. I guess I really do not want to know for I am happy with either answer.

After Roma's death, Katie had to go through many personal items belonging to Roma. She shared some of the things she learned. For one thing, we learned that Roma was a professional tennis player when she was a young woman. She was also an accomplished musician, playing both the organ and the piano. From her scrapbook, we learned that when she was a young woman, she was in love with a young farmer, who loved her very much. This man wrote beautiful poetry to her. We read some of his poems for she had saved them all these years. They were incredibly touching. Roma, and the young farmer, were to be married on January 1st of a particular year. The newspaper article, which Katie shared with me, went on to say that Roma's fiancé had left a New Year's Eve party, at Roma's home, to go to his own farm home. They were to be married the very next day. The newspaper article explained how the young man had unexpectedly died in his sleep that very evening. What a blow this must have been to Roma. She kept this scrapbook all these years. In the scrapbook, she had saved pictures of her young fiancé, a very handsome man, as well as love letters and many memories of a love relationship, which she was not able to fulfill. How this must have hurt her for such a long time and she never told anyone.

Often, I think of Roma, and I wonder if she had a personal relationship with The Good Lord Jesus. At the time I met her, I was not well versed in scripture; nor was I skilled in how to lead anyone into a personal relationship with The Lord Jesus. Our meeting time seemed short! By my actions, I did show her that I loved her and that I had genuine concern for her well-being. The Good Lord did give me the strength and grace to tell Roma that I loved her. She accepted this love, and acknowledged that love by saying, "I know you do!" Just maybe, by my love, the crack in her wall was broken, and this may have allowed The Lord to come in to shower her with His Love. My hope is that after this short life is over, I will meet Roma again, where we can share The Lord's love and joy, for an eternity.

The Lord tells us in His Word, that, "His commandment is this; we are to believe in The Name of His Son, Jesus Christ, and we are to love one another as He commanded us."

28

THE GREATEST GIFT

"All we like sheep have gone astray; we have turned every one to his own way; and The Lord has laid on Him the iniquity of us all."

(Isaiah 53:6)

The Lord 's Word in Isaiah seems to say that each of us is free to make our own decision, free to turn our own way. Since the fall of Adam, each of us has come into the world with a basic tendency toward sin. And, basically, sin is anything that comes between our relationships with The Lord. The Lord says in His Word that each of us has turned to our own way; putting ourselves first, and The Lord second, or third, or farther down in the order of importance to us. And so, "The Lord has laid on Him (Jesus) the iniquity of us all."

In April of 1977, I purchased my own Bible because I had a burning desire to read every Word written about Jesus, and hear every recorded Word said by Jesus. My hope was to be able to read the entire Bible before I died, so that I could learn everything The Lord wanted me to know in order to serve him fully. I didn't want to get to Heaven, face to face with Him and have some weak excuse that I didn't have time to read His Word. It took me four years to complete reading the entire Bible. Not exactly the quickness of a track star but if I had not started, I would never have finished. Now each time I review a paragraph or verse in the Bible, I am taught something new. When I started to read the Bible, I composed two basic statements of belief. First, the Bible is The Lord's Word, and therefore every syllable is true. Secondly, I would trust The Holy Spirit to be my Teacher, so that as I read, He would instruct me concerning what I needed to know to accomplish The Lord's will.

Early in my reading, in the year 1978, well before I had learned even a fraction of what I would be taught by The Holy Spirit, I was asked to give a talk at one of The Full Gospel Business Men's Saturday morning breakfasts. This group of businessmen, members of The Full Gospel Business Men's Fellowship International (FGBMFI) met every Saturday, and had men give a short testimony about their relationship with The Lord. Since I had never been to any of their meetings, I made basic notes to speak from. The notes related to my background in school and church. First, I talked about my childhood, where I went to school, my marriage, and the children that have blessed our marriage. Then I started into a basic discussion about how I came to know The Lord in my life. It was more of a talk than a testimony since I had not, as yet, made The Lord Jesus, Lord of my life.

Something happened while I was speaking, which I will never forget. I met a man who would have a great impact on my life. His name was Tom. Tom was a retired Pentecostal minister, who was in attendance at that first breakfast. I didn't notice him at the table because I was pre-occupied with the notes and delivery of my presentation. Tom was sitting at the left hand side of a horseshoe table. There were about forty men in attendance. After the talk, when I met Tom, I learned that he had cancer. He was very thin, weighing only about 110 pounds. (See another story concerning Tom in # 29 of these writings). As I was talking from my notes, I put in an ad-lib, which I thought would be humorous. I said, "In my case, the only mistake The Lord made in my life, was to give me a free-will, otherwise, I wouldn't be in all this trouble." Tom jumped up like a jack-in-the-box. He hit the table in front of him with his right hand. The table silverware flew! At the same time, He said, "Not so! Not so! The greatest gift The Lord gave us is our free-will, so that we can freely choose Him!" There was a startled moment of silence. I was the speaker! I was just shot down! Almost immediately, without even thinking, I said, "Mea culpa, mea culpa, mea maxima culpa!" They may have thought I was speaking in tongues, and this could have been the case, as these words came out spontaneously. For the first time in my life, I really knew what these words meant. As a young boy, when serving mass, I learned these words since mass was said in Latin. In English, the translation would be, 'through my fault, through my fault, through my most grievous fault.' I knew this was not an area in which to try to be humorous. What Tom said was the truth. The Holy Spirit convicted me and I was truly sorry for my weakness in bringing even the slightest dishonor upon The Lord. The Lord doesn't want puppets. He wants us to choose freely to have a relationship with Him, through His Son, Jesus.

I apologized to the men. Somehow, I finished the talk. The first man up to greet me after the talk, coming at almost a run, was Tom. Through his tears, he tried to apologize to me, but I quickly thanked him for being so courageous to speak out for The Lord. We hugged each other. We became instant friends.

Just a few short months after that first meeting, I learned that Tom was in the hospital recovering from complex surgery. The cancer was in full attack on his vital organs. All who knew Tom were praying for his full recovery. When I visited him in the hospital, his spirit was upbeat, even though he was very weak. I went to comfort him, but his humility of heart ministered to me. After a week or so of treatment, the doctors said they had done all they could for him. Tom had to be taken home by ambulance, to weak to walk. When I heard, I decided to write and try to encourage him. The letter is as follows:

6-29-79

Dear Tom,

I've been meaning to write to you for some time and felt pushed to do so this morning. This short note is written in a spirit of love and concern. If I, as a simple human being, with many faults and failings, am concerned about you, how much more is The Good Lord concerned as He made you and I, and all that is around us? My wish and prayer is to reach out and touch you, as Jesus would, to heal you. In my weak and failing nature, I do not know what God's plan is for His ways are not our ways. I do know that Jesus loved you so much, that He went to the cross to fulfill The Father's will, so that each of us would share in the great treasures He has planned for us. It is His Will that not one of us should perish. Jesus promised us that He would always be with us, and He would not allow us to be put in a position whereby we had no way out. I trust Jesus in His plan for you, even though I do not see His plan, due to my clouded vision. One day, we will know and meet Him Face to face, in all His Glory and Majesty; and all this anxiety and suffering will have been worth it.

As part of a church prayer group, we pray for you every Thursday night. We have only known each other a short time, but I can say humbly that you have ministered to me. The Good Lord has used you to minister to many people, and He is proud of the job you have done. I have admired your tenacity and enthusiasm for the truth. Your life is a pure witness to The Word and Love of God. Jesus does live in you, and your strength in the face of trials and sickness has been an inspiration to me. I feel Jesus' love for you and I see Him in your life. When the going gets tough, the tough get going; and you have strength of faith that is contagious. Jesus said, 'If you do something for the least of His brethren, you do it for Him." You have served many of His brethren, and surely, some were the least. Your rewards will be a thousand fold.

My prayer for you is that you may come to know Jesus more intimately, to serve Him completely, and to love Him with complete surrender in your life, to be with Him for all eternity in the life after.

In Christ's Love, Larry

(Note: attached to the letter addressed to Tom, I had a note to Tom's wife, Betty, as follows;)

"Betty, in not knowing Tom's condition, you can decide if this letter will be of help to him. In Christ's love, Larry."

A few days later, I received the following letter from Tom, dated July 1, 1979, in Betty's handwriting:

"Dear Larry,

It is always a pleasant experience to hear from you. To get compliments of your caliber and character are certainly compliments indeed. You, as well as I, know they belong to God, and I praise Him for you and your commitment to Him.

I am dictating this note to Betty. I have become so weak that I am unable to sustain writing. I'm not complaining. I'm only glad I can communicate. My life has been a pleasant, happy one, with few trials and problems. I have a marvelous family. God has filled me with The Holy Spirit by coming to dwell in me. I would say I'm rich. I'm glad if I can have been of service to anyone for any period of time. I am ready to go if this is my time, for the better life is yet to come. Service to God, I believe, is the highest calling. I see it in your life and in the lives of others in The Full Gospel Business Men, and in other prayer groups. I think I have partaken of the best with God manifesting Himself in my body. What a wonderful thing.

Thank you, Larry, for your care, concern and prayers. God bless you richly.

With all my love, Tom

P.S. Betty told me that you said she was in a position to decide if your letter would be of help. It certainly was. Tom."

Five days after Tom dictated this letter, he died at home. What a man! What a loss of such a good friend! Betty asked me to be a pallbearer at Tom's funeral and I was honored to do so. The Good Lord allowed me to meet Tom, and through Tom's courage, I learned that truly The Greatest Gift The Lord has given each of us, outside of life itself, and the salvation of His Son Jesus, is the gift of a free will. We are made in the image and likeness of God. We can freely choose Him, or reject Him. The choice is ours. He does not want to corner me, or force me into a decision. That would be a controlling or conditional love. He wants me to choose Him freely. I choose God! I choose Jesus, as my personal Lord and Savior. Lord of my life, and Savior of my soul! All praise and honor to His Name!

In my weakness, I have turned to my own way. In God's Mercy, He has drawn me to Himself, through Jesus, His Son, and my sins are washed clean by The Blood Of The Lamb. The Lamb of God – Jesus!

29

IN TONGUES

"If anyone speaks in a tongue, two – or at the most three – speak, one at a time, and someone must interpret."

(1Corinthians 16:27)

In the previous section, #28, entitled 'The Greatest Gift,' we looked at the faith of a man named Tom who loved The Lord. Again, Tom is the main person in this real life happening, for The Lord worked though him in a mighty way to minister to me. Tom was filled with The Holy Spirit, in that The Holy Spirit controlled him. The gifts given to him by The Holy Spirit were manifested freely.

Soon after I had given a talk at a Saturday Full Gospel Business Men's morning breakfast meeting, I became aware of a dinner meeting at a local Holiday Inn. The local chapter of 'Full Gospel Businessmen' sponsored the meeting. An out-of-town guest speaker was scheduled to give the after dinner testimony. I was just starting to reach out in many directions to fill the hunger to know The Lord in a more personal way. Rather reluctantly my wife and I attended the meeting. We sat in the back corner of the meeting room, near the closest exit door, in case the meeting went in a direction we didn't fully understand.

The dinner was excellent. The meeting format was also well done. There was fellowship before the meal, followed by group singing, and a beautiful opening prayer. After dinner, there were short personal testimonies by two individuals about how The Lord was working in their lives. It was very uplifting! Then the principal speaker was introduced. He thanked the chapter of Full Gospel Businessmen for inviting him to speak. Then, quickly, he asked us all to bow our heads for a moment of prayer. Everyone did as he asked. There was a moment of silence. After a period of possibly a half-minute, a man's voice rang out, firmly, clearly, and with calm conviction. I looked up slightly to see a man standing in the middle of the assembly. To me, he looked to be dark complexioned maybe of Spanish nationality. With my ears, I heard two short phrases; sounding like 'Da Nah!' 'Ya Bah!' He sat down. Again, it was very quiet. Inside my spirit, I said, "Lord, I need to know what he said! That message was for me! I need to know what it means!" After a brief moment, another man stood up at the right hand edge of the table. He said, "I call! You come!" Then he sat down. The man was my recently found new friend, Tom. Tom had the gift of interpretation, so he spoke in English what the other man had said in 'a tongue.' My inner spirit jumped! The message was for me! The Good Lord did not want me to stand out on the fringes. He was gently but firmly telling me to get involved; to sell out to The Lord and to risk everything for His sake. I felt a calm and peace about me that was awesome. The Lord worked through a willing vessel, Tom, to touch my heart in a special way. I was given a new zeal to follow Jesus and to let Him work through me.

I've carried the impact of that 'happening' with me to this day. I had attended an actual New Testament Holy

Spirit meeting, much the same as what had happened to the apostles shortly after Jesus ascended into heaven. The Holy Spirit had manifested His power and gifts through two individuals willing to allow Him to work. The one spoke in tongues, the other man, my new found friend, Tom, interpreted through the Power of The Holy Spirit, what the first man had said. It was orderly, very moving, and just what was written to the Corinthians, by The Lord, through St. Paul. I personally received a great gift from The Lord that evening; a Word from The Lord telling me to take my Christian walk seriously. To trust in The Lord and not worry about the results. The results are up to Him. I was reminded of the scripture verse in Matthew, Chapter 10, verse 39; "He who saves his life, loses it, while he who loses his life, for My sake, saves it."

The rest of the evening went well. The guest speaker's testimony was powerful. We were so glad that we went to the meeting. But, the message to me, from The Holy Spirit, is what I took home with me. All I needed do was step out in faith; The Lord would direct my paths. Tom was very weak at the time due to his battle with cancer. In spite of this battle, he had a peace about him, which surpassed all understanding. Now, he is with The Lord, with no human restrictions or limitations. One day, my hope is to tell Tom; "Thank you for being obedient, in expressing your gift – thank you for letting The Lord 'call me' through you."

Since that meeting in early 1979, through The Lord's Grace, I have stepped out in faith. It has been a most joyous ride. The Good Lord has taken me on many trips; some of which are mentioned in other sections of these writings. I have learned The Goodness Of The Lord. How Majestic is His Name! How tender is His caring. I cannot thank You Lord enough for calling me, and then giving me Your Grace to respond. My heart yearns for the day that I will see Jesus, Face to face. My spirit, and the spirit of my wonderful wife,

Elayne, hope and pray that each of our children, and our loved ones, will share in this same, most precious experience – Jesus, Face to face – for all eternity.

30

GROW AND PLANT

"Go therefore and make disciples of all nations."
(Matthew 8:28)

On January 1ˢᵗ, 1967, I entered the insurance business, after fifteen years in the field of engineering. During the first years in the insurance business, I struggled to make the income necessary to raise our family and pay the bills associated with the expenses of ten children. However, during these early years, I did try to expand my knowledge of insurance principles by attending extension classes in the insurance field. After eleven years of study, I was able to pass the necessary courses to obtain the equivalent of an insurance degree through The American College, at Bryn Mawr, Pennsylvania. Extension classes were held in the Quad City area, in which I lived, so that I did not have to travel far to attend classes.

Therefore, in October of 1978, my wife and I went to California, in order to attend the commencement ceremony for all graduates from all parts of the United States. The city of San Diego hosted the National graduation ceremony for all CLU (Chartered Life Underwriter) degree recipients. Elayne had helped me greatly with the studies associated with the ten course insurance degree, so it was very uplifting to have her come with me on the trip. Early in our marriage, we had lived in San Diego for about a year, so it was great to go back to see the area once again. Also, since our anniversary was in early October, we were able to celebrate our 26th wedding anniversary. The flight out to California was excellent, and the meeting was well attended.

Following the Commencement Weekend, we went to Los Angeles, by airplane, to see my six brothers and sisters living in that area. We had a wonderful visit with each of them, as we shared old times, and caught up on the new happenings in their families. My brother Bob drove us around as we traveled to see each of my brothers and sisters. Since Los Angeles is like New York City, or Chicago, spread out ranch style, there was considerable driving done to get to each of their homes. On one such trip across Los Angeles, Elayne and I were in the back seat of Bob's car, while Bob and his wife Sheila, were in the front. I was relaxing while Elayne, Bob, and Sheila, were involved in a long conversation. I was in deep thought, centering upon how much I missed my brothers and sisters. Each of them moved out to California when I was quite young, and I did not get the chance to see them very often. Due to jobs and family commitments, they were not able to travel back to our area where they had previously lived. Therefore, the only way we were able to see them was if we went out to California. This happened only about once every 5 years, or so, as we too had many family commitments with the children. As we traveled across the freeway, I was thinking about the possibility of us moving to California, so that we could be closer to my immediate family. Would that be fair to Elayne and her family? What would The Lord want? If we did move to California, would I really get the time to see my brothers and sisters, and further, would I ever get the chance to help them in their walk with The Lord? At the time the conversation between

Elayne, Bob, and Sheila, was in full progress, I was asking
The Lord for His will in this situation. "Lord, what is it You
would have me do? Whatever you want, Lord, I'll do it!" At
this point, as I was looking out the rear side window, a car
pulled up along side of us, in the next lane. In the rear left
side window of the car next to us, was a window sticker,
showing a plant in full bloom. The caption on the sticker
read, 'Grow Where You're Planted.' At first, it didn't catch
my attention, but as I looked at it, the car moved slowly out
of view, and it finally hit me. I didn't move to Davenport,
Iowa. I didn't choose that city. Neither did my brothers and
sisters. Some forty-eight years earlier, our parents moved
there from Chicago, Illinois. My dad worked for The Rock
Island Railroad. He was transferred to Davenport, Iowa in
1930. I was only five months old. I didn't have a choice. It
came to mind that maybe The Lord put me there for a reason.
Maybe Davenport is where He wants me to be. There certainly are a lot of people in the Davenport area. They need
help too. Just maybe, The Lord wanted me to be obedient to
His will in Davenport; to reach people for Him through the
insurance business, in Davenport, Iowa. All these ideas were
rushing through my mind.

After about a half-hour, having traveled a good distance,
a most unusual thing happened. We had changed two freeways, with many thousands of cars having passed, in both
directions of traffic. A second time I was startled. As I was
looking out the right rear passenger window, the same car
I had seen before came slowly alongside, in the next lane.
We were going about sixty-five miles per hour. There, in
full view, was the same sticker on the window of the car
alongside; 'Grow Where You're Planted.' It was a confirmation of my thoughts. How did that same car come alongside,
after we had changed at least two freeways and traveled over
thirty miles? Maybe it was not a coincidence! Just maybe,
it was God-Instance! At this point in my conversation with

The Lord, I said,"Okay, if this is what You want Lord, I'll do it" immediately, a thought came to mind, which seemed to make the decision more pointed. I thought, Yes, and I can 'plant' where I am growing. I felt at peace. The Lord had touched my heart! We have stayed in Davenport, Iowa all these years.

From that day until today in 2001, I have felt that The Lord wanted me to stay in the insurance business in the Davenport area. He directed me to the people He wanted me to meet and serve. As I reflect on these last twenty years, I recognize that sometimes I would only plant a seed. Sometimes, I would only provide the water of encouragement for a seed planted by someone else. Sometimes I would be privileged to be present when someone would bloom, in full color, to accept The Lord. It is all His work! The Holy Spirit does all the prompting. We as disciples of The Lord, grow where we are planted. And, we plant seeds, for The Lord, where we are growing. What a wonderful plan The Lord has! We are the laborers in His Vineyard. The Lord gets all the glory! Then, The Lord reaps the 'Harvest,' for His Honor and Glory. Praise be His Holy Name! Praise be The Name of Jesus!

31

"I LOVE YOU"

*"If a man say, 'I love you,' and hateth his brother,
he is a liar; for he that loveth not his brother, whom
he has seen, how can he love God Whom he has not
seen?"*

(1John 4:20)

W hy are these three words, "I love you," so difficult to
say? The answer has probably eluded man since the
first sin of Adam. By nature, each of us, has a sinful nature
due to the fall of our first parents, Adam, and Eve. Since each
of us have fallen short of The Glory Of God, then I guess it
follows, that each of us can see the flaws in the character of
another person, making it impossible, on our own, to unconditionally love another person. Since God Is Love, (1John
4:16), then maybe we can't love another person, unless we
can see that person as God sees him or her. God overlooks
our sin and sees the soul and spirit, of each person, made in
His Image and Likeness. We have value, because He made
us to have value in His eyes, and therefore, He loves us
unconditionally.

The word 'Love' is used in our language for so many
things. I love your dress! I just love this bean soup! I love

the way my new car handles on the road! I love this game! We've all heard the word 'love' to explain all kinds of feelings and emotions. But, it is certain that love can only be expressed by one person, be it a human person, like all of us, or a spiritual person, like God. Love isn't love, unless it is given away, freely! I can't love the automobile I drive, because the auto can't receive the love, and further, it cannot return the love, even if it could receive it. As mentioned, 'God Is Love,' and therefore God is an 'action God,' for 'love' is an action word. In scripture, The Good Lord talks about love; "For God so loved the world, that He gave His only begotten Son, that whosoever believes in Him, will not perish, but will have eternal life!" (John chap 3:16). This sounds like we are not naturally lovable in our fallen state; but God, in His Goodness, loves us in spite of that, so much that, He gave His only son, Jesus, Who is our Saviour. Then, it follows that, for me to love someone, in the truest sense of the Word, I must accept Jesus, Who is the only answer given by God The Father, as 'The Way' to accept and receive God's love. In the purest sense then, it seems to really love someone is to wish that person to be in The Kingdom Of God, and to do all I can through prayer and service, to lead that person into a relationship with Jesus, Who is The Way, The Truth, and The Life. Maybe this is why the reason it is difficult to say "I love you," is so elusive. We have to surrender to Jesus, overlook the faults of others, and then we are able to see others as Jesus sees them. When we see another as Jesus sees that person, our desire to see that person in The Kingdom Of God, is kindled; and this is to really love that person.

To love someone means we must be able to forgive that person for any wrong doing to others, or, to us directly. It's not an option. It's a command. The Lord said, "Love one another" (1John 4:11). Forgiveness is not easy, but rather, is an act of the will. I choose to forgive someone. It does not come naturally. Forgiveness doesn't come naturally, due to our sin nature, but not forgiving someone is probably the greatest 'illness' in the world today. Once, I heard a man say, "Not exercising forgiveness is like swallowing poison, and hoping that the other person dies." When we don't forgive, it holds us, and the other person in bondage.

My four sisters, and four brothers, and I, grew up in a family where the words, "I love you," were not heard; nor were they used by any family member. Each of us knew what love was, and we held each brother or sister in a special place in our heart, but the words expressing this love, were never used. Our father had a drinking problem when we were growing up, with his own resultant set of problems. None of us were very close to him. Our mother didn't have a good relationship with him either. In later years, she admitted that she was emotionally disturbed for a good portion of our childhoods. I know, for example, that she did not go out of the house for many years when I was a child. Even in this tough family environment, The Lord helped us. His Grace worked in our lives, so that each of us grew in the knowledge of The Lord, feeling His presence in each of our lives.

One day, when my dad was in his late 80's, and I was in my 40's, I came to the realization, that I had never told my father that I loved him. He lived in California at the time, having been retired for some time. The only contact I had with him was an occasional letter or when I would call him on the phone. I called him most every week to see how he and my mother were getting along and to show him that I cared. During one such call, when we were talking about things in general, I knew that this was the day I would have to swallow my pride, and tell him that I loved him. It was so difficult. It had never been spoken by either of us to the other. One of us would have to be the stronger of the two. It needed to be said. Most probably, it would have to be me. I knew in my heart that his ears needed to hear these words.

Quite probably, he had never heard the words from any of his children. Just as I was about to sign-off, I got up the courage and sandwiched the difficult words in a phrase, by saying; "Well, I love you back here, Pop!" There was just a slight pause on his part. Then, he said, "You better, or I'll choke you!" That's okay. His spirit took it in! It must have hit home! His spirit needed to hear the words, mull them over, and finally digest them. I didn't need to hear him tell me that he loved me; he needed to hear that I loved him. Jesus had taken care of the 'love' problem in my life, and I could see my father as Jesus saw him. At the time, he couldn't respond with "I love you too, Larry"; but, that was okay. From that day on, our relationship grew. Pop would ask me questions about the Bible. He would ask me where a certain passage was that spoke about a particular promise or parable. I would copy that page in the Bible and send it to him. When we love someone, The Lord can work through that love to bring that person to a saving knowledge of Jesus.

During one particular telephone call to my dad, after our 'love' conversation, it came to sign-off time, and I said, "Well, take care of yourself, Pop!" Quickly, he answered, "If I didn't do that, I'd have been dead forty years ago." Then, a few weeks later, before I could catch myself, I used the same sign-off, saying, "Well, take care of yourself, Pop!" He said, "I tried that once, it didn't work!" Then, a week later, at a time when Pop was in his 90's, I caught myself in the sign-off, stopping short of the full phrase I had used two times previously. Instead, I said, "Take care, Pop!" Pop said, "I tried that, and found out I needed a 'Caretaker,' and now I've got One!" Pop had accepted Jesus as his Caretaker! My dad died a few months before his hundredth birthday. During the years before his death and after his statement about having a 'Caretaker' I noticed in our conversations that he talked freely about Jesus and his relationship with Him. One time, he said, "Larry, there is only one Person Who could have saved me!" I said, "Jesus." Pop said, "Right on!" Would my dad have come to the Lord without my saying, 'I love you'? I don't know. I do know however, that if I love someone, as The Lord commanded me to do, and if I pray for that person, The Lord can work through this love to lift that person up to His level. Do you agree with me? It is so important to say, "I love you."

32

BETTER TO GIVE

"I have always shown you that it is by such hard works that you must help the weak. You need to recall the words of The Lord, Himself, Who said, 'There is more happiness in giving than receiving.'"
(Acts 20:35)

The other day, when Elayne and I were driving down the highway, on our way home from East Moline State Prison where we were visiting the prisoners, we felt the presence of The Lord in a very personal way. It was so peaceful! We were both very tired, but it was a good kind of tiredness. We had just been to an excellent meeting with the prisoners who had completed a 'JOY' weekend. A 'JOY' weekend is one where volunteer prisoners come to the chapel on the prison grounds to participate in a very spiritual weekend of talks and sharing. Some of the prisoners had given testimonies that evening that The Lord had blessed them on the last JOY weekend, which was the previous weekend. Their talks were very inspiring. We were so happy for them, because they had accepted The Lord Jesus into their hearts as their personal Lord and Savior.

As we traveled across the highway, we noticed that the car we are currently driving (1998) was running so smoothly. I said to Elayne, "Honey, doesn't the car sound good?" Elayne said, "Yes, It runs so quiet. The Lord is so good to us." Then I said, "Lord Jesus, we thank You for the use of this car while we are here." Elayne said, "Amen." This incident started us talking about all the cars we have owned in our married life. Or, rather, I should say, the cars we have used in our married life, as The Lord is the "Owner" of all. In our forty-eight years of marriage, we came up with seventeen vehicles, which had been titled, in our names.

When we were married, in 1952, I owned a 1941 Pontiac, 4-door maroon roadster. It was a good car. We took it on our honeymoon. When we bought a 1949 green Pontiac Coupe, we sold the 1941 Pontiac for a very low price. On a business trip to Ohio, I bought a 1950 Buick Special, which had 40,000 miles on it. We drove this car for many years. It took us to California in 1956, when we moved there to work for Convair Aircraft Company. This Buick took us back, with four children, when we moved back to Davenport, Iowa, to work for Bendix Corporation. When we needed a larger car for our growing family, we gave the Buick to a technician who worked in my department at Bendix. We had purchased, from a dealership, a 1958 nine passenger Plymouth Station Wagon, which gave us good transportation on many vacation trips. This station wagon was very large, so Elayne didn't feel comfortable driving it. We then purchased our first new car, a 1964 Volkswagen Bug, as it was much smaller, and Elayne could drive this type of car. We gave the 1958 Plymouth Wagon to a young man who worked with me, but couldn't afford the purchase of a car for his family. He was so joyful at receiving the car that this added such fun to the giving of the car. Since our family was getting even larger, we could not all get in the VW Bug, so we purchased our second new car, a new 1966 Volkswagen Bus. Elayne really liked this car. She could sit up high, allowing her good visibility. Elayne drove this car everywhere, taking the children to their many meetings and other functions. She took it shopping, took the children to school, as well as all the general errands. This car really helped us out because we could all get into one vehicle. We took all ten children with us on vacation to New Jersey one year, and then the next year, we took them all to California. This VW Bus provided much family fun. We finally gave the 1964 VW Bug to our oldest son, Chris, for his transportation to and from school and work. We gave the 1966 VW Bus to a young family who needed a vehicle, but could not afford the purchase price. We bought a 1967 Pontiac which the girls used for transportation to high school. They called this car "Old Blue." Then we gave this car away to a young needy family. A business client gave us a 1970 Subaru, which didn't run. We gave this to our son, Daniel, who helped pay for the parts to get it running. Dan and I had fun getting the car running. It required a complete engine overhaul. Dan used the Subaru for work and school. I had purchased a 1969 Volkswagen Karmen Ghia to use for business. When Dan sold the Subaru, for a low price, we sold him the Karmen for what he received for the Subaru. The Karmen Ghia was Dan's Sportster. He fixed it up to look super and it ran great after he overhauled the engine. We were given a 1977 Ford Pinto, which became Elayne's car. The full story on the 1977 Pinto is covered in these writings, in #14, entitled "First Class." We gave the Ford Pinto to one of our nephews, who needed good transportation for his family. We purchased a 1973 Ford LTD, at a low price, from the estate of a former client, named Roma. This story is covered in #27, entitled "Love One Another." Of all the cars we have owned, the 1973 LTD is Elayne's favorite. When we sold the 1973 Ford LTD to our son, Chris, we purchased a used 1970 Chrysler Imperial from an individual owner, who was introduced to us by an insurance client. The Imperial provided us with excellent transportation for a long time. This was a dream car with many extras. We eventually sold the Imperial to our son Peter who needed an extra car. We purchased a 1969 Buick Century which was not operating. After fixing it up, we sold it to our daughter, Felicia, and her husband, David. We purchased a 1980 Dodge Omni from a business client at a low price, since it was not working. After an overhaul, we sold this car to our daughter, Anita, at a low price.

Then, we started getting into some really fine automobiles. One of the men in our gospel quartet would get a new car every year and one half, to use in his position as a traveling salesman. Tom would have the opportunity to buy the used car when his employer would provide him with a new one. On most occasions, Tom would buy the cars for himself or someone else in his immediate family. Through Tom, we were offered his 1985 Chevy Celebrity for about 60% of the retail price. Naturally, we grabbed this opportunity. In the Celebrity, we went to Florida, as well as into many other states, on other trips, without any problems. When our daughter, Anita needed a car, we sold her the Celebrity. We used that money for the down payment on a 1989 Ford Taurus, which became available through my friend, Tom, when he again got a new company car. We got the 1989 Taurus for about 60% of the regular retail price. When we got the chance to buy a 1990 Ford Taurus from Tom's company, we sold the 1989 to our son, Chris. This money provided us with the down payment on the 1990 Taurus. Then we were offered a 1995 Ford Taurus through Tom's company. We sold the 1990 Ford Taurus to our daughter, Anita, at the price she received when her 1985 Chevy Celebrity was totaled in an accident. We then used this money for the down payment on the 1995 Ford Taurus. Now, in 2001, we are still driving in the 1995 Ford Taurus, when we had the experience first mentioned in this section. And then, just to show

how The Lord works, a few months ago, my friend Tom mentioned that he had a new 1999 Dodge Intrepid, which could be available, if we wanted it, when he gets a new car next year. Isn't The Lord Good!

In all, we have had the use of seventeen automobiles in our married life thus far. Every one of the vehicles has given us good service. All have given us over 100,000 miles of operation each. We are still driving the 1995 Ford Taurus, and it has just turned over 130,000 miles. Except for the 1964 and 1966 VW's, we have never sought after a vehicle. The cars seemed to come to us at the right time and at either no cost, or certainly, a very low cost. And, in turn, we either have given the cars away, or sold them at very low prices.

We are told that this is not the typical way of doing business of buying and selling cars; but, this is the way we were led to do it. In thinking about The Lord's Word, when He said it is better to give than to receive, we certainly find this true in our lives. There is real joy in giving. There is real joy in giving someone a better bargain than they would have thought possible. This gives real joy. We also find that The Lord does not mean that in giving, we will not receive. We should feel free to give, whether or not we receive. We should not give, with the idea that we will receive, but in The Lord's way, we usually receive, when we give. The Lord looks for the attitude of heart. If we give freely, He takes notice, and He blesses. And, in our lives, we find the blessings coming as surprises, when we least expect them. That's just how The Lord is! He is so Good! Elayne and I have been blessed in so many ways throughout our married lives; but, I wanted to share with you this one particular way in which The Lord blessed us with good automobiles to drive. When I think about the wonderful car we now drive, the 1995 Ford Taurus; that came to us, and the low price we paid for it, I marvel at how good The Good Lord has been to us. We thank You Lord for the use of this fine car while we are living here in Your World. Give us Your Grace to always realize that it is You Who is in control of all things, and we who are dependent solely upon You.

33

CONFESS OR DENY

"Whosoever therefore shall confess Me before man, him will I confess also before My Father which is in heaven. But whosoever shall deny Me before man, him will I also deny before My father which is in heaven."

(Matthew 10:32-33)

In 1977, I was asked to give a talk at a Full Gospel Business Men's Breakfast. Note that this story was covered in detail in section #28, entitled "The Greatest Gift." Following that talk, I started to attend the meetings regularly, because I was hungry for every way in which I could learn more about The Lord Jesus, and I wanted as close a relationship to Him as possible. At one dinner meeting of Full Gospel Businessmen, the guest speaker was a man named George Otis, a former executive of a company called 'Lear Aircraft.' His testimony was powerful. He related how The Lord had worked through him to witness to many people, even owners of large corporations.

He told the detailed story about how The Lord impressed upon him to call a particular company president, whom he knew very well. While he was on an airplane, en route to a business appointment, he received the urge to call this man as soon as possible. At an interim stop, he got off the airplane to use a telephone in the airport terminal. Even though it was in the evening, he called the man at his office. To his surprise, he found him in. After many rings, the man finally answered the phone. George could tell that the man was very tense. After some conversation, George learned why. The man had a gun to his head. George continued to talk to him and finally persuaded him to at least wait until he could see him. He told him if after they talked, if George hadn't made any sense to him, then he could go ahead with his plans. The man agreed to wait. George changed his flight plans and returned to the area from which he had come. He went to the man's office that very evening. When George explained to the man the love of Jesus, and how He had come to this world, not to condemn sinners, but to save them, the man came to a saving knowledge of Jesus Christ and asked Him into his heart as his personal Lord and Saviour.

This witness really ministered to my heart. It impressed me that George would take such an interest in this man, and that he had the courage to go to him with just the hope that he could talk about Jesus, and if he could, he knew he could be of help. At the end of George's talk, he did something which really surprised me. He asked if there were any in attendance that evening who would like to have a personal relationship with Jesus. Further, he asked if that person, or those people, who wanted a personal relationship with Jesus, would acknowledge this publicly. He said, "You know about Jesus, but maybe you have never asked Him into your heart in a personal way." I knew in my heart that he was talking to me. I knew a lot *about* Jesus at that point in my life: I loved Jesus, and I believed that He was truly God in the Flesh; that He rose from the dead, and He was with His Father in heaven. But, I had never acknowledged this publicly. I had never demonstrated in public that I needed Jesus in my life.

George said, "The Lord would like us to do this, in public, as a demonstration of our commitment to Him." A war was going on inside me. A lot of people in attendance knew me very well. They knew, that I was a 'Christian.' Also, I knew that most considered me a very religious person. And yet, in my heart, I also knew that I had never admitted, in public, that I was a sinner who needed a Personal Saviour. I had never admitted publicly that I wanted a personal relationship with Jesus as my Lord and Saviour. Finally, I swallowed my pride. I raised my hand, as George asked. George prayed for those whose hands were raised. In my heart, I felt accepted. I felt good about my decision. I knew that The Lord had read my heart. Jesus came into my heart that evening in a personal way.

Soon after that evening, I came across the verse in Matthew where Jesus asks us to confess Him before men so that He may confess us before His Father in Heaven. On our own, we are nothing before The Father. Our works are but filthy rags. But, by accepting Jesus as our personal Lord and Saviour, The Father looks at us through the Blood of His Son, Jesus, and he sees the Righteousness of Jesus, Who then confesses us to His Father. We become adopted sons and daughters. If, however, we deny Jesus before men, by our words and life style, then Jesus, by His promise, must deny us before His Father, which is in Heaven.

I pray, in Jesus Name, the Name above all names, that we can swallow our pride, and ask Jesus to come into all our hearts, to cleanse us from all sin, and make us acceptable to God His Father.

34

TRUST IN THE LORD

"Trust in The Lord with all your heart and lean not upon your own understanding. Acknowledge Him in all your ways, and He will direct your paths."
(Proverbs 3:5,6)

In 1985, Elayne, was working part-time, as a secretary, for a businessman, in Bettendorf, Iowa. Our daughter, Anna, was looking for full-time work and contacted a man, seeking employment. This businessman needed someone who would work on Mondays, Wednesdays, and Fridays. Anna needed full-time summer work to help with her college expenses but she told him that he should be talking to her mother. Even though Elayne wasn't looking for work, the man called her. She was taken by surprise, but agreed to an interview. Suddenly, Elayne was working part-time. It was temporary but Elayne reasoned that the extra money would come in handy to help with upcoming wedding expenses for one of our children.

On April 26th, of 1985, I was driving along the highway, on the way back to the office after an appointment. Hoping to hear some good Christian music, I turned the radio on. I always have the radio tuned to station WDLM, at 89.3 fm, a Christian radio station, in East Moline, Illinois. That day, at quite a distance from the station, the reception was very clear. The reason my car radio is always tuned to WDLM, is that I have learned so much about The Lord's Word, through the programs on this radio station. When I first turned the radio on, I heard the announcer's words, something about 'trusting The Lord with all your heart.' The words pierced my heart and my mind. Then, the announcer started giving the news for the day. I asked The Lord to help me find that spot in The Bible that talked about what the man had said. I prayed, "Lord, those words were for me! I need to know where these words are in The Bible. Help me to remember enough of these words, so that when I get home, I can look for the verses." I knew that if I could remember enough of the key words, I could use my concordance to find the verse I wanted. (note: a concordance is like a dictionary, only instead of explaining the given word, the concordance gives all the verses in The Bible which use this word.) With half an ear, I continued listening to the station, but I was trying to remember as much of what I heard as I could. Then, at the end of the newscast, the man said, "Remember now, the Bible verse for the day, "Proverbs 3:5 and 6, 'Trust in The Lord with all your heart, and lean not upon your own understanding. Acknowledge Him in all your ways, and He will direct your paths.'" Quickly, I jotted the verse identification down on the back of an envelope lying on the front seat. I was so relieved to know where the words were in The Bible. I thanked The Lord for letting me hear the words, and for letting me know where to find them so that I could study them.

When I arrived home, I looked in my Bible, and copied the words onto a 3-inch by 5-inch file card. I wanted to memorize and meditate on the words and apply them to my life. Just a few days after hearing these words on the radio, on April 30th, 1985, I picked up Elayne, after work, to bring her home. Shortly after coming into our home, she remarked,

"Oh, by the way, this is for you!" Elayne handed me a small piece of paper she had taken out of her purse. Jotted down on this small corner of an envelope, Elayne had written two bible verses ; first was 'Proverbs 3:5,6, and second, was Matthew 19:26. I said, "What do you mean, this is for me?" Elayne went on to tell me that since she had a lot of free time at work, she had taken quite a few Christian books to work, so that she would have good material to read. In one particular book, she came across these two verses. As she was reading, she thought to herself, this is for Larry, so she jotted the verses down to tell me about them. I asked her what day and time she was reading the particular book, and she said the day was April 26ᵗʰ, and the time was 11:30 a.m. This is the exact day and time when I heard this verse mentioned on the radio. I pulled the card from my pocket to show it to her. Also, I told her that I was memorizing the verse, and further, that this was the exact time I was listening to the radio, when I heard the words spoken. Elayne simply answered, "See, that's a confirmation."

My goal is to live out these words in my life; to trust in The Lord with all my heart. Not to look at the circumstances, but instead, look at The Lord Jesus. I want to acknowledge The Lord in whatever direction I go, since, in The Bible, it is written 'ways,' not way. The word is plural; there are many ways in which I can go. What I must do, is to acknowledge The Lord in whatever direction I go. Also, The Lord will make my 'paths' straight. Again, the word is plural. The Lord is so good. As I step out in faith, He will direct my path. Eventually, I will be at peace in the direction I go, and I will be in the perfect will of The Lord. Complete freedom! Perfect unconditional love!

Sometimes, when I am down in spirit, I'll put my name in this verse to make it personal. When I'm tempted, or when the problem looks too big for me to handle, I will say out loud; "I, Larry Lyons, trust in The Lord with all my heart. I,

Larry Lyons, will acknowledge You, Lord Jesus, in all my ways, and I, Larry Lyons, trust in You, Lord Jesus, to direct my paths." This action makes the Word of God, come to life. When I make such a personal response, The Lord's Peace, which surpasses all understanding, again comes into my heart. Isn't the Lord Good!

35

THE POTTER'S WHEEL

"Then Jesus said to them again: Peace be unto you;
as My Father has sent Me, even so send I you!"
(John 20:21)

I n the year of 1976, I came across a small flyer which outlined a Catholic conference being held in St. Louis, Missouri. I didn't know anything about this spiritual movement, but somehow, in my heart, I knew that Elayne and I should attend. The meeting was held in the Fall. When I mentioned the meeting to Elayne, she was not in favor of attending. I felt that as time would go on, Elayne would come to the position that she would agree with us going, so I completed the application and sent in the registration fee. In all our married life, I had never done anything like that before. Always, I would get agreement before taking any action, but I guess because I really wanted to go, I figured I would be able to persuade Elayne before the time came. A week or so after making the registration, I did explain to Elayne that I had made the application, and that we had about two months to prepare for the weekend meeting. As the departure time approached, Elayne reminded me that we would have three daughters out on the first night of the meeting, a Friday night, and it would not be good parenting to be gone with three children out late attending a high school 'homecoming dance.' Of course, Elayne was right! But, what could I do? I really wanted to attend the meeting. After much deliberation, I figured out a possible solution. We could wait for the girls to be home in bed and then we would leave early Saturday morning in order to get to the meeting for the opening session on Saturday and Sunday. Elayne's older sister agreed to stay with our children while we were gone, but still, we wanted to be there while the three of them were at the homecoming dance. Elayne mentioned that we had made hotel reservations for both Friday and Saturday evenings, so we would still have to pay for Friday evening, even though we did not come. I decided to call the conference center in St. Louis, to explain our problem. With all the conference material in front of me, I called the headquarters in St. Louis. My hope was that we could get out of the reservation for Friday evening, and stay only Saturday evening, returning after the closing session on Sunday afternoon.

I called the 800 toll-free phone number listed on the material. The first sound I heard was a woman's voice. The voice said, "As the Father has called Me, so I am calling you. The correct number is _ _ _ _ _ _ _ (a different number than what I had called). I hung up the phone, rather startled by what had happened. In my heart, I felt it was a message from The Lord, telling me to come to the meeting, without apprehension or tension. Then, I dialed the new number just given to me. A man's voice came on the line, saying, "St. Louis Catholic Charismatic Conference." The man was very polite and very helpful. When I explained to him that we had a problem concerning our arrival time, he said that this would help him out. People were clamoring for hotel rooms and if we would be willing to give up the Friday evening, we would not be charged for the early room reservation fee. How good The Lord is! It worked out that we saw our daughters safely in bed, and we left about 4:00 a.m., Saturday morning. We arrived in St. Louis about 8:45 a.m., and parked in the driveway of the Hilton Hotel, across the street from the convention center. It was very crowded at this Saturday morning rush hour. Elayne waited in the car while I went in to the hotel to register. The attendant at the desk was very helpful. When I told him we were to attend the meeting across the street, and it was starting in a few minutes, he seemed genuinely concerned. I asked him what to do about parking since we were very late. He pointed to a doorman across the driveway, who was dressed in red, and he told me tell 'Charlie,' that 'George' said he was to get us a place to park. Charlie moved a barricade aside, and Surprise! We had the first parking spot, directly across the street from the entrance to the convention center.

Since we arrived late, we had to sit in a bleacher section toward the top. There were over 8,000 people in attendance. As we were sitting down, all in attendance, were finishing the opening songs of praise and worship. The first speaker on the program was an older white-haired priest from Boston. As if it were yesterday, I can remember his first statement. He said, "The Lord is The Master Potter" as he gestured upward with his right hand. At that point, I would have to say, that I had what could be described as a vision. I wasn't asleep and I wasn't in a trance. Yet, in my mind, I saw a picture of ten potter's wheels, turning, with one of our children on each of the wheels. I don't remember another word of the speaker's presentation because I was so caught up in what was happening. My focus was on one particular potter's wheel. Upon that wheel was placed one of our children with whom we were having some difficulty. I guess you could call it youthful rebellion. As parents, Elayne, and I were having concern over this situation; in fact, we carried this problem with us on the trip, hoping to get some help on a direction to reach this child. As I looked at the wheel, I could see a

Large Hand, molding and shaping the image of the child. I could also see my hand in the picture, for I too, was trying to form the image of our child on the wheel. There was another Hand, on my arm, restraining me, as if to say, 'Hands off!' My interpretation of what I was seeing, was that the 'shaping hand' was The Lord's, and the other restraining Hand, was also The Lord's, telling me to 'let go.' I was overwhelmed. I remember saying in my spirit, "You mean, Lord, You want me to step aside? But, this is our child, I'm the father. Isn't that my job? It would be a cop-out, if I just let go."

Then, a peace came over me which I cannot describe. I sensed, in a very real way, the Love that The Lord had for this child. His Love is unconditional! My love is conditional! Our child could read in my actions that there were things I could not accept. I was humbled! The Good Lord let me see the intensity of His unconditional Love which He has for each of His created beings. His Love is so perfect! I was able to see that the track that this child was on, was the only track possible in order for salvation to take place. In my human approach, I wanted to change things. I wanted to keep this child from being hurt, with the hope this would cause this child to turn from the present life-style of rebellion, to a position of wanting to serve The Lord. The Lord showed me that His Love was so perfect, that He knew this child perfectly, and He was willing to let the child go free, so that in desperation, at the end of a blind way, there would be a turning to The Lord for help. The Lord let me see that the makeup of this child was such that He knew the child would dig a hole, fall into the hole by mistake, and try every way possible to climb out of the hole, without success, before there would be a turning to The Lord for His help. In this way, and only in this way, would there be an eventual acceptance of Jesus as Lord and Saviour. Such a perfect Love! Not a sentimental love; but a true unconditional love of The Father of all. It was a great spiritual experience which

I will remember forever. I felt the warmth of The Father's Love—A touch from "The Master Potter."

Later, I shared with Elayne what had happened. We talked about this experience for the rest of the weekend, as well as on the trip back home from St. Louis. While traveling back from St. Louis, by car, there was a moment of silence as we were reflecting on the experience of the weekend. Elayne broke the silence by saying, "You know Larry, there is one thing we have to add to that!" Since we had been discussing the potter's wheel experience, I knew she meant that we would have to 'add' something to our 'letting go' as far as the children were concerned. I answered, "Honey, what could be added to that!" Elayne replied, "We have to be there to pick up the pieces."

"I like that," I said.

We were both filled with such gratitude for the spiritual touch from The Hand Of The Lord that weekend in St. Louis. When we arrived home, we put this experience into practice. We shifted our roles as parents. We gave our children as much free rein as we could from that point on. From then on, our love was 'tough love.' We didn't allow disrespect to anyone, nor did we allow a wrongful lifestyle while living under our roof, under our direct responsibility. Even today, our children know exactly where we stand. They know we love them dearly. We tell them so. Our children have honored us as parents, both while living under our roof, and now, when each of them are out on their own with their individual families. When the falls and hurts come, as they do in every life, Elayne and I are there to help pick up the pieces; pointing our children back to The Lord.

Now, for Elayne and I, The Lord is asking us to be 'prayer warriors,' to help Him Love our children into "The Kingdom." I think back to the message on the answering machine to the telephone call I made. It reminds me of what Jesus said; "As The Father has sent Me, even so, send I you."

36

LORD OF ALL

"Who has claim against Me that I must pay?
Everything under heaven belongs to Me!"
(Job 41:11)

Jesus is Lord of all, or Jesus is not Lord at all.

In April of 1966, I was in Fairlawn, New Jersey, on a business trip. As Technical Director for a company in Moline, Illinois, I was commuting regularly to New York City, as we were involved in the preparation of technical manuals for J. C. Penney Company. The Penney Company was establishing Auto Service Centers around the United States, and our company was involved in technical writing as well as illustrations for the necessary repair manuals to be used at these centers. Specifically, the work involved all the art-work, mechanical drawings, photographs, and technical writing associated with service manuals for automotive repair. While in the Northeastern part of this country, I also contacted other companies in the general area, in an attempt to obtain additional business for the Moline based company.

During one such business trip, while in my motel room one evening, I searched within myself for what type of work

I wanted to be involved in, for the rest of my working-career. At the time, I was thirty-six years old. Since my aptitudes were in the area of products and engineering, I was called upon to travel often, in my present and all previous employment positions. Because The Lord gifted me with technical abilities, I excelled in engineering, product development, and communications. Since I did a good job, my travel time increased, because I was able to bring more business into each company I worked for. I didn't want to travel because I wanted to be home with our family. That particular night, I longed to be home, and so I was looking at my future working-career with focused determination. In desperation, I started to list every type of occupation in which I felt I could succeed. Additionally, I looked at all the variables associated with each occupation. The general types of occupations I listed were: a large corporation; a small company; a sales company; sales with salary plus commission; my own company; civil service; engineering company; and, a product company; intangibles – ideas and service. These were the areas in which I felt I was gifted. After listing the various occupations, I developed thirteen different variables which would be present in these occupations, in various degrees. These variables were as follows: Retirement Benefits, Immediate Income, Long-Term, Interest, Security, Fringe Benefits, Location – No Travel, Free-Time, Taxing To My Health, Return For Input, Development, Recognition, and Do-Good. I assigned 10 points to each category. Subjectively then, I looked at each category, and came up with a point distribution across each occupation. In looking at just one such category, as an example of point-distribution, let us consider the category, 'Location-No-Travel.' The highest point total of ten, was given to three occupations, namely; Small Company, My Own Company, and Intangibles-Ideas & Service. If I were to work in any of these areas, travel would be non-existent, or at least at a minimum. In contrast,

I assigned the lowest point total to the occupation 'Sales With Salary Plus Commission,' because this endeavor would probably involve much travel to obtain the sales necessary to support our large family. In similar manner, I looked at each category, assigning point totals in a subjective manner, as they applied to me. There were papers all over the table in my motel room. So that I could not steer the outcome, I would cover up each point category point distribution, as I went along, and I thereby could not predict or slant the outcome. Finally, I made a chart compiling all the data on a single page.

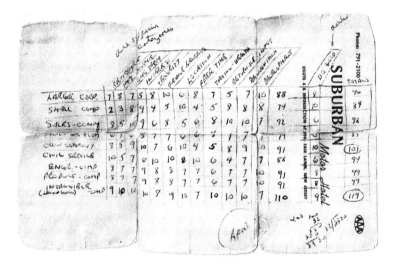

Note: The edges of this chart are in worn condition because I carried it in my wallet for many years, before taking it out to frame it. The framed chart hangs on the office wall in our home as a reminder of what I did that night, and the career decisions I have made since.

Much to my surprise, the totals came out as follows: the highest total was 119 for the occupation 'Ideas And Service'; the next highest total was 109, for the occupation 'My Own

Company'; and the lowest total was eighty-four, for 'Small Company,' with the other totals dispersed in between. In my mind, I kept scanning the chart in an effort to discern what it all meant. What could I do in the area of 'Ideas And Service,' which could do good, while at the same time be fulfilling? Could this also be 'My Own Company'? While flying home, I had the idea that I would do work for a hundred different people, at a fee of $100 per year, for a total annual income of $10,000. At the time, this would have been just enough income to support our family. It would be up to the hundred individuals to use my time to their benefit, to justify the $100 annual fee. I felt I could help them in many ways, such as; designing a home, finding a better job, consulting with them in their business, fixing their car, doing home repair, tutoring them or their children, doing electrical work, doing plumbing, or any other service function which could be of help. To me, at that time, it seemed like a plausible idea.

Soon after my return home, I was contacted by an insurance person, who had recently purchased a life insurance agency. This man had done some insurance work for my employer, so I felt I had to agree to meet with him. After a couple of appointments, he asked me to take an aptitude test to determine my compatibility with the insurance business. My scores were very high. So, after much discussion with my wife, I agreed to go into the insurance business, with my starting date, January 1, 1967.

Starting out was extremely difficult for two reasons; Basically, I am not a so-called 'salesman,' and secondly, I didn't fully understand the compensation arrangement. In my haste to start a new endeavor, I didn't check into all the aspects of the compensation package. The business looked like it was in line with my basic desires; I would have 'My Own Business,' working for people in the areas of "Ideas And Service." The compensation system was not a salary as I thought, but rather, a combination of one half company training allowance, and one half draw against commission earned. Since I approached the business from a 'service' standpoint, I ended up doing a lot of work for people, for free, while the actual sales did not produce commissions that matched a pre-set 'validation curve.' I didn't know about this validation curve. Soon, I learned that my income was dropping due to lower than targeted commission earnings. We had to borrow in order to stay in the business, and be able to pay the family bills. To further complicate the problem, I learned, after a year and a half, that I was in debt to the agency, since the half income from the agency was based on actual commission earned. It was a most difficult strain on Elayne and me. But, I did enjoy the part of 'helping people.' Every day, I was on my knees in a small church in downtown Davenport, Iowa, asking The Lord for help. Just to earn enough to pay the bills and raise the family – that's what I asked for. And, The Lord did honor my request. Even through tremendous financial struggle, our needs were provided.

It took about ten years before we were able to get our income up to what we had before coming into the insurance business. We were completely on our own, working in the areas of life and health insurance. I can recall as if it were yesterday, late one particular evening, being at home working on an insurance study for a very wealthy man. He didn't need any insurance. As a service to him, I was going through his existing policies to see if the policy provisions and beneficiary arrangements were in line with his needs. If not, I would contact the companies to make the changes for him. There was no charge for this service. Somehow, I hoped that all this effort would work out in some way for us. I remember how low I felt at the time. We needed money to pay bills, and the particular work I was doing would not bring in any immediate income. It was about 1:00 a.m.! Elayne came out to the small study where I had set up a desk to do my home service work. Having just gotten out of bed, she was rubbing her eyes as she stood there. "Larry, when are you coming to bed," she asked? I replied, "Pretty soon, I have one more policy to review as I have to give this to Fran" (my secretary) "in the morning for her to type." Elayne didn't leave. I turned to see Elayne standing in the same place. Again she asked, "Larry, why don't you come to bed?" I put the policy down, totally frustrated. We had bills to pay, no money, and this work was for free. Caught off guard by Elayne's remarks, without even thinking, I said, "Why don't I quit trying to prove a point – why don't I get back into engineering – something I understand?" If Elayne had said something like, "Boy, have I been waiting for you to say that," the next morning, I would have crawled back to one of three companies, to plead for a position in one of the departments of which I had been in charge. I was feeling pretty hopeless –a failure. Instead, Elayne came over to where I was seated. She sat down, took my hand in hers, and said, "Larry, would you quit now, when you are that close (as she held up two fingers, with a small space in between) to having what you want? I'm not asking you to quit! I'm asking you to come to bed! You don't have to work that hard! People will understand what you are doing, and one day they will be coming to you. Now please come to bed!" I remember clearly how it felt like someone had poured warm oil over me. I thought to myself, Lord, this woman actually understands me! She has trust in me. In face of all these obstacles, she has blind faith that things will work out okay. The next day I called that man. I was supposed to see him that evening with the completed study. Instead, I told him that something had come up, and I would not be able to see him until the following week. Because of what Elayne had said to me, I decided to cut back on my working hours in order to devote more time to the family. Knowing my family better, became a priority for me. To trust in The Lord became a mode-of-operation for me.

The business grew gradually. Soon, we were handling all areas of insurance: life, health, auto, homeowner's, group, and business insurance. Even though Elayne was helping me, we couldn't handle all the paperwork associated with the business, and at the same time perform all the service needed. Eventually, our oldest son, Chris, joined us as a partner. Shortly after that, our youngest daughter, Anita, began as a part-time secretary, under a high-school co-op program. After graduation she worked full time. A few years after that we added our youngest son, Paul, also as a partner. As of this writing, late in 2001, we have a small building for the business in downtown Bettendorf, Iowa. We have been blessed by The Lord beyond measure. The business has tremendous potential for growth.

Elayne and I are now semi-retired. The business is incorporated. I am not a stockholder or owner. The children own the business. In addition, Chris' wife, Sheryl, has come into the business as a secretary. Not being an owner in the business seems almost contradictory. It seems all my life, that I wanted my own business but now, I have given this up. Someone said to me, "How difficult it must have been." But one day, some years ago, I realized that the business wasn't really mine. I realized that The Lord owned everything, including the insurance business. The question I had to answer was, 'Am I operating The Lord's business properly?' Was I truly allowing The Lord to help me and guide me in the building of the business? Immediately, I shifted gears, and from that day on, I looked at everything with the idea – 'If Jesus were in this position, what would He do?' In Hebrews 3:4, it is written; "For every house is built by some man, but He that built all things, is God." God really is "The Owner" of the insurance business. One day I asked myself, "Larry are you a good steward of the business The Lord gave you to run?" At that point, I had to do some changing in my approach to the operation of the business. That is why it was easy to 'give up' ownership, to the children. The business was not ours! In fact, our children are not ours! The home we live in is not ours. The cars we drive are not ours. The body I live in is not mine. In fact, anything I feel I own, really owns me, because in effect, I have not given up control of these items or situations to The Lord. "Jesus is either Lord of all, or He is not Lord at all!"

Often while driving, Elayne and I will thank The Good Lord for having the use of our excellent Taurus automobile, while we are in this world. "Thank You Lord for letting us live in such a wonderful home while we are here. Thank You Lord for such beautiful children! Help us to be the parents You want us to be, while we are here!"

I would like to share with you one 'good example' of the ownership question that came up in my life. One of my good clients, who is now with The Lord, asked me a question while we were riding along in his car. Bob said he wanted to ask me a question. Immediately I asked The Lord to help me. Bob asked, "Larry, do you think it's okay to own an expensive car like this?" He was driving a new German AUDI automobile. The soft leather cushion kind of wrapped around me as I sat in the front passenger seat. Almost at once, I said, "Could you give it up?" Bob thought for a moment and said, "Yes." I said, "Then it's okay to own it." Bob truly loved The Lord and knew in his heart that all things are owned by The Lord. We only use them, while we are here.

Then, as The Lord said, when he talked to Job, in the midst of Job's trial – "Who has claim against Me that I must pay? Everything belongs to Me." (Job 41:11)

37

A NEW HEART

"Thy Word have I hid in my heart, that I might not sin against Thee."

(Psalm 119:11)

For many years I sang in a comedy quartet with four other men who became as close to me as my own brothers. Our quartet was together for eleven years. This is long time for such a group to remain together, as the usual duration would be only a couple of years. Tim sang Bass, Norm sang Baritone, Denny sang Lead, and I sang Tenor. We called ourselves "The Four Bits Of Fun." Our routines were good, our comedy was genuine, and consequently, we were in demand. We sang for just about anyone who would listen. Each of us did so enjoy singing close barbershop harmony. Mostly we sang at barbershop shows, variety shows, contests, and conventions. As one might imagine, the hazard of these events is that the beer and liquor flowed freely. We were well liked wherever we went. Usually we were offered drinks as a sign of appreciation. As a consequence, I developed a drinking problem, which became most difficult to control. Sometimes I could have several glasses of beer without affecting me, but on other occasions, just one drink would remove any inhibitions. Some of my barbershop friends said they liked me better after a couple of drinks, because I was not so quiet. Eventually, the problem carried into my personal life. I started to drink at home more often. When out for an evening meal with Elayne, my wife, I would pick a place where I could order a drink. Elayne recognized it as a problem, I didn't.

The whole problem came to a head for me on Saturday, July 8th, of 1978. On that day, I arrived home to find out from Elayne that my two closest childhood friends were in town. Both were neighborhood buddies of mine for most of our early childhood. In fact, when we were age eighteen, one went into the Marines, one went into the Air Force, and I went into the Navy. Both were out of the service at this time, having put in enough years to retire. They were at a nearby restaurant type night-club, and they were waiting for me. Elayne told them that she would alert me when I arrived home. Well, the three of us got together to share old-times, over a few drinks. In fact, the few grew into quite a few, over a period of four to five hours. During that meeting, one of my friends told me about his experience years before, as he dated a previous girlfriend of mine. (The complete story relating to this girlfriend is covered in the section number eighteen, entitled 'Desire Of Our Hearts'). My friend told me that when he came home on leave from the Marines, he would date this girl. The relationship became very serious. The girl said she would marry him if he would join her religion. So, while he was stationed in San Francisco, California, he made an appointment with a priest to take the necessary instructions. At the outset, the priest said he wanted to ask him a few questions, before starting the in-depth instructions. First, the priest asked him if he believed the Bible story of Adam and Eve—that they were the start of human creation. He told the priest that he didn't know how life started, but he didn't believe the Bible story. Then the priest asked him if he believed the Bible story about Noah and the ark. Again, he said 'No, that's a fiction story.' Finally, the priest asked him if he believed in life after death. Again, my friend answered, 'No!'; saying that no one knows where we came from, nor do we know where we are going, so you get the best out of life, as that's all there is. The priest told him that they had nothing further to talk about. The interview terminated. The girl did not marry him. He was now married to another girl he met in the service. Our minds were dulled by the drinks we had, so we all laughed as my friend shared this experience with us.

Sunday, the next day, my family and I went to a church service together. My two friends had both left town to return to their homes in other cities. Thoughts about the previous day kept coming to mind. Did my friend still believe this same way? Almost fifteen years had passed since he had dated my previous girlfriend. Why didn't I talk to him about this further, when we were together? Why didn't I witness to him about the truth of scripture? When we arrived home, our family members went to other parts of our home, and I found myself alone in the kitchen. I started to walk, back and forth, across the kitchen floor, mulling this over in my mind. In retrospect, I know I was under conviction by The Holy Spirit of God. I had to admit to The Lord that the drinking was wrong – at least it was in my life, as it was getting in the way. Without the drinking I could have clearly discussed with him the truth of scripture, and possibly helped him to see and accept the truth. After a while came the most difficult part of the encounter with The Holy Spirit of The Lord. I had to admit to The Lord that the drinking was wrong in my life. More than that, I had to admit that I could not quit on my own. Even the thought of quitting was too difficult to handle. So, first, I tried to bargain with myself. "Okay, Larry, you will have to limit yourself to one drink!" But sometimes with one drink I would be hugging people, "Well, then I'll only drink at home!" But I had to admit that the liquor at home disappeared rather quickly, even though we didn't have that many guests visit us. I was consuming it! Elayne had cautioned me regularly about what she was seeing, but I was strong and macho and I could handle anything. Finally, I called out to The Lord. My prayer was more of a conversation – "Lord, I agree the drinking gets in the way, and I ask for Your forgiveness. Help me Lord! I can't quit! The only thing I can come up with is that You will have to take this drinking problem from me."

I then went over to one of our kitchen cabinets, in which I kept the liquor supply. I took out my Meyer's Catawba Wine, Smirnoff Vodka, Black Velvet, and Johnnie Walker's Red Label Scotch. I poured all the contents into the kitchen sink. Inside, I felt completely helpless. My thought was that by the time Tuesday came, I would probably go to purchase more to replenish my supply. If someone, even a close friend, had come to me at that point and tried to encourage me by telling me that they had confidence in me, I wouldn't have believed them. I felt it was impossible. In fact, I felt that on Monday or Tuesday I would feel defeated when I would go to get some more. I was 'helpless' but not 'hopeless,' for my hope and trust, was in The Lord Jesus, for His strength.

The strangest and most surprising thing happened. When I awoke on Monday morning, I didn't have to quit. The Good Lord had taken it from me! I didn't want to sin against The Lord, not even in this most common way – drinking to excess. The Good Lord honored my request by giving me a new heart! A renewed heart to serve The Lord – no matter what. Now, some twenty-three years later, I still do not have the desire to drink. I am confident I could drink without drinking to excess, but since The Lord did this great work for me, I choose not to drink, to honor what He did for me. I have been healed by a Good and Loving God. His Word is true: "Ask, and you will receive."

As proof of my healing, I would like to share with you an interesting event which took place five years after my healing. The Pastor of our church asked me if I would become a communion distributor. First I searched my own soul to see if this would be something I should do. I talked with Elayne to see if she thought I should be involved with this. I prayed to The Lord for direction. The Lord gave me peace about it, so I accepted the Pastor's invitation. Soon there-after, I was invited to a particular morning service to be installed. I thought there would be several people installed at this service. As it turned out, I was the only one to be installed that morning. I was caught completely off guard when I was called up to the altar during that service. At communion time, I was handed the chalice, from which I was to take a drink of wine. Inside, I said, "Lord, I told You I was not going to do that anymore." Behind me, I heard something like a voice say, "It's not the same thing." Now, I can receive communion, a special blessing from The Lord, and I don't have a desire to return to my old habit of drinking wine. My 'wine' drinking is reserved for this special 'Communion' with The Lord.

Another footnote to this story is that The Lord has allowed me the privilege of redeeming my error with my childhood friend. This same man came to town about four years ago to visit his mother. When he was in town, I was able to spend a full day with him. Twenty years earlier I did not witness to him about The Lord, His truth, and how He was working in my life. But during our visit, I was able to tell him about my love for The Lord and how The Lord had healed me of the drinking problem. Following our day together, I sent him a copy of a thirty-nine page healing letter I had sent previously to my brothers and sisters. This letter contained a 'Salvation Message.' I thanked The Lord for not letting me be a stumbling block in his life any longer. I did not know his heart, but I did pray for him. I asked The Lord for His Grace in his heart, so that he could see any sin in his life which would separate him from The Lord's perfect Love; for The Lord's Grace that he could repent of that sin, and that he could see Jesus as his personal Lord and Savior. Also I prayed that my friend would be saved and part of The Lord's Kingdom. All this I prayed 'In Jesus Name.' I was so thankful to The Lord for giving me this chance to see my friend.

The Lord allowed me another chance to visit with my friend. In August of 1998, he came to town for his mother's funeral. We shared precious time at her funeral. In addition, we met several other times when he was in town. On one occasion, while visiting in his mother's apartment, I came under conviction to witness to him. I told him how guilty I had felt for not telling him about the truth of The Lord's Word when we were together some twenty years earlier. When the time seemed right, I asked him if I could ask him two personal questions – not to hurt him but to help him. He agreed. First, I asked him if he believed that Jesus was truly dead, when they buried the Body He lived in when He was here. Then, I asked him if he believed that His Father raised Him from the dead, and that He was with His Father now in heaven. His answer to both questions was, "Yes!" I explained to him that because he believed both of these truths, he would be saved. Only God could have put these truths in his heart. No man could convince him of this. Also, I was able to give him a small Bible booklet that contained the Bible verses to cement his belief. I shared the main verses with him from Roman's 10: 9-10 – "If you confess with your mouth that Jesus is Lord, and believe in your heart that His Father raised Him from the dead, you will be saved. For with the heart, man believeth unto salvation, and with the mouth, confession is made unto salvation." My friend was at peace with this truth. I was touched in a special way by The Lord, as He let me be an instrument to pour His Love into my friend. He too, received 'A New Heart'!

Lord, I need no further proof that You are real! That You are alive! You did something for me that I could not do for myself! You have given me a new heart. I thank You with all my heart – my new heart.

38

Pam's Day

"For He says, 'In an acceptable time I have heard you; on a day of salvation, I have helped you.' Now is the acceptable time! Now is the day of salvation."
(II Corinthians 6:2)

P am said, "That little card you left with my tip was so nice; it made my day!"

On Tuesday, November 28th, 1995, I had to go to Cincinnati, Ohio, to attend a 'Compliance Meeting' for one of the companies I represent. Once each year, I have to attend a meeting of this type to maintain my 'Equities' or 'Securities' license. There was a meeting in Chicago, Illinois that year; however, I hadn't been notified in time to make the meeting. When I heard about it, I was angry because Chicago was a lot closer than Cincinnati. The company informed me of another such meeting in Minneapolis, on Monday, November 27th, and I had made plans to drive to this meeting. This would be about a seven hour drive. Elayne was going to come with me. Arising early Monday morning, we were greeted with freezing rain and sleet. When I called the hotel in Minneapolis where the meeting was to be held, I was told that they had experienced a foot of snow. The Highway

Patrol told me that Interstate 80 West, and Interstate 35 North, were 100% ice and snow covered. I was told, "Unless it is an emergency, stay home!" Frustrated, I called the home office of the company in Hartford, Connecticut, to get the name of the person conducting the meeting in Minneapolis. I called this person in Minneapolis to tell him of my predicament. He told me that if I could not make the meeting, I could catch another scheduled meeting in Cincinnati, on Tuesday, the following day. That meeting would start at 3:00 p.m. in the afternoon. This meant even a longer drive. As I checked further, I learned that the storm was moving that direction. To complicate things, I learned that this would be the last meeting of the year, and if I didn't attend a compliance meeting that year, I would lose my equities license. I was getting angry. Why didn't they notify me of the meeting in Chicago? That would have been so simple! At wits end, I made many phone calls in an attempt to figure out what to do. Finally, I found an air flight, which would leave early Tuesday morning, November 28th, with a returning flight that same evening. This flight would put me in Cincinnati some five hours before the afternoon meeting.

Reluctantly, I went on the trip, trusting The Lord for His protection, guidance, and purpose. The pressure was on, and I was truly humbled. I had little control. I had to admit that morning that I like to control things. Sometimes in the midst of the storm, I can't see The Lord's purpose, but afterward, I get a glimpse of His plan. That day, I saw His gentle Hand at work! For years I had procrastinated in the preparation of these writings. On that Cincinnati trip, I took with me a pad of legal size writing paper. I thought I would use it to take notes at the meeting in Cincinnati. All the way on the plane, my mind was racing. Ideas were coming as fast as I could think. All during the trip and in the hotel lobby of The Hilton Hotel in Cincinnati, ideas kept coming to mind. One after another, a real life happening would come to mind, along with a scripture verse, as the underlying power behind the experience. On each separate page of the writing pad, I would put a title, a verse, and then notes to cover the main points of the story. My plan was to write the details of each story at a later time. The time on the planes, and the time waiting in the hotel lobby, was reserved for the outline of these fifty-seven stories. What a blessing! In my humanness, I was upset at the inconvenience of flying to Cincinnati at Thanksgiving time. But, The Lord had set this time for me to get going on the one thing I really wanted to do at that time in my life.

The airplane trip from Moline, Illinois, to St Louis, was about forty minutes. In St. Louis I had to change planes. The trip from St. Louis to Cincinnati was only about forty-five minutes, so I did not get breakfast on either of these flights. Instead, I had a late breakfast in the 'Atrium' of the Radisson Hotel near the airport in Cincinnati. The meeting I was to attend was held in the same hotel. A very nice waitress, named Pam, waited on me. I was the only one in the open area. As I usually do, I left her an "ASK" card, along with a nice tip. This card has printed on it The Lord's written Word.

After breakfast, I found an easy-chair at the end of the lobby, away from any action. I wanted to be alone to think about the titles and notes of my writings. It was a beautiful, peaceful time alone with The Lord. With my head down, mulling over my notes, I didn't see anyone or hear anything to distract me. All of a sudden, I heard a woman's voice say, "That little card you left me with the tip – It made my day. Thanks!" I looked up to see "Pam" smiling at me. I was in awe! She had apparently looked all over the hotel lobby to find me. What a blessing. Many times I have left "ASK" cards. Sometimes I do hear that the card has made a difference in someone's life. In a way, it's not a 'big deal' to me, but to Pam, it was The Word Of The Lord, sharper than a two-edge sword, able to penetrate the heart and soul.

I thought at that time, sitting in the lobby of the Radisson Hotel that morning, what if The Lord had groomed me my whole life just to meet Pam that morning. That would be a "Big Deal," because it is The Lord's Will that not one should perish, but that all should come to a saving knowledge of Jesus, as Lord and Savior. Maybe, this was Pam's day! All praise, honor, and glory be to Him! He does the work. All we need be is sensitive to the needs of others as well as available, teachable and not easily offended. Then, He can work through us to accomplish His Work. For, "Now is the day of salvation."

39

LADDERS AHEAD

"He told them a parable on the necessity of praying always and not losing heart!"
(Luke chap 18 :1)

On Saturday, April 6th, 1991, Elayne and I were driving back from Chicago, Illinois, when a most unusual thing happened. It could have easily resulted in a disaster. When one thinks about it, we are all just a breath away from a 'near disaster,' as far as our earthly life is concerned. It's just that most of the action is in the spiritual realm, and we do not see it. So, we are not fully aware of what is happening all around us. There is a devil; Jesus said there is. The devil's main goals are to kill, to steal, and destroy. Jesus tells us in John, chapter 10, verse 10: "The thief (devil) comes to steal and slaughter and destroy; I have come that they might have life and have it to the full." The devil comes to steal the truth, The Word of God – the truth of scripture. He comes to kill, of course, the body, which we live in. And he comes to destroy relationships. First to destroy relationships between members of a family, so that each member's relationship with The Good Lord is impaired. In John, chapter 3, verse 8, it is written: "The man who sins belongs to the devil, because the devil is a sinner from the beginning – it was to destroy the devil's works that The Son Of Man (Jesus) revealed Himself." In fact, it appears that the word 'devil' is mentioned only in the New Testament of the bible. In the Old Testament, he is referred to as Lucifer (Isaiah, chap 14:12). In the Bible, devil, devilish, or devils, is mentioned in over ninety-five verses. The Good Lord must want us to be aware of his presence and his tactics. In the original Greek, he is referred to as 'Appollyon,' which means destroyer. It is important to know certain things about the enemy in order to be able to handle enemy contact. The enemy cannot read our minds. He is not omnipresent, and therefore can only be in one place at a time. He does not know the future. And, he cannot make us do anything, as each of us have a free-will. In contrast, The Good Lord is omnipresent, He can read our minds. In fact, He reads the attitude of our hearts. He does know the future, and He can make us do something, but, He chooses not to for He wants us to exercise our free-wills to freely choose Him. We who are believers in The Lord Jesus, are aware of the devil's existence, but in humility we turn to The Lord as our Protector. The Lord and His angels do our fighting for us. We fear The Lord for as a just God, He must punish evil. Then, we accept Jesus as our personal Lord and Savior. He has provided us with salvation so we need not fear the devil. For it is written in James:4 7 & 8: "Therefore, submit to God; resist the devil, and he must take flight. Draw close to God, and He will draw close to you." Again, in Proverbs1:7, it is written: "The fear of The Lord is the 'beginning' of knowledge; wisdom and instruction fools despise."

Before leaving the home of our daughter and son-in-law in Chicago, I took Elayne's hand as we sat in our car parked in their driveway. We prayed: "Lord, please protect us as we travel home today, in Jesus' Name we pray." Elayne reaffirmed, "Amen." Away we went. We had just finished a joyful visit with our daughter Anna, her husband Hal, and the three children, Matthew, Michael, and Mary. As we traveled, we were visiting in the car about the wonderful time we had with them. About a half-hour into the return trip home, we had reached the exit to Aurora, on Interstate 88. We were in the center lane of three lanes and had our cruise control on. We were traveling at the speed limit of fifty-five miles per hour. There was a strong cross wind from left to right, so I had a tight grip on the steering wheel to keep the car in the center lane. Traffic was heavy on that Saturday afternoon. Elayne and I were sharing about how good The Lord had been to us. About how He bestows so many blessings upon us even though we do not deserve them. A white panel truck started to pass us in the left lane. Strapped to the top of the truck was a double-extended aluminum ladder. When the white truck was about fifty feet ahead of our car, the ladder suddenly was blown off the truck into our path. The ladder was dancing up and down like a pencil, right in front of our car. It bounced at eye level several times. Normal reaction would be to swerve or hit the brakes, but, for some reason I did neither. Instead, because of heavy traffic, I gripped the wheel tightly, heading straight at the bouncing ladder. It happened so quickly; neither of us had even a fleeting thought to pray. At the last second, before certain impact with the ladder, it seemed to be slapped flat down on the pavement, cross-wise in our lane of traffic. All four wheels hit the ladder. It was about seven inches in height. From inside the car, the noise made a sound like we were inside a drum as the ladder rolled underneath the car. Immediately, I looked into the rear view mirror. Behind us, lengthwise in our lane, the ladder looked like a twisted aluminum pretzel. No other vehicles hit the ladder. All the other vehicles quickly changed lanes to avoid contact. Surprisingly, I was still able to control the car. I eased through the traffic and parked the car on the right hand shoulder of the highway. Looking back, I saw the driver of the panel truck, pick up the twisted ladder, and throw it into the center median grass. The panel truck continued on past us. I looked under our car for any damage. To my surprise, I could see no oil, antifreeze, or gasoline leak. The tires were still inflated. We drove the rest of the way home to Davenport, Iowa, without any problems.

On the Tuesday before taking the trip to Chicago, I had a new set of tires put on our vehicle. Therefore, when back in Davenport, I went to the Goodyear tire store where we purchased the tires. The manager carefully inspected the tires and found no damage. Since we did not purchase 'road-hazard' protection for the tires, if there was damage, it would have been at our expense.

About two weeks after this incident, our son, Paul, said that he saw me driving past the post office, near our office, and he saw something hanging from under the car. That evening I got under the car to see what I could find. To my surprise, I found a piece of the aluminum ladder wrapped around the emergency brake cable. Still today I have that piece of the aluminum ladder, in a plastic zip-lock bag, as a reminder of the close call. It also reminds me of how good The Lord is, and the unrealized power of prayer. We asked for protection; The Lord, The Provider of everything, gave us His Protection. Elayne and I will always have the feeling that a couple of The Lord's angels slapped the ladder down, at the last instant in order to avoid an otherwise certain disaster. That is probably what the devil had intended. Once in a while, The Lord will let us see the spiritual action going on in our lives. Most often this is going on without us even knowing it. When we do see His action, we come to understand better Who He is. We see His unconditional Love for us. He is The Great Provider of all that is Good!

40

FAX PLEASE

"Take delight in The Lord and He will grant you your hearts requests!"

(Psalm 37: 4)

O ften times in my life, when faced with a decision, I will simply say, "Lord Jesus, please help me with this decision." Or, I might say, "Lord Jesus, help me." I wish I could tell you that I do this with every decision, as this truly is my desire, but this is not the case. Quite often I go off on my own to solve my problems without first asking for help.

This story centers on a relatively simple business decision. It illustrates how The Lord gets involved with even the small details when we ask Him to help. He shows His caring, mercy, and kindness.

In our insurance business, we were receiving many requests for us to send information to others by 'fax' Many times attorneys, banks, clients and other service organizations ask us to fax information to them. When we had to use this process, we would use the fax machine at a nearby printing company. They would charge us a nominal fee for this service. As we were doing more and more insurance work involving real estate closings, the need for fax use became frequent. We had to look closely to see if we should own our fax machine.

Soon it became apparent that we would have to get our own machine. With this particular decision, I did the right thing. I asked The Lord for His help. After researching companies in our local area, I came up with three machine brands that could fit our needs. I called these companies to get general information and prices. On the day after this search, I planned to go to these companies to decide which machine we would actually purchase. We had pretty much settled on the Sharp machine. We had a Sharp copy machine that was providing us with excellent service. That morning, as I was getting ready to leave the office, a female salesperson came in to tell us about a fax machine. She did not have an appointment, nor did she represent any of the companies I had called. She knew her material. We learned a lot about fax machines that morning. The machine she wanted us to buy was priced over $1,000, which was more than what we wanted to spend at the time. It did have many extra features, but we did not need them for our limited use. Since she had stopped by, I had no more time, so I decided to go out the next day to get the fax machine. The next day was a Friday. My plan was to see the machines in operation to help us firm up our decision. We felt we could get a machine for around $400 to satisfy our needs. On that particular Friday morning, I was called to a special insurance meeting in Iowa City, Iowa which was no problem because I could go looking that afternoon when I returned to the office. During a morning break at the meeting, I called our office in Bettendorf, Iowa, to see if everything was okay. Anita, our secretary, explained to me that a problem had come up regarding a claims adjuster representing a firm in Illinois. He asked Anita to fax a claim report to him in order to expedite the settlement of the claim. The man said to Anita, "Why don't you fax the loss report to me so that I can get going on the claim right away." Anita said, "Well……," as she was going to tell him that we were in the process of getting our own machine, so we wouldn't have to go down the street to use the printing company's machine. This would take a little longer. The man interrupted her. He asked, "You mean you don't have a fax machine?" As Anita tried to explain, he told Anita that he had just purchased a new machine that used single sheet regular paper, rather than the roll paper. He could send and receive material much faster with this type of machine. He explained that he had many fax copies to send out each day, so he needed a machine that used regular paper. He told her that there were a few problems with the machine he was replacing, but he would sell it to us for $50. When Anita told me that it was the same make and model we were thinking of buying, I told her to call him back and tell him we would take it. He said he would bring it to our office sometime Monday morning.

On the following Monday, when I got into the office, the man had already been in. Anita said that he had decided to give us the machine at no cost. We were able to correct the minor problems with the machine. It was somewhat smudgy on the receiving end, and we were able to correct this by giving the machine a good cleaning. We used the machine in our office for over six years until we needed a fax machine that uses regular paper. We purchased another Sharp machine. It is performing beautifully.

Even small details are important to The Lord. We take delight in The Lord – seek His Righteousness, and His Kingdom, and he will grant us our hearts requests. "For as the heavens are high above the earth, so surpassing is His Kindness toward those who fear Him." (Psalm 103:11)

41

A SIGN

"Do not be anxious about anything, but in every-thing, by prayer and petition, with thanksgiving, present your requests to God."

(Philippians 4:6)

In March of 1992, Elayne and I purchased a small residence in downtown Bettendorf, Iowa. In November of that same year, we relocated our insurance business to that location. After I had exhausted myself, looking on my own for many years, I finally asked The Lord to help us find a suitable spot for the insurance business. It seemed like there were complex problems with everything I touched, and we were not able to find a building in line with our needs and limited funds we had available. We did not want to go into huge debt to obtain a building. Elayne had her heart set on a separate building to give us individual identity. She pictured a small bungalow, located in a business district, which could be rezoned commercial. When I finally stepped back to wait on The Lord, a most wonderful location and building seem to come out of nowhere. It had provided us with a peaceful spot to conduct our insurance service business. In fact, as of the time of this writing, we are still located in this most peaceful of spots. What a blessing!

There are many signs that this location is truly from The Lord—as has happened so many times, The Lord provided for our needs through someone we had helped in the past. We hadn't communicated at all with the realtor who found this building for us. This fine woman had not been long in the real estate business, when she heard from her husband that we were looking to relocate. She and her husband were two of the very first clients I had after coming into the insurance business in 1967. She showed us a couple of places, but they were not in any location we wanted. We preferred to keep our business phone number (355-5555), for that number was very important to us (see story #13 - titled 'Fleece Of Wool'). She then showed us a building which was exactly what we were looking for. A small Cape Cod type bungalow, located in downtown Bettendorf, Iowa. A single mother, and her two children were renting it. The owner had the property for sale. It was in a commercial location, so we could have it rezoned for office use.

We could see The Hand of the Lord present as we worked through the purchase and remodeling of the building. The young woman and her two children were able to move just two doors west, so they were not handicapped by our taking possession. Funds became available, as we needed them. Physical help came, as we needed it. Everyone who worked on the project enjoyed helping out. All of our children helped on the project. Some helped us move the business from our home to the newly furnished building. Some helped in the total reconstruction, the painting, the cement work, the removal of trees, the installation of a fence, and the many other details that came up during the eight month rebuilding project. Our family provided almost all the labor associated with the renovation of the building as we changed it from residential to commercial use. The City of Bettendorf cooperated with us in the rezoning of the property. The City accepted our design of a ramp to allow handicap accessibility. The City approved a cement parking lot in the rear of the building. We didn't have any problem getting the necessary permits for the mechanical, plumbing, and electrical work to be done, even though we were doing most of the work ourselves. We took possession of the building in March of 1992, and we moved into the building the day before Thanksgiving of the same year.

Another sign of The Lord's Hand came in the form of an unexpected shipment we received from Florida. A client friend, named Dave who was in the office furniture business, moved to Florida some years before we purchased the building. One evening, a few weeks before we moved into the building, a trucker called me at home to tell me he had a shipment from Florida for our insurance company. Even though I told him we were not expecting any shipment from Florida, he insisted the material on his truck was for Lyons Insurance. Thinking it might be some small item, I finally agreed to have him drop it off at our residence. An 18 wheel semi-truck backed into our driveway at about 9:00 p.m. that evening. They unloaded almost a complete compliment of office furniture for our business. It filled up half of our garage. It was amazing! We had cushioned chairs, a conference table, desks, credenzas, file cabinets, a typewriter, a copy machine, and many other office items. All this came at no cost to us, with shipment expenses pre-paid. I was asked by my publisher, why Dave sent this furniture. Did he have surplus? Was he opening a new office…so not having a ready answer, I called Dave in Florida to ask him. This is what he said: "Larry, you can tell her this. We had grown so close. I felt that since you had done so much to help other people, it was about time that someone did something nice for you. If you want to know the truth, I felt the Lord pushing me in that direction." When I did insurance work for Dave before he left for Florida, we had many discussions about the Lord and he accepted the Lord into his heart, so we became pretty close…like brothers. And I guess we are—Brothers in Christ. We are still using these items today, and often I think of my friend Dave. One client came to us to do a complete landscaping design and installation, at no cost to us. We received a special write-up in the Sunday edition of our local newspaper. The story in the paper covered all the reconstruction details and the fact that it was a 'family' project.

One particular Saturday during the rebuilding project, I went into the building tired and frustrated at the amount of work left to be done. No one else was available that day, so I would be on my own. As I approached the front door, I noticed a small clump of leaves on the door threshold. Before opening the door, I thought to myself, I don't want this tracked into the building. So I picked the clump up and tossed in over the railing into the front yard. A while later, as I was inside working on the electrical outlets, I remembered the small clump of oak leaves. It was most unusual in that the clump of leaves was green. I thought that a squirrel must have dropped the leaves, as he was building his nest in our front tree. Out of curiosity, I went out to find the leaves. When I picked up the clump, I noticed that there were seven small leaves all attached to a short stem. Immediately I thought of the Bible and the use of seven as a sign of completion. The Lord completed His creation of the universe in seven days, and then He rested. "This project will one day be completed," I said. This thought and the oak leaves gave me a boost of great joy and energy at how Good The Lord is. I kept the small sprig of oak leaves as a sign from The Lord, showing His concern for even the small details and problems in our lives. The framed sprig of oak leaves hangs on our front office wall, with the bible inscription – "And God blessed the seventh day, and sanctified it; because that in it He rested from all His work which God created and made

(KJV)." As He showed me that day, the project was completed. At the time of this writing, in 2001, we have enjoyed the building for these past nine years.

Just prior to moving in, we knew we had to come up with a sign for the outside of the building. We had to tell our clients and passersby's, who we were and what we did. I had my own ideas for the design of the sign. My plan was to design our own sign, and then find a sign company to make up the lettering to show our company name and services. Shortly after opening day, without solicitation, a client came into our office with a most unusual presentation. He said he wanted to give us his recommendation for a sign to put in the front yard. At first I was reluctant, because I had strong ideas of what I wanted in a sign. But then I thought it might not hurt to get a proposal from someone in the sign business. It might give us some ideas on how to proceed. Of course, I immediately started to tell him what my ideas were. I drew sketches and explained construction details. He pointed out areas in my design that he disagreed with. This irritated me. I thought to myself, if I am going to commission someone to design a sign for me, and pay for the design and installation, at least I should have a say in it. I started to raise objections to some of his design concepts. His total approach differed from mine. He interrupted me saying, "Look, you know the insurance business – I know the sign business; let me show you how it should be done!" Wow! My mind started racing! In a nice way, how could I tell him that he was offending me? Before I could collect my thoughts, he completely surprised me. He said, "Anyway, this is at no cost to you – The Lord told me to do this for you." How could I answer that? I swallowed my pride. This man came back with a surprisingly good mechanical design and a good logo and wording. The Lord had so humbled me, that I let this man come up with every detail of the design, including the colors. The sign has stood tall and well for all these years. There has been no fading or discoloration of the lettering. The sign still looks as new as the day it was installed. The Lord has provided a "SIGN" for our business, at no cost to us, and even better than what I had envisioned originally. The sign stands as a reminder of The Lord's Love for and concern for us. It serves as a reminder for us to provide Godly service to our clients – to treat everyone who comes to us the same. To let the Love Of The Lord pass through us, to touch His people. The sign in our front yard reminds us of our mission; "May the favor of The Lord rest upon you; establish the work of our hands for us – yes, establish the work of our hands." (Psalm 9:17)

42

WHO IS THE GREATEST?

"'I am the Alpha and the Omega' says The Lord God. 'Who is, Who was, and Who is to come, The Almighty.'"

(Rev.1:8)

Throughout these past thirty-five years, I have been involved in many insurance meetings and seminars. There is always a need to have updates since the products change dramatically with time. At one of these meetings, there was considerable time spent in the discussion of new insurance products. There was a prominent Vice President of one of the companies I represent, as the keynote speaker at the dinner that night.

After an introduction, he came to the podium and paused for quite a while before speaking a word. The silence was so long, that most of us thought he had forgotten how he was supposed to start. Finally, he spoke, by asking us a question. He asked, "Who is the greatest fighter who ever lived?" Then he waited. I knew what he wanted, but I would not have given the answer he expected. At the time of his talk, Cassius Clay, the prizefighter was the leading boxer. He had changed his boxing name to Mohammed Ali. In my heart

I knew The Greatest Fighter Who ever lived was The Man Christ Jesus, for He defeated the enemy without throwing a single blow. With all my strength, I wanted to stand up and say, "Jesus Christ," but because of fear of rejection, I couldn't even get the words out while seated. Finally someone said, "Mohammed Ali." I felt so convicted and ashamed for not getting to my feet to speak for The Lord. The speaker of course went on to explain that Cassius Clay was the greatest because he believed he was the greatest, said he was the greatest, and was in his mind, truly the greatest.

Not speaking up for The Lord Jesus hurt me for a long time. I decided to write something about how great The Lord is and send the message to this man. Also, I would confess to him that I didn't have the courage to express myself when he asked the question at our meeting. Usually at the end of each year, I would try to catch up on all my insurance paperwork. At first I thought I would finish the paperwork and then start the writing, but I had to be honest with myself, and admit that I probably would not get to the writing. Already I had procrastinated for two years, so I didn't want to put it off any longer. Writing the message about Jesus being The Greatest, became the priority item.

It was so rewarding to me to spend the Christmas Holidays on this writing. I felt so relieved that I had stopped in the hectic pace of business life, to speak out for The Lord Jesus. The writing turned out as follows:

WHO IS THE GREATEST

Who is the greatest fighter Who ever lived?
He defeated the enemy without throwing a blow!
Who is the greatest mariner Who ever lived?
He calmed the sea with a stroke of His Hand!
Who is the greatest orator Who ever lived?

His Word is sharper than a two-edged sword!
Who is the greatest salesman Who ever lived?
The entire world has heard of His unselfish service!
Who is the greatest fisherman Who ever lived?
He skillfully lands even the most stubborn,
and then He cleans them!
Who is the greatest shepherd Who ever lived?
He laid down His life for His friends!
Who is the greatest carpenter Who ever lived?
Even now, for His people, He is building
mansions in His Father's House!
Who is the greatest Father Who ever lived?
He never married but adopted children
throughout the world!
Who had everything and set it aside
for a glorious cause?
And yet the recipients
are a rebellious unworthy people!
Who came from another land
to adopt a chosen people?
Even His own would not accept Him!
Who is the greatest friend a person could ever have?
He freely laid down His life
and then picked it up again!
Who is the greatest defender
a person could ever have?
He is before the throne day and night,
standing in for those who trust Him!
Who was killed by His enemies
and laid in a borrowed grave?
And yet is alive today!
Who is the greatest King Who ever lived?
And yet His enemies crowned Him with thorns!
What King gave 800 years
advance notice of His coming?

And yet all that was prepared
was a manger in a stable!
What King is coming back with the shout of trumpet?
And will gather His people who believe on Him!
Who is the greatest? What is His Name?
Why His Name is Wonderful! Great is His Name!
His Name can move mountains!
His Name can melt hearts!
His Name is 'Lord Jesus!'
For God is with us.

I had this writing printed on five by seven inch cards. The first card was sent to the person who gave the talk at the meeting I attended. This man wrote back to me to tell me he appreciated the card and the letter of explanation. The second card was sent to Mohammad Ali, in hopes that he, as well as any other person who may read the writing, is led to accept Jesus as personal Lord and Savior.

43

WITNESS TIME

"But you shall receive power, after The Holy Spirit
is come upon you; and you shall be witness unto Me,
both in Jerusalem, and in all Judea, and in Samaria,
and unto the uttermost part of the earth."

(Acts 1:8)

Often times I learn important principles of life from our own children. One such learning example came up in life when our daughter, Anita, was a senior in high school. The story was told to us by one of Anita's friends, and it exemplifies the principle of 'respect for one's parents.'

One fall evening, Anita was out with her girl friends attending a football game. After the game, the whole carload of girls wanted to go out to 'The Butcher Block.' This was a spot where the young people hung out. One of the problems for Anita was that beer was served at this place of business. On the way to The Butcher Block, Anita said that she either wanted to be let out of the car or be taken home, as she was not going to a place where there was beer being served. Of course, there was great pressure put on Anita to go. The girls came up with many reasons to prod her into going. Finally, one of the girls said to Anita, "Give us one good reason why you can't go out to The Butcher Block?" Anita told them that there have been times in the past that the young people there had been 'carded.' And neither she nor her friends were of legal age, they could get into trouble. "So what!" was the response. "All they could do is to take us down to the police station and try to scare us!" they responded. She said this was the main reason why she was not going. Anita told them that the police might call her parents, and she did not want to 'embarrass' her parents. What a powerful witness to these other children. What a powerful witness for The Lord! Yes, and what a powerful witness for the 'Lyons' name, and the 'Lyons' family.

This illustrates to me that Anita loved her parents such that she did not want to do anything that would hinder the relationship we have, nor did she want to bring dishonor to our name. Hearing this story about her also reminded me of my relationship with The Lord. Protecting this relationship motivates me to do the things I'm supposed to do as a believer, as a witness for The Lord Jesus. In my heart, I do not want to do anything to embarrass my Father in Heaven, nor Jesus, nor The Holy Spirit. I pray that with The Lord's Grace, I do not do anything in my life to embarrass The Lord Jesus or grieve The Holy Spirit.

One area of temptation for me is to speed while driving a car. And yet, to this date, after 55 years of driving, I have never had a speeding ticket. I have asked The Lord Jesus to help me in this area, and He in His love and mercy, has helped me, over and over again. Even though speeding while driving an automobile is an attraction to me, The Lord Jesus wants me to obey the laws of the land, as long as these laws do not conflict with the Lord's commands.

As an example of this principle, that of keeping the laws, I will share with you a time when it seemed like the proper thing to do, was to speed. Early one summer morning, just as I arrived at our insurance office, I received a phone call from one of our client contractors. He wanted to bid a construction job for The Corps Of Engineers, at The Rock Island Arsenal, in Rock Island, Illinois. In order to bid the job, he needed a 'bid-bond.' Since the bid-bond was of special type, we could not prepare the bond in our office. It would have to be prepared by the home office of the bonding company in Des Moines, Iowa, about one hundred and sixty miles away. The distance was too great for us to drive to Des Moines and return in time for the contractor to make the bid-opening at The Corps Of Engineers, because the bid was due that same day. After much discussion with the bonding company, we came up with one possible solution. We would have to meet someone from the bonding company, mid-way. I was off. The maximum speed limit at the time was 55, so since I didn't want to speed, I kept the car right at the limit. I was to meet a representative from the bonding company at the entrance to The Holiday Inn, on Interstate 80, at the Little Amana exit. We were to meet at 11:30 a.m. I arrived at 11:15 a.m. Anxiously, I waited at the front entrance, looking for the messenger. Quickly the time passed; soon it was 11:30, then 12:00 noon, then 12:25 until I was frantic. I wanted to be of service to our client. In desperation, I ran into the motel to make a phone call to the company. Once inside the building, I saw a young man sitting in an easy chair, beside the indoor swimming pool. He was calmly watching the swimmers enjoying themselves in the pool. In his right hand he was holding a white envelope. Without even introducing myself, I asked him if he was from the bonding company. He was! How could he have gotten past me, I wondered. I thanked him, grabbed the envelope, and ran for the car. Once on the highway, I glanced at the dashboard clock to see that the time was about 12:30. By quick calculation, I figured that at 55 miles per hour, I would get back to the contractors office at about 2:00 p.m. That was the exact time the contractor was to be at the bid opening. I was in deep trouble!

If I drove at 55, it would take about one and a half hours. What was I going to do? I wanted to provide good service to the contractor as a witness of our caring, but I also wanted to be a good witness for The Lord, by obeying man-made laws. I concluded that I would have to stay at 55. It almost seemed that I should bend man-made law to go slightly over the speed limit.

Instead, I talked to The Lord about it. I told The Lord that I wanted to provide the service to the contractor which he expected. And yet, I did not want to transgress the speed limit law that governs the land. I told The Lord that I would stay at 55. I then asked The Lord to help me in whatever way He felt was best, and I would accept the outcome. I watched the speedometer closely so that I could stay as close to 55 as possible, and take the least time for the trip back. Many cars passed me as I traveled back to Davenport. I thought, 'that's not my problem'; so I kept the car at 55. Much to my surprise, I pulled up to the designated meeting place at exactly 1:40 p.m. The contractor's wife jumped out of the pickup truck to meet me in the middle of the street. She grabbed the envelope out of my hand, without any conversation. They were off! There was enough time for them to make the bid opening. The Lord had come through for me.

To this day I do not know what happened. Maybe I was going faster than 55 miles per hour, while the speedometer registered only 55. But then, if that were true, how did so many cars pass me on the return trip? Maybe The Lord shortened the distance, so that I could still drive at 55, and thereby cut the driving time to one hour and ten minutes, instead of the normal one and half hour driving time. Or just maybe The Lord slowed the time down so I could arrive on time to provide the 'service' my heart desired. I don't know what happened. But this I *do* know: The Lord Jesus wants witnesses, "Unto the uttermost part of the earth," and He will help in the carrying out of this mission.

44

FIRST FRUITS

"Bring the best of the first fruits of your soil to the house of The Lord you're God."
(Exodus 23:19)

For all of our married lives, Elayne and I have always contributed to our church at every Sunday service. However, we have never had a formal system for giving to The Lord. We would always give a set amount to the church, and if there happened to be a special collection for other ministerial needs, we would give to that if we had any extra funds available. Since we had to satisfy the varied needs of a family with ten children, there were seldom any extra funds to help with special needs.

It had always been a problem for me to make a giving decision. I had to balance between the desire to give and deciding if the funds were really available to give at all. While the children were growing up, we always had more direct family needs than we had income or funds to satisfy these needs. One evening, in the year 1982, I was up late at home, working on some insurance papers for a client. On the corner of the desk, there was a pile of requests for contributions from various Christian organizations. I was under

243

conviction to do something about these requests. That night I made the decision to do something about these requests. I put the insurance papers aside and started to sort through the pile of requests. Requests from 10 Christian organizations had accumulated. Each of the organizations looked good to me, and the work done by each group was commendable. In looking at our family checkbook, I found that we had only $28.00 in the account. In so many words, this is as close to being 'broke' as we could get. After long deliberation, I decided to write a check for $2.00 to each of the organizations. Twenty-eight dollars is broke! Eight dollars is broke! Even though small, each could benefit in some way from the $2.00. It could at least give them hope of maybe more to come.

The next day, Elayne happened to look at the checkbook balance. She was very disappointed, and she let me know how she felt. Within her rights, she asked me why I did such a thing when I knew we had bills to pay, and so little money available to pay these bills. Elayne was right, and I was very wrong. I should have discussed this with her before acting. We should have been in agreement. Inside, I had two problems: first, I felt inadequate as a provider for the family; and secondly, I felt weak as a contributor for The Lord's work. Plus, I was struggling in the insurance business, and I had no idea where the next sale was coming from. After fretting over this for about a week, I decided to talk to a Christian business associate of mine. My hope was that he could help me come up with an approach to proper giving to The Lord. In my heart, I wanted to give, and I didn't want to have the feeling of guilt that we couldn't give because we didn't have the money.

While driving out to my friend's place of business, I asked The Lord to help me with this problem of giving. I really didn't want to ask him, even though it may be well to do so. I decided to ask The Lord to show me a way that would be right for Elayne and me, not anyone else. Just before reaching his place of business, a thought came to mind that made me turn around to return to my office. What came to mind was that Elayne and I should open up a separate special checking account to hold the funds for Christian contributions. Just the thought of having this special account gave me a feeling of relief and peace. I thanked The Lord for His Grace. Later that day, I talked the whole subject of giving over with Elayne. Elayne thought the idea of a special 'giving account' was a good one. She agreed! I didn't go to see the man about giving.

From my Bible reading, I remembered in the Old Testament, where The Lord described what He wanted from His people. He wanted their 'first fruits.' He wanted the first produce of their work effort. Basically, He asked for the best. Not because He is needy, or greedy. He wants His people to give off the top, and then trust Him to supply all their needs. If we hold back, then we are saying that we feel we are independent, not truly dependent, and therefore we must hold back to satisfy our needs, or we might be caught short. In fact, He asked the Old Testament people to give Him the first 10% of their produce, off the top. The Lord called this produce, "First Fruits." If the people would give The Lord the first 10%, this would show that The Lord was first in their lives. It was not to be given grudgingly, but to be given freely, out of love, honor, and obedience. The Lord could then bless His people without them becoming so independent that they didn't need Him any longer.

Elayne and I named our special giving account, the "First Fruits Account." Then we decided upon a percentage of income we would put into this account. We applied this same percentage to every bit of income we put into this account, no matter what the source. Whenever we put a deposit into our family checking account, the first check we would then write, was for an amount to deposit into the "First Fruits

Account." What a relief! What a sense of freedom! No longer did we have to worry about what we had to give. Whatever was in the First Fruits Account, was what we had to contribute, spread across all solicitations. What was in the First Fruits Account, was specifically The Lord's money, for His work. At the time of this decision, we were struggling in the insurance business, so the actual dollar amount we put into this account was not very large. However, we did have a formal giving plan for every bit of income we would receive. At the same time, we looked forward to the possibility that The Lord might bless our insurance business in the future, so we decided upon different percentages of contribution according to increasing income levels. First of all, we decided on a certain percentage of the first $25,000 of income. Then we made a chart, which would show a gradually increasing percentage, as our income would advance. So, if The Lord would bless us with what the world would call, 'Big Income,' we would know what percentage we would put into the "First Fruits Account." What a blessing. The Lord has given us a way - a way that fits our thinking and our desires. How The Lord has blessed us for being obedient. Our income has increased from sales not even attainable on my own. I know without a doubt that The Lord out of His Love and Trustworthiness has helped me build the insurance business. He keeps His promises! Always! We do not give to the First Fruits Account in order to receive from The Lord. We give because we really want to give, and because we love The Lord and want to demonstrate our love and dependence. Because The Lord is kind and merciful, He gives in return. He uses our little bit to bless us abundantly. Just as The Lord Jesus multiplied a small amount of bread and fish in order to feed a large crowd, so too, He multiplies the blessings from a small amount of giving. He is most deserving of our love and service.

When we first opened this special account, I found that we had to keep a minimum balance of three hundred dollars in the checking account, or we would incur a service fee. I did not want to have a service charge taken out of the money we had earmarked for The Lord's work. Also we did not want to have an idle balance of three hundred dollars sitting in the bank account. We wanted all the money out at work in the Lord's ministries. We wanted to be able to run a 'zero' balance in this special account. After a few months of operation with this new giving system, I went to a branch office of the bank we were using for the special account. I talked to a young woman at the counter inside the bank. I told her that I wanted her to contact one of the officers at the main bank building, and tell that person this: "Tell that person that this account is for our special charitable giving; that it is for The Lord's work, and we would like to have a 'zero balance' account – with no service charges." Even though the woman told me of the standard bank practices of checking accounts and charges, I still asked her to tell the bank officer what I had told her and then call me back later in my office. About an hour later, when I returned to my office, I found that she had already called. I called her back at once. With a cheerful voice, she said, "Mr. Lyons, he said okay." I was overjoyed. We still enjoy this special account today, without service charge or minimum balance. If fact, even though we are now with another bank, the new bank honored our requests for zero balance and no service charges. Elayne and I enjoy freedom of giving, along with Mercy and Kindness from our Lord and Savior, Jesus Christ!

45

THE WAY

*"There is a way that seems right unto a man, but the
end thereof are the ways of death."*
(Proverbs12:12) and (Proverbs 18:25)

In January of 1982, Elayne and I ordered our first 'ASK'
cards from a company in Nashville, Tennessee. An 'ASK'
card is a witness card, which contains some printed scripture
verses, including a salvation message. We use these to hand
out to individuals as a witness to The Lord's Word. Our first
order was for fifteen hundred cards. As our supply would
diminish, which early on would be about every year or two,
we would reorder. Through the years, we would gradually
increase our order quantity. This was for two reasons: first,
because we were handing out more and more of them; and
secondly, because we could get a better price per card by
ordering a larger quantity. To date, we have ordered sixty-
five thousand cards. Our last order was for a quantity of ten
thousand. This is the largest quantity we have ever ordered.
Some or the stories outlined in these writings, tell of some of
the incidents involving the handing out of ASK cards.

Most of the cards have been handed out to individuals
met in the course of business dealings or personal contacts.

I would hand them out at places where we shop, in restaurants, on vacation, or anytime I felt prompted to do so. In all these years, I can only remember two instances when anyone refused to accept a card. The first instance was when an older woman rejected my offer to give her a card. She was standing across from me at the mail table, inside the post office. As I was leaving the table, I tried to hand her a card and said, "This is the only good news there is – have a good day!" Immediately, she responded, "I don't do that to you at my church!" She didn't even reach toward accepting the card. It seemed as though she was expecting me to do this, and she was waiting with her answer. Maybe she had seen me before, in the post office, doing this same thing with other people. At any rate, I told her that I was sorry, and that I did not want to offend her. From that day on, whenever I would see her, I would smile and greet her, but she would never respond to me. I do remember praying for her.

The second time happened in 1998, when I was leaving a supermarket where we purchase groceries. This rejection really startled me. I didn't see it coming, nor did I have a response, because I was so saddened by what had happened. When I was passing through the checkout lane, I noticed a young employee at the end of the counter. He was bagging our groceries. He was bright looking, and in his early twenties. I picked up a few plastic bags of groceries and started for the door. The young man stopped me and insisted on carrying the bags for me. I assured him that I could handle it okay, but he took the bags from me and insisted upon carrying the bags for me. As we continued out of the store, I took an ASK card from my pocket to give to him at the car. He was pushing the groceries in a two-wheel cart. He was a handsome young man, with very good manners. He showed me respect and was very polite. He talked about things of current interest as he was putting the groceries into the trunk of our car. Just as he was putting the last bag into the trunk, I offered him a card. I said, "This is for you – have a good day!" He first reached for the card, and after taking a closer look, backed away. He quickly said, "Do you preach the kingdom?" I was completely caught off guard. I thought of The Kingdom Of God, with Jesus as The Head, so I answered, "Yes!" Instantly, he replied, "Do you also preach the kingdom on earth?" I thought, 'Jesus said that My Kingdom is not of this world," so I answered, "No!" Again, he quickly responded, "Well, it is - - hope to see you on earth!" He turned his back on me and went back into the store. The conversation was over. I stood there stunned. Again it raced through my mind what Jesus had said: "My Kingdom is not of this world!" What on earth was this young man talking about? Why did he not want to discuss this with me? I hurt inside for him. But, with an emphatic closure, he was gone.

For a long time, I just sat in the car – hurt by what had just happened. I thought, 'Here is a bright young man, who has his mind set on a principle that does not line up with scripture.' We didn't even get to the real issue of Jesus. Questions like; Who is Jesus? - What did Jesus say? - Where is Jesus now? – Where is the Kingdom Of God? – or, Where is the Kingdom Of Jesus? Oh, how my heart hurt for the young man, with his apparent rejection. I did pray for him as I sat in the car. I prayed that he would somehow be given the opportunity to hear the truth, and be able to make a free decision, unencumbered by the enemy.

Sitting in the car, the verse that came to me was, "There is a way that seems right to man, but the end thereof, are the ways of death." The truth of this scripture rang loudly in my ears! One, like this young man, can really feel that he has the right answer, but, if the answer does not line up with scripture, one is 'dead' (spiritually speaking) wrong.

In scripture, in John, chapter 8, verse 32, Jesus said, "You shall know The Truth, and The Truth shall set you free." Again, in John, chapter 14, verse 6, Jesus said, "I am The Way, The Truth, and The Life; no one comes to The Father, except through Me!" To further prove this point, let's look at simple mathematics. One principle is that if two entities are equal to the same thing, they are then equal to each other. For example: if 'a' equals 'c' and 'b' equals 'c' then it follows, that 'a' equals 'b.' Further, in the two verses above, we see that the word 'Truth' is used. First, 'The Truth shall set you free,' and then 'I am The Truth.' So, we can substitute 'Jesus' for 'Truth' in verse 32, and scripture would then read verse 32 as follows: "You shall know Jesus, and Jesus shall set you free!" There is a saying often seen on bumper stickers and car windows.

No Jesus, no freedom!
Know Jesus, know freedom!

The most critical question we can answer is the question Jesus asked of His disciples; "Who do *you* say that I am?" Peter answered correctly; "You are The Messiah!" Thomas answered correctly; "My Lord and my God!" When we think about the circumstances of Jesus' death, we find that He was actually killed because He claimed to be "GOD." In John, chapter 8, verse 58, Jesus said, "I solemnly declare it; before Abraham was, I AM!" After this statement, they plotted to kill Him. If we look at this statement by Jesus closely, we have to say that He was either right, or He was Wrong. If He, for the sake of discussion, was wrong, then He was either insane or a liar. He would be insane for 'thinking' He was God, when He was not, or He was a liar, for saying He was God, when He knew He was not. It is unbelievable to hold that anyone would lie in order to be killed, especially by such a cruel death such as crucifixion. Again, this could only happen if the person was insane. And, if Jesus were, for the sake of discussion, insane, then His mother would not have stood at the foot of the cross to watch her Son die such a cruel death. She would have asked for her Son to be turned over to her, as He would not be responsible for what He was saying. Naturally, she would have rescued Him. But, she did not! Nor did she even open her mouth to change the outcome. So, we must conclude that Mary knew her Son Jesus is Who He said He is! Jesus said, "The Father and I, are One!"

We have to look to the fact that Jesus was right. Jesus is GOD! He is 'The I AM'! We really then have only two choices: either I must accept Him as personal Lord and Savior; or, I must reject Him, and He becomes my Judge. There is no 'in-between.' In light of this, let's look at the young man I met at the supermarket. As I sat in the car that day, I wondered if someone had misled this fine young man. Or, had he come to this position completely on his own? Had this young man, who apparently rejected the ASK card I offered him, also rejected The Man, Christ Jesus? Did he reject, for all eternity, the One Who was foretold in Isaiah, chapter 7 verse 14, wherein it is written: "Therefore, The Lord Himself, will give you this sign; the virgin shall be with child, and bear a Son, and shall Name Him Immanuel?" I pray this is not the case in his life, because 'Immanuel' is translated 'God is with us!' The penalty for making the wrong decision is too great…that of being separated from God for all eternity. As scripture tells us, there is a wrong way, and there is a Right Way, and that is Jesus – The 'Only' Way.

46

BY HIS GRACE

"For by grace are you saved, through faith; and that not of yourselves; it is a gift of God; not of works, lest any man should boast."

(Ephesians 2:8-9)

As mentioned in other sections of these writings, I have moderated CCD (Christian Education) classes for many years. Often times I would tell personal stories to the young people, to show them how The Lord has worked in my life. Hopefully they could see how The Lord was actually working in their lives, even though they were unaware. Often times when I would meet these young people at a later time, they would tell me how much they enjoyed the stories.

One of the stories I would mention to every class, was how I can remember being baptized as a small child, and how special this was for me. During one of these classes, one of the students challenged my statement. "Mr. Lyons," he asked; "How could it be possible for you to remember being baptized; as a catholic, you were baptized as a little baby?" This caused me to question if my recollection was really correct. So, I called the rectory of Sacred Heart Cathedral, in Davenport, Iowa. This is the church I attended as a small child. Since neither of my parents attended church, the woman could not find my records under their names. I explained to the woman in the church office, that I had attended Sacred Heart School for eight years. During grade school, I received First Holy Communion and Confirmation at Sacred Heart Church. If I were not baptized, I could not have received either of these church sacraments. The woman then asked me a surprising question. She asked me if could remember the names of my baptismal sponsors. For some reason, I always remembered that two neighbors were my sponsors. An older lady, living a few doors down from us, was one of my sponsors. Her name was Mary Powers. The other sponsor was a relative of our next neighbor, by the name of Tom Harney. Under the name of 'Tom Harney,' she found my baptism records. I was baptized on April 9th, 1933. I was baptized just four days after my third birthday. The event is still vivid in my memory. My parents probably forgot about having me baptized, but, when my third birthday came around, my guess is that one of my older sisters remembered, and had an appointment set up for me.

How well I can remember – my baptism was filled with personal excitement. I recall walking down the alley and up a half block to the church entrance. I remember walking up the many stairs into the church. Somehow, even at this young age, I knew this was 'my day'! I knew it was going to be important to me. Maybe my sisters filled me with great expectation. I can remember having on a red felt coat and black leggings.

The baptism was performed just inside the church entrance, in the vestibule. At the right side of the entrance doors to the main body of the church was a statue of an angel. The angel was holding a large sea-shell in a horizontal position. Also the angel was crouched in a kneeling, almost sitting position, on top of a pedestal. Since I was too short to reach the baptismal font, a stool was placed alongside for me to stand on. From the stool, I could see into the sea-shell baptismal catch basin. They had me bend over the basin, placing my head in one of the indentations at the sea-shell edge. Vividly, I can remember looking into the face of an older, white-haired man, who poured water over my forehead. Later, I learned his name was Monsignor Cone. He was a priest at Sacred Heart for the eight years I attended school there. While pouring the water, he repeated the standard words used at all catholic baptisms of that time period: "I baptize you, Larry, in the Name of The Father, and of The Son, and of The Holy Spirit."

How well I can remember a feeling of peace and acceptance. In our neighborhood, I was not accepted. Nor was any member of my family accepted. We didn't believe that it was bad to be poor, but being poor was certainly looked down upon by the people in the neighborhood. Each one of my brothers and sisters, and there were nine of us, felt this put-down, at an early age. But, on the day of my baptism, I felt a closeness to The Lord. I felt 'acceptable.' This was not based upon anything I had done. The neighborhood had helped me understand that I did not measure up, so to speak. My feeling of acceptance was not based on anything I felt I could do, or even had to do. It was just so wonderful to know that The Good Lord had touched me in that special way on that day. Even at this early age, I knew The Lord existed, and I wanted to know Him in a more personal way. From that day until this, I have come to know the Mercy and Kindness of The Lord. In spite of my faults, failings, and my sins, I learned through the years, that I could come to The Lord to ask for His forgiveness, and His limitless help. Even though unmerited, He would restore my damaged relationship with Him, time after time.

This relationship carries through to today. Now I know that it is The Grace Of God that bestows these special blessings upon me. Grace is defined as: "the unmerited Love and

Favor of God toward man"; and, "Devine influence acting in man to make him pure and morally strong" (Webster – 1964 edition). It is then, by The Grace Of God, through faith in Him, wherein we are saved. Grace is a gift, and faith is a gift. God, being Caring, Generous, and Loving, freely gives these gifts to anyone who seeks Him. As it is written in scripture, we cannot work our way into an acceptable position with the Lord, and thereby <u>earn</u> our way into Heaven. The very 'good works' we perform, were created in us before we were made by our Creator. We can't take credit for any of the good. We can however, in contrast, 'work' our way as a free choice, into hell. For, it is written; "The wages of sin is death, but the 'gift' of God is eternal life, through Jesus CHRIST, our Lord" (Romans chap 2:23). And it is written in Ephesians, chapter 2, verses 8 and 9: "For by Grace are you saved, through faith, and that, not of yourselves; it is a gift of God; not of works, lest any man should boast."

No one can go into hell by accident! Such a happening is 'earned' by sins, which are not covered by The Blood Of The Lamb – our Lord and Savior Jesus Christ. All I need do is ask The Lord Jesus into my heart, and He will do the rest. I must turn the doorknob of my heart to allow Him to enter.

On April 9, 1933, I was baptized. The enemy tried to steal my relationship with The Lord, by attacking me On April 9th of 1996 (see section #12 relating to this attack). Today, my trust is in my Lord and Savior, Jesus – that He will carry me throughout life. If I live to the Rapture, when He comes to gather His people, He will take me with Him then. Otherwise, He may call me to be with Him earlier, but eventually to be with Him for all eternity in heaven. This is all by His Grace.

In closing this story about The Lord's Grace, I would like to share with you what happened to me at Sacred Heart Church, on December 11, 1998. On that evening, Elayne and I were attending a Healing Service at the church. Following the service, we went to the back of the church to look at a book and gift table. There were Christmas items for sale. Much to my surprise, I noticed the same angel, still on the pedestal in the church vestibule. The angel was still holding the sea-shell. I put my head in the same indentation, where sixty-five years earlier, I had placed my neck. It was so interesting to be able to tell Elayne, and a few others who were standing there, about my earlier baptism experience. The angel was a little scratched and chipped, but it is still standing. I too, am a little scratched and chipped, and a little older, but I am still standing – on The Lord. My memory of how The Lord touched me so many years ago is still front and center. It has not diminished. The Lord is faithful to complete the work He has started in us!

47

TRUE OR FALSE

*"All scripture is inspired of God, and is profitable
for doctrine, for reproof,for correction, for instruction in righteousness; that the man of God may be
thoroughly equipped for every good work."*
(2 Timothy 3:16,17)

Our daughter Anna, attended college in Dubuque, Iowa.
During each of her four years, she was a cheerleader
at every game for all sports. Elayne and I made many trips to
Dubuque to attend the various games and other school func-
tions. We would bring Anna home for short visits at Spring
Break, Easter, Thanksgiving, Summer Break, and Christmas.

During Anna's junior year, Elayne was not able to come
with me at Christmas time, so I went alone to pick Anna up
and drive her home. The drive usually took about one and a
half hours. After a short distance out of the city of Dubuque,
Anna asked me a most unusual question. She asked, "Dad,
what parts of the Bible do we have to believe, and what parts
are stories, subject to our own interpretation?" Her question
caught me off guard. Quickly, I asked The Lord for help!
My answers to her even surprised me, as I had never considered the possibility that parts of the Bible were not true.

Instead of answering Anna's question directly, I first asked her a question. "Anna, why is it that you are asking me such a question," I asked? Anna then described her situation at college. Her teacher, who headed the religion department at the college, was in the middle of an in-depth study of scripture with her Bible class, when the Christmas break came up. During his presentation, he told the students that the book of Genesis was not an actual account of how life started on earth, but rather, it was a story, which was not true, nor should it be taken literally. Also, there really wasn't a flood to take all life except Noah, his wife, and their three sons and daughter-in-laws. He said that too was a story or an allegory. Anna continued on to relate to me that the teacher, who was ordained, said it wasn't true that Jonah was actually swallowed by a large fish. This was a story to show us what can happen if we do not do what The Lord intends us to do. The story of Jonah could not be taken literally.

At this point in Anna's conversation with me, I interrupted her, and asked: "Anna, would you accept what Jesus would have to say about any particular subject?" Only The Lord could have given me this revelation of truth, and the question to ask her. Anna answered, "Yes, sure!" I was so happy to have come up with the question from the perspective of Jesus' treatment of scripture. When Anna first brought up the subject of The Bible, I was asking The Lord to help me explain it from a position of truth. In my mind, The Bible came alive. Then I said to Anna: "Let's look at what Jesus said about Jonah, for example!" I related the conversation Jesus had with the Pharisees, as written in Matthew 12:38-41. When Jesus was confronted by the scribes and Pharisees, with the question: "Teacher, we want to see you work some signs," Jesus answered them by saying an unfaithful age is eager for a sign, but no sign would be given it but that of the prophet Jonah. Jesus said: "Just as Jonah spent three days and three nights in the belly of a whale, so will The Son Of

Man spend three days and three nights in the bowels of the earth; At the judgment, the citizens of Nineveh will rise with the present generation, and be the ones to condemn it. At the preaching of Jonah, they reformed their lives; but you have a greater than Jonah here (meaning Himself)." I then asked Anna: "Does this sound like Jonah was just a story, or was he real?" Anna, responded; "Wow Dad, that makes Jonah a real person, and that really did happen to him." The good part is that Anna believes in Jesus, and anything He says is good enough for her. It seems that her teacher may have a doubt about the deity of Jesus. Scripture says, "Unless we become like children, we cannot see the Kingdom Of God." It doesn't say become 'childish,' but 'child-like.'

It was beautiful to see that Anna had a personal relationship with Jesus, and would accept anything He would say. I told her that she should pray for the man who was teaching her because he was on thin ice. Evidently he had not read scripture for himself, but rather, he had accepted an error told to him by someone else. Then I mentioned to Anna, the very last verses in The Bible. In the book of Revelation, chapter 22:18-19, Jesus is speaking: *"I, Myself give witness to all who hear the prophetic words of this book; if anyone adds to these words, God will visit him with all the plagues described herein; if anyone takes away from the words of the prophetic book, God will take away his share in the tree of life and the Holy City described here!"* I mentioned to Anna, that if this applied to the book of Revelation, it also pertained to every book of The Bible, for all scripture is inspired of God.

Anna and I had a great visit the rest of the way home. We were at such peace as I could sense the presence of The Lord in our midst. It was such a precious time together. I was so glad that Anna had enough confidence in me that she felt I could shed some light on her questions about scripture. Through my reading of The Bible, The Holy Spirit had taught me much truth, and He gave me recall of what was necessary to help Anna in her search for the truth.

It was about twenty years ago that we had that special visit about scripture on the way home. During that trip, we talked about many other areas of scripture such as: (1), If The Bible *is* the inspired Word of God, then all written therein is true – if there is one false statement, then we can discount the entire Bible; (2), We cannot judge The Bible – as the Word of God, judges us; (3), We can't pick and choose, cafeteria style, the parts we want and reject, as subject to interpretation, the parts we don't want to accept; (4) If we can't understand the meaning of some area in The Bible, we simple can't just reject it, but instead, we must ask The Holy Spirit to teach us, as we read what we need to know, in order to carry out The Lord's Will; (5), Often we hear references to some part of The Bible in this way – 'the writer of this book, or the writer of this letter,' but in reality, The Holy Spirit is The Writer, Who inspired many men to write it down; therefore, instead of saying 'The letter of Paul to the Romans, one should properly say 'The letter of The Lord, through Paul, to the Romans'; (6), The bible is written 'to' and 'for' the believers, not the unbelievers, so we should not be surprised when an unbeliever challenges the truth of scripture; (7), Jesus often quoted The Old Testament of The Bible, so 'this' speaks to the accuracy and infallibility of 'all' scripture; and (8), Just as we were arriving home during that Christmas season so long ago, I said to Anna; "Anna, if Jesus said that Jonah swallowed the whale, I'd believe it! – I would ask Him to help me understand the truth of His statement, but I would believe it"

If Jesus said it, I believe it! That settles it for me! 'All' scripture is inspired of God! 'All' is true! And there is no need to look to anyone else as a teacher of scripture. We need only to turn to The Writer, The Holy Spirit. This is explained in The Bible, in The Lord's first letter, through John 1:26-27.

"I am writing these things to you about those who are trying to lead you astray. As for you, the Anointing you received from Him remains in you, and you 'do not need anyone to teach you.' But, as His Anointing teaches you about all things and that Anointing is real, not counterfeit – just as He has taught you, remain in Him."

Don't take my word for it. Don't take anyone's word for it. I pray you will go into the Word of God! Ask The Holy Spirit to teach you what it is you need to know. Start in The Lord's Gospel through John, or start where The Good Lord leads you but if you are not in scripture, I pray that you do start. For "All Scripture Is Inspired Of God............"

48

IS GOD INTERESTED?

"Call unto me, and I will answer you. I will give you
knowledge great beyond your understanding."
(Jeremiah 33:3)

For many years, I operated the insurance business out
of our home on Maryview Lane, in Davenport, Iowa.
Prior to that, the business's first location was in downtown
Davenport, and then uptown in Bettendorf, Iowa. Moving
home was supposed to be temporary, but it actually extended
into a period of ten years. During the time at home, I was
trying to find a permanent business spot that would give us
individual identity, rather than only a small part of a multi-
office building (more on the subject of insurance location
can be found in section #13 – titled 'Fleece Of Wool'). One
of the greatest benefits of the move home was that I was
able to develop a more personal relationship with the members of my family. Most often I would go to the office away
from home, in the evening, to do the preparation of the insurance studies for my clients. When I got to be home in the
evenings, I could still do the paperwork, and be around my
wife and children. If something came up, I would be there to
help out. There was much less strain on me, because I would

much rather be with my family than alone in a remote office location.

While working on a study for one of my clients one evening, our daughter Anita, came into the office with a problem on her mathematics homework. She was really upset with the presentation of a particular problem in Algebra. She placed her mathematics book right on top of my paperwork and started to explain to me her dilemma. "Look at this, dad," she said; as she was pointing to a particular spot in the book. Then as she pointed to another page, she said, "They expect me to get from here, to there, by using this formula, and they don't even tell where the formula came from – it can't be done!" Anita was upset. The terrific thing to me was that she felt she could interrupt me in the middle of the task I was doing. She must have known me well enough at that point in our relationship, to be able to break into the middle of my work, without it being a big deal. She concluded first that I would be interested in helping her, and secondly that I would be able to help her. The work I was doing at the time was important in that I had to complete it that evening in order to get it to my secretary the next morning for typing. Anita probably didn't even think that her asking for help would be a problem for me. It felt good to know that she would ask me for help, and that my response would be done with unconditional love. It was a complement to me that she had asked. It indicated to me that we truly did have a 'personal' relationship. I remember how special it was that evening as Anita talked to me from her heart, letting me in on her personal emotions. I realized how much I truly loved her.

A big plus is that I <u>was</u> able to help her. We went through the Algebra problems without too much difficulty. After she left my office, I pondered what had really happened. Anita had faith in my ability to help her with the mathematics. How thankful I was for the relationship we had. Anita taught me that night how The Lord must feel when I come to Him with my personal problems in life. Just as I wanted to help Anita, The Lord must want to be included in even the most incidental details of our life experiences. It must please The Lord when we call on Him for help, since this is the 'business' The Lord is in – helping and saving His people. In reality, we can't interrupt Him. But even though He is always working on complex matters across the whole universe, He is still very interested in even our smallest requests. In Matthew 7:7, it is written: "Ask, and you will receive; Seek, and you will find; Knock, and the door will be opened to you."

How wonderful it is that The Creator Of The Universe is caring enough that He will respond to every request asked of Him, when asked in accordance with His Will.

It has been said that Jesus does have a phone number. If He does, it must be "JEREMIAH 33:3 – Call unto Me and I will answer you – I will answer you – I will give you knowledge great beyond your understanding." Without a doubt, The Lord is interested!

49

ARE ANGELS REAL?

"Do not neglect to show hospitality, for by that means some have entertained angels without knowing it."
(Hebrews 13:2)

In 1975, Elayne and I, traveled with our four youngest children, Anna, Felicia, Paul, and Anita, to visit my sister, Angie, and her family, living in the State of Virginia. They lived in the city of Waynesboro, which is not too far from our nation's capital, Washington, D.C. One of the highlights of the trip was that we drove from Angie's home, to see the Capitol building, and the Washington monument. It was inspirational to see the many buildings and monuments near the Capitol dome. We spent quite a bit of time at the Washington Monument before leaving for the return to Angie's home, where we were staying. After our sight seeing tour, the children wanted to go to McDonald's. As we walked to the cars, one of our children said, "Let's go to McDonald's for lunch." I cut the request short by stating that there is no McDonald's restaurant in downtown Washington. Just as quickly, my brother-in-law corrected me by saying, "It turns out, Larry, there is a McDonald's nearby – it's only a few blocks from here."

Soon, we were all walking into the McDonald's fast food restaurant. The design of this restaurant was totally different than any we had seen before. It was a converted downtown retail store, located in the middle of the block, with a small entrance and the store itself rather narrow. The entrance to the store was at the right hand side of the storefront. At the rear of the store, the ordering counter extended across the full width. There was a short partition going down the middle of the store, almost the full length of the store. While my brother-in-law and I ordered the food for our families, the rest of the group found two corner booths at the front left of the store. My brother-in-law's order was ready before mine, so he left to distribute food to his family members, while I waited for my order to be served. Finally, with a large tray, I headed to the front of the area where my family members were seated. I was looking down as I walked between the booths. I didn't want to trip, and I didn't want to spill the milkshakes. I came to the front booth, still looking down, and I came face to face with a man standing in the middle of the aisle. He was blocking my way. The first thing I noticed was that his pants were soiled, and his toes were protruding from openings in the sides of his shoes. As I raised my head to look at the man, I saw that his tan colored shirt was stained with liquid marks and splotches of dried food. His teeth were in need of extensive repair. He had on a baseball cap, which had seen better days. The man was an African American. From his appearance, I would guess him at from seventy to eighty years of age. Our faces were only about two feet apart. He spoke to me softly, "You can't expect me to walk." I answered, "Where?" "To the hospital," he said. Then I asked, "Where is it?" "Clear across town – I could take the bus," he answered. Without hesitation, I asked, "How much does it cost?" "Anything will help," he said in reply. I put the tray down on one of the tables, and reached into my right hand pants pocket. Usually, when we travel by car, I end up with a large amount of loose change in my pocket. That particular day was no exception. I grabbed a sizable amount of coins from my pocket and put them into the man's outstretched hand. As best as I can recall, the man said, "This will bring you good fortune for life, son." I was so startled by his comment, that I can't say where he went or what he did from that point on. I probably gave him about four dollars in change. Before I got seated, one of my nieces, to the left of our booth, blurted out, "Uncle Larry, why did you give him that money?" "He asked for it – he said he needed it to get across town to the hospital," I replied. "You know what he's going to do with that money, Uncle Larry? He's going to buy booze," she said. "That may happen, but I don't know for sure that this is what he is going to do," I answered. With this remark, my niece seemed really upset with my actions, so she said, "If he wants money, he can work for it like everyone else!" This encounter with my niece came rather unexpectedly, so my reply to her even surprised me. I said, "Would you hire him – Or for that matter, do you know of anyone who would hire him, or even give him a chance?" Silence fell over everyone in both booths. The children sat very quietly, mulling over in their minds what had just happened. Maybe they were thinking this was a con-man who took advantage of their uncle, or their father. Or maybe they reasoned this really was a man in need, overlooked and shunned by a selfish society. How could one know for sure?

After a long duration of time, I broke the silence by asking this question: "Did anyone see this man come in the front door, walk clear to the back of the store, cross over to our side, and then come back to where we are seated?" No one could say they saw him come in, or where he came from. "Okay, then let me ask you even a tougher question than that – I had my back to him – he was in your plain view – after I gave him the money, did anyone see him leave – can you tell me where he went, or where he is now?" No one could answer me. Again, there was a long silence. I do not know who this man was. I do know that I liked him. His eyes were compassionate. Never will I forget this incident. In thinking about it later, I wished I had taken out my wallet to give him a much larger amount of money. The chance was gone, as our encounter was brief. I did feel good though that my heart was 'right' when I met this man – or was he a man? Would that my heart could be 'right' in each of my encounters with every person I meet in life. Since I don't know this man's name, I am going to call him "Joseph." Just maybe, Joseph was one of The Lord's angels, who came to teach us a lesson in not being judgmental, I don't know. But, the Bible is clear about one thing regarding strangers: "…….some have entertained angels without knowing it."

50

BECOME LIKE CHILDREN

"And Jesus called a little child unto Himself and sat him in the midst of them:'Verily I say unto you, except you be converted, and become as little children, you shall not enter into the kingdom of Heaven. Therefore, whoever humbles himself like a little child, is the greatest in the kingdom of Heaven.'"
(Matthew 18:2-4)

On Tuesday, January 2 1996, I was sitting in our sunroom in our home. I was relaxing while waiting for a special lunch my wife, Elayne, was preparing for us. Our daughter Anna, her husband Hal, and their three children, Matthew, Michael, and Mary, had been staying with us for a four day New Year holiday. After lunch, they would be returning to their home in the Chicago, Illinois area.

The sunroom was warm and peaceful. I was very much at peace. It had been a beautiful visit with them in our home. Mary, one of our young granddaughters, came out into the sunroom, and sat on the edge of the coffee table. As the sun shone on her, she looked up at me with a questioning gaze. She said, "Grandpa, do you remember when you and Gramma came to our house to stay with us, when mom and dad went to California?" "Yes I do," I replied. Mary said, "You told us lots of stories. Would you tell me a story now?"

Having just celebrated Christmas, with all the singing and family fellowship, my heart was still in the Christmas spirit. I was warmed by a special touch from The Lord. I asked Mary, "Would you like to hear a story about Jesus?" Mary nodded and said, "Yes."

"Well you see," I began, "when Mary, Jesus' mother, was expecting The Baby Jesus, she had to go to the city of Bethlehem, with her husband Joseph, to register for the census. The census required that everyone in the area had to go to Bethlehem, where they would have to register by giving their name and their address. Mary had to ride on the back of a donkey. The trip was long and tiring. When they arrived in Bethlehem, they found that all the sleeping rooms were taken. The only place they could find available was a stable, in a manger. This was such an unfit place for a King to be born."

"When Mary and Joseph brought The Baby Jesus back to their home in Jerusalem, they found that a plot was unfolding that could cause Jesus to be killed. The bad king, Herod, had ordered all young boys, age two and under, to be killed. In a dream, an angel appeared to Joseph, Jesus' father, warning him that Herod was jealous of Jesus. He heard that Jesus was supposed to become a King, and he thought Jesus would try to take his place as king. So, the angel told Joseph to take Mary and Jesus to a far away land called Egypt. Mary interrupted, and asked, "Grandpa, did they kill all the little girls too?" "No," I answered. "It was the small little boys he was afraid of, because he didn't know which one would grow up to be king, to take his place."

I continued the story, by telling Mary: "Joseph, Mary and Jesus, stayed in Egypt for a long time, until one day an angel appeared to Joseph in a dream, to tell him king Herod had died, and it was safe to bring Jesus back to live in a small town named Nazareth. Jesus worked with His father and became an excellent carpenter. He built furniture, houses, and all kinds of wood working. Jesus stayed with His parents for many years. His father died and then He only had His mother left. At age thirty, Jesus left home to start His ministry. He wanted to tell everyone in the area about His Father in heaven, His Father's love of all people, and about the Kingdom which was to come."

Some older men, who were teachers in the temple, grew to hate Jesus because when Jesus taught in the temple, all the people would come to hear Him. These men became jealous of Jesus because they thought Jesus was becoming more important than they were. So, they tried to trick Jesus by asking Him questions they thought He could not answer. But, of course, Jesus could not only answer their questions, He could read their hearts, and put these men in their place. Soon they realized that they could not trap Jesus, so they plotted to kill Him. One time when He was talking to these men, He told them that He and His Father were One; this made them angry because He was telling them that He was God. Another time when He was talking to a large group in the temple, He said, "Before Abraham was, I am!" He used the sacred word, "I am," which was reserved only for God. In that way, He claimed to be God, which of course we know to be true. They hated Him so much that they finally captured Him and handed Him over to the Roman ruler, named Pilate. Pilate condemned Jesus to death. Then, as we have heard, they nailed Jesus to a cross, and He died."

At this point in the story, Mary interrupted me again, and asked, "Why did they kill Jesus? Why did they nail Him to a cross? I heard that before. Why did Jesus have to die?" I asked Mary, "Have you ever done anything bad – Grandpa sure has!" Mary thought for a bit, and with sincerity, said, "Yes!" "Well, I have too, honey. All of us have. We don't want to do bad things, but we do. Each of us has the same 'sin nature,' which we inherited from our first parents Adam and Eve. And of course, when we do something bad, or sin, we cannot be in God's presence, because God is a Holy God, and cannot accept wrongdoing. 'All' wrongdoing has to be punished. God realized that there is no way anyone can pay the price for their sins, so out of Love for His people, He sent His Son Jesus, to take our place. Jesus never sinned, and yet, He suffered and died on the cross to take the punishment for us. Now, if we believe that Jesus is truly God, and believe that His Father in Heaven, raised Jesus from the dead, then when we die, or if Jesus comes back to take us with Him, before we die, we can be with Jesus for all eternity."

Mary then said, "I want to see Jesus." Her innocent face gleamed in the sunlight. I told her that Jesus is so awesome, that if He did appear, we might just vaporize and disappear, because He is so bright and Holy. With the tenderness of a child, Mary said, "I still want to see Him!" I told Mary that Jesus did appear to His Apostles, and many other disciples, after He rose from the dead, so it is not impossible that He could even appear to her sometime. "Also," I said, "when we accept Jesus as our personal Lord and Savior, then He comes to live in our hearts, through The Holy Spirit, Whom He sent to be with us after He went back to heaven."

Mary put her hands over her heart, and said, "I still want to see Him!" Gazing off into the sunlit yard, Mary thought for a while, and said: "You know what Grandpa – I want to go to Heaven right now." How precious this little girl was to me at that moment. In a way, I inwardly hoped that at that moment, the Lord would come to gather all His people to be with Him in Heaven. I thought to myself, Why can't we all be that simple – why can't we see the truth as easily as this small child? Is it our pride that gets in the way?

Mary was so excited about this story, that she asked me to tell the same story again. I wanted to tell her so much more about Jesus, but I was not able to. It was lunch time.

Elayne called us all to come to the table. The sharing at lunch was really great. True, honest love, was bubbling in every heart. As they drove out of our driveway, I could see Mary waving to us through the van window. Following their departure, I reflected on my meeting with Mary. She taught me so much. Jesus doesn't want us to become 'childish'; He wants us to become 'child-like.' He wants us to become 'as little children' – like Mary! Simple faith and confident belief in a loving Lord, named Jesus, that's what He wants. He wants to love those who become His disciples.

'Lord Jesus, that we could become child-like! Innocent! Trusting! Not proud! Not haughty! Not arrogant! Just like Mary.

Remove our blindness Lord; we want to see Jesus.
We want to reach out and touch Him.
We want to say that we love Him!
Remove our deafness Lord; and teach us of Jesus.
Remove our blindness Lord; we want to see Jesus.

51

EARS TO HEAR

*"Everyone who calls on The Name Of The Lord will
be saved. But, how shall they call on Him in Whom
they have not believed? And how can they believe
unless they have heard of Him? And how can they
hear unless there is someone to preach? And how
can men preach unless they are sent?"*
(Romans 10:13-15)

Whether I talked to Hal on the phone, or visited with
him in person, he was always polite giving me a
kind word or pleasant greeting every time I talked to him.
Hal's job was answering the phone for a small contractor in
downtown Rock Island, Illinois. Dick, the owner of the company, had Hal as his right-hand office man for six years. Hal
worked only half days because he was semi retired. Dick's
company specialized in furnace repair and installation during
the winter months, and did the installation of new gutters for
residential dwellings during the warm months. Hal's manner
on the phone gave every customer a good image of the company. Most of the calls involved setting up appointments
for the field people to contact customers directly in order to
prepare estimates to satisfy the individual needs. He would

also help prepare customer bids, and schedule the outside workers on the installation or repair jobs. Hal was a definite asset to the company. One of the most valuable assets Hal had which made him a natural on the phone was that he had an excellent speaking voice, and could be easily understood. Hal had a way of putting every caller at ease when they called. Since I did insurance work for the company owner, I was in their office a few times each month. Even if you were under a lot of stress or facing unusual problems, Hal had a way of lifting you up. In the year 1995, he turned 70 years of age. I grew to like Hal a lot, and even though I didn't tell him this, I'm sure he knew it.

Hal was a heavy smoker and in 1995, he had to take a leave of absence because he was battling cancer. Whenever Hal's condition would worsen, Dick would call to ask me to pray for him. One August day, Dick called to tell me that Hal was back in the hospital, and this time the outlook did not look good. He asked me if I would go to the hospital to see him. From the reports given to Dick, he was afraid that Hal might not live too much longer, and Dick didn't know where Hal stood in his relationship with The Lord. Dick thought that if I could see Hal, maybe I would get the chance to pray with him. Even though I felt very inadequate in this situation, I agreed to see him later that afternoon. I remember going to the hospital that day. The hospital was located in Moline, Illinois. The day was cloudy, overcast, gloomy, and to make it even more dismal, it was drizzling. As I walked from the parking lot of the hospital, I wondered what I would actually say to Hal. I asked The Good Lord to give me the words to use that would encourage him. Arriving at the elevator, I was surprised to see Dick, the company owner, and one of his employees named Mike who were going to visit with Hal too. Hal's room was quite crowded. One of his daughters was there, along with the head nurse, and the three of us. Hal's daughter was joking with him, and I guessed she was doing this because she wanted to disguise her anxiety over Hal's serious medical condition. Hal couldn't talk! I believe the cancer had attacked his throat and lungs, making speaking and breathing extremely difficult. After being in the room for about fifteen minutes, I realized that there would not be any one-on-one time with Hal, nor would there be a chance to pray with him. Hal's daughter was controlling the conversation. Dick, Mike, and I wished Hal our best and left his room. We told him that we would be back to see him later. We stood in the parking lot talking over what we had just seen in his room. At that moment, none of us knew what to do. We did pray that The Lord would raise up the right person to talk to Hal, if this witness was needed in his case. We did not know if Hal had accepted The Lord into his heart.

Early the next morning, as I was shaving, the inspiration came to me that maybe I should try to see Hal that very morning. Maybe if I got there early enough, no one would be in the room with him, and I might get the chance to see him alone. No one questioned me as I walked through the halls and into his room. Once again, I asked the Lord to help me with what to say, and to fill my heart with compassion. When I entered the room, I found Hal alone. He appeared to be sleeping, in a semi-sitting position, with his bed tilted upward. I sat by his bed for quite a while, waiting for him to awaken. Finally, I noticed that his right eye was open, but his left eye was closed. "Hal," I called out. He didn't respond! I thought he was either in a coma or heavily medicated. When I came closer to him, I was able to determine that his right eye was a glass eye. This is why the right eye remained open. After about ten minutes, I just started talking to Hal, in the hope that even if he were in a coma, he could hear me. I spoke kind words to him; about how we were all concerned for him, and that we were all praying for him. Still, he did not respond. I asked The Lord to bless him, and in His Mercy, to give Hal The Lord's Peace.

After a bit, I felt it was time to leave. It was amazing to me that no one came into the room all the time I was there. As I was leaving the room, I moved from the window-side of his bed, to the door-side of the bed, which was at his right hand. Placing my hand on his right shoulder, I talked with Hal as if he were awake. "Hal," I said: "I do not want to be presumptuous by thinking you may not have a personal relationship with The Lord Jesus, nor do I want to assume that you do, and let this opportunity go by, without you having the chance to ask Jesus to come into your heart; so if you can hear me Hal, and you would like to have Jesus come into your heart, as your personal Lord and Savior, please pray in your heart these words, after me." I leaned down close to Hal's right ear so that I could speak softly and he could hear me. I prayed, "Lord Jesus, forgive me for I am a sinner – I believe You died for me Lord Jesus, and Your Precious Blood, will cleanse me from all my sin – By faith, I now receive You Lord Jesus into my heart, as my Lord and Savior, trusting You only for my salvation – Lord Jesus, help me to do Your will each day, in Jesus Name I pray." Hal was motionless, but as I looked into his face, I could see a large tear fall from his right eye, down his cheek. He didn't move; nor did he respond in any other way. Only the tear!

As I left Hal's room, I was so thankful for having been able come. I thanked The Lord for being able to share in His work. When I arrived at my office, I called Dick to check in with him. Dick was so joyful when I related to him what had happened in Hal's hospital room earlier that morning. Later that day, as I reviewed the visit with Hal, I thought how good The Lord is to give everyone the chance to accept Him. It appeared to me that even though Hal's body was shutting down, his hearing was still in tact. The Lord, in His Mercy, gives everyone the chance to accept Him, down to the end. Maybe hearing is the last of the senses to leave us at the time of death.

Hal lived but a few days after that. I read in the newspaper that he had been a self-employed carpenter before working for Dick's company as receptionist and a work-scheduler. The article in the paper also indicated that Hal served in the Merchant Marines during World Was II. The write-up told that Hal enjoyed helping others, and working crossword puzzles. I had always liked Hal a lot. Even though I didn't get to know him well in this life, I have a hunch that I'll get the chance to spend a lot of time with him in The Lord's Kingdom. Dick did his God ordained part by calling me and urging me to go see Hal. I'm so thankful I was sent. I'm thankful Hal could hear. "And how can they hear unless there is someone to preach? And how can men preach unless they are sent?"

52

MAJESTIC EAGLE

"But they that wait upon The Lord shall renew their strength, they shall mount up with wings as eagles; they shall run and not grow weary; and they shall walk, and not faint."

(Isaiah 40 :31)

With great anticipation, we looked forward to our annual fishing trip in the fall of 1991. Usually, we would get away in early summer of each year, but in the year 1991, we just couldn't seem to make the break until later in the year. In that particular year, it was in mid-September when Elayne and I took a week to go to our favorite spot in Wisconsin. We had found a spot called Spider Lake, and we adapted to the surroundings like butter goes on bread. We both felt that we needed to take the time away, as it had been a hectic year in many ways, and we do so enjoy our time together. When we are on an outing like fishing, neither of us gets out of sight of the other for the whole time we are gone. We talk in the car, both coming and going; we prepare meals together, we fish together, and we just have plain fun, enjoying each other's company.

We arrived mid-afternoon, on the Saturday before our week of fishing would begin. After unloading all the gear, food and clothes, from our car, we spent some time getting the cabin and boat ready for the week of fishing ahead. Following this, we went into a nearby town by the name of Birchwood, to do our grocery shopping for perishables needed for the week. While in town we attended a Catholic church service, before going back to the cabin to prepare supper. With all this behind us, we sat back relaxing, in anticipation and excitement of the start of fishing early the next day. It was a beautiful evening, with all the peace and quiet of a cool Wisconsin welcome. Just before bedtime, it started to sprinkle lightly. By morning, the sprinkle grew into a torrential downpour. The heavy rain continued all day Sunday, in to Monday, and throughout Tuesday, Wednesday, and Thursday. When we went to bed Thursday evening, it was still raining. There was no fishing to be done. It was just too wet, and it would have been too dangerous on the water in this major storm.

There are a total of seven cabins at this resort. With such a storm, we didn't see much of the other people staying in the other cabins, although it was our understanding from the owner, that all cabins were occupied. We could see the cars parked outside of each cabin, so we concluded that the others were just like us; holed up in their cabins, waiting for the rain to stop. Apparently, all the others became totally frustrated, because one by one, they started leaving during the daylight hours of Thursday. Elayne and I, being the die-hard fisherman and fisherwoman that we are, ended up being the only people at the resort on Thursday evening. Adell, the owner of the resort lived a few miles from the resort, so we didn't even have her company. The sky was pitch black throughout the night, with only the pitter-patter of rain to be heard on the cabin roof, keeping us company. There we were, way out in the country, next to a lake, without another person within three to four miles of us! It was most unusual!

We awoke early the next morning, expecting the familiar rain. It was Friday, the 13th day of September, and since this is suppose to be unlucky, one would have expected the weather to be unusually unfriendly so as to again hinder our attempt at fishing. But, to our surprise, as we looked out the window of our cabin, toward the lake, we could see the warm sun rising in the East. The rain had finally stopped! It was a most peaceful day and beautiful day. So we decided do what we came to do – we decided to visit our 'friends' in the lake. After a nice breakfast, we headed out. Spider Lake is actually a chain of five lakes tied together by little waterways, a 'chain-of-lakes,' making it a most unusual and breathtaking experience for fishing. Since there is only one resort on the chain of lakes, and everyone else had gone home, we had the entire area to ourselves. In looking at all the many fishing trips we had ever taken, including all the places we had been, and under all conditions, this was without a doubt the most perfect fishing weather we had ever seen. It was just perfect, not too hot, a slight breeze, and sunny, with the lake so still, it looked like glass. The water reflected back a beautiful reflection off the trees along the bank of the lake like a mirror. On that particular morning, we decided to do something we had never done before. We decided to 'troll' for Northern Pike. To troll, we ran the boat motor very slowly, and dragged our fishing lure behind us as we went through the water. In this way our fishing lures would be near the bottom of the lake where the Northern Pike are supposed to be feeding. Usually Elayne and I would only use live bait, such as minnows or dew-worms, but on that morning we used artificial bait. We only had three artificial lures with us on the trip. I gave Elayne a large spinner bait to use, which I had found on a fishing trip, years before in Colorado. It had a multi-colored 'skirt' covering the treble hook at the end of the lure. I used a smaller spinner, I had found while fishing at another lake. The lure I was using had a white brush type skirt covering a small treble hook at the end, hanging somewhat below the spinner. We positioned the back end of the boat almost up against a small island, and then we started to troll away from the island, down a narrow, but deep channel. We hadn't gone but about fifty feet, when Elayne told me her lure was dragging in the weeds at the bottom of the lake. I stopped the boat so that we could free Elayne's lure from the weeds. Tug after tug, Elayne pulled what she thought was a weed clump, closer and closer to the boat, so that I could grab hold of it and get the lure loose from the weeds. So that I would not get my fingers caught in the hook, I used a large fish net with which I could pick up the whole mess, and then try to figure out how to untangle the lure. All of a sudden, Elayne exclaimed, "It's moving!" It must have been a huge Northern Pike that attacked the lure and then got all tangled up in the weeds while trying to get away. Elayne kept trying to drag the whole mess of reeds and the fish up to the boat. Just as I was about to net the large object coming to the surface of the water, the fish suddenly decided to turn and go the other way, and the fishing line snapped. To say that Elayne was 'upset,' would definitely not be an exaggeration. She hated losing the fish, but more than that she was angry for losing the large fishing lure. We still had one other lure left. It was a small multi-colored fish, called a 'Rapella.' I put that lure on Elayne's line and we again started to troll. We didn't go very far, maybe forty to fifty feet, and Elayne caught and we landed a 23 inch long Northern Pike. It was a beauty. Since the fish was too large for our fish basket, I put it on a hook-type stringer, so that we could drag the fish in the water along side the boat, as we continued to troll. Within a distance of another 100 feet, I caught a twenty-four inch long Northern. Now we had two large Nothern's on the stringer alongside the boat, as we continued to troll.

After a few minutes, we saw the most unusual sight we have ever seen, on any fishing trip. A large eagle flew very low over our boat, coming to rest on a shore-line tree limb, about two hundred feet away from us. The eagle was so beautiful! As we continued trolling, moving along the shore-line, the eagle would move from tree to tree, keeping his eye on us. Soon we came to the end of the channel. I asked Elayne to keep an eye on the eagle, while I made a large turn, to begin trolling back down the channel in the opposite direction. As we were turning, this put my back to the eagle. But, it put the two Northern's on the side of the boat toward the eagle. Just then Elayne shouted, "Laaaarrrrry!" Coming right toward the boat was our eagle friend, with his wings spread out, looking as broad as a four by four sheet of plywood, against the sky. His feet were extended toward the boat with claws out full. He was coming in to claim 'his' two fish. After all, they were in the water, and that was his territory. Elayne was waving our net wildly in the air, trying to get our new found friend to change directions. I joined in, wildly waving my fishing pole back and forth. The eagle was truly majestic, but he was also frightening because he was so huge. With his wings extended, as he was slowing down to make a strike at the two fish in the water, he made an ominous silhouette against the sky above. Fortunately, our frantic waving did discourage him, and he veered off to the left, just before reaching the side of our boat. He came within ten feet of our boat, before he went back to stand again on a tree limb. My legs were shaking! I had to sit down. Only Elayne and I saw the eagle that day. We were all alone on the lake. As I sat in the boat, trying to collect my thoughts, I continued to gaze at the eagle in the tree. In a situation like that, you really don't know what to say. The words that first came out of my mouth shook me to the core. I loudly said, "Who says there's no Jesus – come talk to me – I'll tell you about Him!" In my spirit I sensed the magnificence of The Lord

Jesus' creation. I thought to myself; 'This eagle does what he wants to do!' Then a verse came to mind in the Gospel of John, chapter 1, verses 1 through 3: "In the beginning was The Word, and The Word was with God, and The Word was God – He was with God in the beginning – Through Him all things were made; without Him nothing was made that has been made." Jesus is the designer of all things, and yes, He made that huge eagle. Then again, in John 1:14, it is written: "The Word became Flesh and made His dwelling place among us." At that moment, I felt such a closeness to The Lord. Just being able to see the eagle that close – to witness the uniqueness of his design, was such a treat. Elayne and I were both thrilled.

We talked about the whole episode for quite a while, just sitting in the boat. Soon, we started to troll again, all the while keeping an eye on the eagle. It remained perched on a tree limb. As we moved along in the water, apparently a tree limb would get in the way of the eagle's view, so he would move his head from side to side, to keep his 'eagle-eye' on 'our' fish. I'm sure he was plotting how he was going to make his next strike. Since we did not want to risk another encounter with the eagle, we had to pull in our fish and return to the cabin to clean them. We were run-off from our fishing spot by an eagle! Somehow though, we didn't really mind. We got two nice fish, and the experience with the eagle was breathtaking. Jesus allowed us to get a glimpse of the breadth and depth of His creation. And the Northern Pike were two of the largest fish we had ever caught. My guess is that not many people have come that close to an eagle in the wild, and lived to talk about it. In retrospect, it seems that the whole week had built up to that perfect time when we would be visited by this 'Majestic Eagle.' Even though it had rained the whole week, we weren't in a bad mood. We enjoyed it. We were together, it was peaceful and we were able to share a lot. We conversed about many areas of concern in our lives at that particular time. One day, I used the rain-time to prepare some of the general outlines for these writings. And then, after a long wait, The Lord had this special surprise awaiting us – a look at one of His most marvelous creations – The Eagle.

Like the eagle, if we wait upon The Lord, we too will renew our strength; we will run and not grow weary; we will walk and not faint.

53

HOUSE OR HOME

"For every house is built by some man, but He that built all things, is God."

(Hebrews 3:4)

A ll ten of our children were raised in our home on Maryview Lane, in Davenport, Iowa. For the first four years of our marriage, Elayne and I lived in an upstairs apartment on Scott Street, in Davenport. Just after our third child, Carla, was born we moved into our new home on Maryview Lane. This was in December of 1956. Elayne and I designed the home; we even did the drawing of the house plans, and did most of the finishing work, such as wiring, plaster board, siding, painting, and exterior landscaping. The original home was built of rectangular shape, with a flat roof. The width was twenty-four feet, and the length was forty feet. The home stood on an acre and one quarter of prime land, in the Northeast corner of Davenport. Because of the flat roof, it looked to some like a 'root beer stand.' We had decided to start with a flat roof, so that we could either add 'up,' or 'out,' whichever would be needed, depending upon our family size. In addition to the single story we also had a full basement. As it turned out, we needed both 'up' and 'out.'

Since The Lord blessed us with ten children in a period of thirteen years, we needed additional room 'out' in order to provide living area, and we needed more room 'up,' to allow for more bedrooms. In 1963, we had grown to a family of eight children, so we added on a large dining room, so we could all sit together, and we added a small den and a two car garage. How exciting it was to get a large dining table with twelve matching chairs, for our new dining room. We could now all eat together where before we had to eat in shifts. Before long, we had ten children, and all the chairs around the table were occupied during family meal times. These were indeed special times of learning and sharing. With the addition of the dining room and den, we had about fifteen hundred square feet of living area, plus the garage. In each of our two bedrooms, we had two sets of bunk beds. We had four children sleeping in each bedroom, two children on a hideaway sofa in the living room, and Elayne and I in the third bedroom. With only one bathroom, it took quite a system which Elayne developed to get ten children ready for bed in the evening, and then off to school in the morning. With these restrictions, in order to be fair to Elayne and the children, I knew we had to do something to make more room.

So, in 1971, we started to look into purchasing a larger home, with four or five bedrooms and hopefully more than one bathroom. We were not able to find a home in good shape, to satisfy our needs that was within our price range. Both Elayne and I liked the area of the city we lived in, so the prospect of moving to a different area was not appealing. One evening, after dinner, as we all sat around the dining room table, we started to explain our predicament to the children. We talked about the prospect of a move, but the children objected to this alternative, because they wanted to stay where we were. They said not to worry – they would make do. We told them we had been thinking of another option, that of adding a second story on to the existing house. We explained that this would mean a lot more work for Elayne and me. We told them that such a move, would mean that we would have to take out a large loan to cover the cost, and if we did this, we would expect a commitment of cooperation from each child. After much discussion, with input from each child, we took a vote. It was unanimous – each child raised his or her hand in favor of the new second story addition. We drew up the plans, secured prices on materials and labor, obtained financing, and then in March of 1972, we proceeded to add a second story. It was definitely a family project. All the boys, Chris, Peter, Daniel, and Paul helped in the actual construction. The older girls, Maria, Carla, and Laura, helped in carrying the materials for the construction of five new bedrooms and two additional bathrooms. Each of the children really pitched in. There was a spirit of sincere cooperation. Before Christmas, we were all in our new rooms. Chris took over the master bedroom downstairs, formerly used by Elayne and me. Upstairs, we had Maria and Carla in one bedroom, Laura and Anita in another bedroom, Anna and Felicia in another bedroom, and Peter, Daniel, and Paul in a larger bedroom, which we called 'the boy's room.' Elayne and I had a master bedroom upstairs, with a separate bathroom. There was plenty of room, with plenty of just plain 'good old living' going on. And, very important to Elayne and the children, we had three bathrooms.

When Chris got married, Peter moved into the downstairs bedroom. And so it went. As each of the children would marry, we would go through room shuffling. Eventually, we ended up with one child in each bedroom. This was of course a dream come true for the ones remaining. Eight of our children stayed with us until they married. For some, this came at a later age. One of our children didn't marry until age twenty-six. This was truly a blessing to have children with us for so long a time. Laura stayed with us for a while after her four year enlistment in the Air Force, before leaving to go off on her own, and then marry. Carla went into an apartment with two of her girlfriends before she married. It seemed to go so quickly. Each of our children eventually went off to be on their own, to marry, and start their own families. Elayne and I ended up living all alone in a twelve room home, of 2,892 square feet living space, plus a full basement, with two car garage. In 1985, we had added on a sunroom and a large deck, off the rear of the house, making up the total living area. It was a lot for two of us to maintain, and on top of that, we had over an acre of grass to trim. During the years, Chris, Paul, and Anita, had come into the insurance business, and since we used the three downstairs rooms for our business, we were not alone during the day.

Anticipating our eventual move, we knew we would first have to find a permanent location for the insurance business. In 1992, at Thanksgiving time, Lyons Insurance Service moved into a renovated building, in downtown Bettendorf, Iowa. At Christmas time of that year, Elayne and I had a long talk about what we would do. We decided to stay in our large home because we were at such peace there, plus, it was great to have the extra bedrooms when our 'out-of-town' children came home to stay with us for the holidays. We also thought that if one of our children should ever have financial difficulties, it would be good to have a place for them to come until they could get back on their feet. After two years of handling the upkeep by ourselves, we decided to tell the children we would be looking for a smaller home. We actively started to make plans to sell our Maryview Lane home at Christmas time of 1994 and look for a smaller bungalow. We spent the first six months of 1995 remodeling our home, in order to give the prospective buyers a home in the best shape possible. This turned out to be a major project, which included new exterior siding, exterior painting, replacement of some windows, paved driveway, a new furnace, air-conditioning of the downstairs, ceiling fans in each bedroom, waterproofing of the basement, as well as extensive interior painting and decorating.

In July of 1995, we put a 'For Sale By Owner' sign in our front yard. Many people called to make appointments to see our home. Everyone who saw the home, raved about it but once they were inside they were surprised at how large it was. Most were a little apprehensive about the task of mowing such a large lawn. We hoped, and prayed, for just the right buyer. We wanted a large family to purchase our home; a family who could experience the 'peace' we had throughout all the forty years we had lived there.

During the first week of September, a young man, the son of one of my best friends, called to express an interest in seeing our home. This young man made at least five trips over to go through the home. His wife came along on two or three of these visits. Sometimes they would bring relatives to look at what they were considering. On one occasion, an architect came to make measurements, as the couple contemplated some changes of their own. They had a contractor come to look at the house design, to see if the changes were even feasible. Soon after all these visits, the young man called to say, "We want your home!" It was so great to hear him call it a home, because there is a great difference between a 'house' and a 'home.' He went on to tell me that when they would come over to check out a particular idea, that when they got within a couple of blocks, they could feel the "peace" from our home. They wanted our home for their family! The young man said that since we had the home for our family for forty years, now he wanted this home for his family for the next forty years. It seemed to us that The Lord had provided the perfect buyer for our home. They had four children and were expecting their fifth. He said the only problem he had was that he could not take possession until March of the following year. This would put us into 1996. He needed that time for his wife to complete pregnancy. He

291

didn't want her to have to go through selling their home, then dealing with the modifications they had planned to the new place while she was carrying her baby. We told him that this would be no problem for us, since we didn't have a place to move to, as yet. Also, I told him that it would be great to have a winter in our home when we could take advantage of our new concrete driveway. In other winters, we would spray gravel all over with our snow blower when we cleared the snow from our old driveway. He asked if we would need a contract or down payment. I told him that wasn't necessary. If he wanted our home, it was his. They had a relatively new home in Bettendorf, Iowa, but they really liked our area, and our home was exactly what they were looking for. Since they were expecting their fifth child, and their present home did not provide enough room, they wanted a permanent home where they could raise their children, and then stay there into retirement. The young man said that his wife had some late-term difficulties in prior pregnancies, so he did not want to risk moving until March of the following year. Again, I said to him, "If you want the home, I'll take the sign out of the front yard." He replied, "The only way we won't take this home, come March, is if this heart (pointing to his heart) isn't pumping blood anymore!" What a wonderful husband and father. We were so pleased that they decided to purchase our home.

We arrived at the price for our home by first getting an appraisal to be done by an independent appraiser. Then we subtracted the normal 'realtor' commission, and we offered them our home for the net price. They didn't even try to bargain. Isn't The Lord good! The home was theirs. They trusted us, and we trusted them. No paperwork! Many told us that we were crazy to go this route without a contract. They told us that these people would surely back out of the handshake, leaving us in the lurch. When he made his declaration over the phone one day, about his heart 'pumping blood,' I told him the sign was coming out of the yard. That is exactly what I did – as soon as I hung the phone up, we took the sign down. In our conversations with them, we could easily see that they loved The Lord as we do, so we had nothing to be concerned about.

Now, we had a problem though. We had only five months to find a home. We did consider building a new, smaller home, but building costs were much too high, in comparison to what we would get for our home. We would end up putting everything we got out of our Maryview Lane home, into the building of a smaller home. That didn't make sense to us. One evening, in late fall of 1995, while we were sitting in our family room, I caught Elayne off guard by asking her two questions: first, "Where do 'you' want to live – in what part of town;" and secondly, "What main features do 'you' want in a home?" Elayne responded quickly. She said that she wanted to live generally in the same area we were living or she could live in North Bettendorf, if we couldn't find anything in that area. My main goal was to find a place where Elayne would be happy, for wherever Elayne is, I will be happy with her. Then, as far as features in the home, she said she hoped we could find a single level home, with a full basement, attached two car garage, three bedrooms total, including a Master Bedroom with separate bath – and finally, a basement that could be finished later. She added as an afterthought, that it would be nice if the basement would be of the 'walk-out' style. This gave me something to search for. Every day Elayne would scan the newspapers. We checked out homes for sale by local realty firms. Nothing seemed right! Then, I'm sure, as an answer to prayer, I came up with the idea to drive Elayne around in the area of her choice, just to see if we could find a home for sale that she liked. There was nothing for sale that appealed to her. So, we just started looking at homes that did appeal to her, even though they were not for sale. We took down the addresses of twenty-two homes in the general area of choice, where Elayne felt she could live. In the City Directory, I looked up the names of the owners to match the addresses of the homes she had chosen. Even though the homes were not for sale, we sent letters to each of the twenty-two homeowners. I composed the letter, but to make it personal, each letter was hand-written by Elayne. In the letters, we described our situation and told them that we needed a home by March of 1996. We told them that we had sold our home on Maryview Lane, and that closing was in March of 1996. We mentioned that our children were all married; that we had to scale down; that we wanted a three bedroom bungalow on one level; with an attached garage. We explained that we had no reason to believe that their home was for sale, but, if they were thinking about it, we would be happy to talk to them. We added, that we did not want to offend them, but we were set on finding a single level home in their area. To our surprise, we had twelve responses to our letters. Some responses were by phone, and some were by letter. Some said that they would be interested in talking to us, but their time of sale would be beyond our time of need. One woman called to tell us that she had checked us out to see if we were truthful in every aspect of our letter. She went to the courthouse to see if we had actually lived at the Maryview Lane address for forty years. She found of course, that we were completely truthful in every detail. She was skeptical of our approach, but since we checked out, she decided to contact us. She said she had planned to retire from teaching in June of that year, but our letter made her reconsider to move her retirement date up to March. She was planning to move to a city near Des Moines, Iowa, to be close to her mother. She agreed to have us come to see her home.

When we visited her in her home, she gave us a tour, along with a complete history and background. She was the only owner of the home which was built for her in 1965.

And isn't it great how The Lord works. The home had all seven characteristics that Elayne had mentioned to me as her desires. It even had the 'walk-out' basement which was completely finished. It had a large family room, large bedroom, attached bath, workroom and laundry room. There was a small kitchen area. When we had first looked at the home, we couldn't see the back of the house, since there was no alley behind, so we didn't know if there was a basement or not. The back yard of the home backed up against a large school playground, so we couldn't get a look from any angle. It happened quickly – we made an offer – she accepted. In October of 1985 we had our new home picked out. At Maryview Lane, we had 430 feet of property depth, with a whole lot of grass to cut, but at this home, there was 800 feet of grass but we would only have to cut our grass to the depth of 50 feet, the rest was playground. Elayne came from a farm background, so this wide-open space behind the house was really appealing.

The woman had to find a home in Ogden, Iowa, before she could arrange a closing date for spring of 1996. She did find a home, without going through a realtor with the exact features she wanted. On March 9, 1996, we had back-to-back closings. We closed on the sale of our Maryview Lane home in the morning, and then we closed on the purchase of our new home in the afternoon. The woman closed on her home the following day in Ogden, Iowa. The Lord has been so good to us. It is not that we are deserving; it is that He is so Kind and Merciful. At the time of this writing, we are in our 'new-to-us' home, and we find it hard to believe, but we are even more 'at peace' here, than we were at our Maryview Lane home of forty years. In a way, when we handed the keys over to the young family at our Maryview Lane home, The Lord must have let us 'turn a switch,' so to speak, so that our hearts turned immediately to our new home. Often we marvel at how much we like it here. In these past fifteen years, we have never made the almost - automatic statement of, "Remember back home when…" Whenever we talk about where we used to live, we always refer to that home as our 'other home.' Many times Elayne has said, "That home was for when we raised the children – this home is for you and I – like when we first started out in our marriage." The young couple that purchased our 'other home,' hired the architect who had come to make measurements before they purchased the home. They hired the contractor who had come to check out the construction feasibility. They added a third story. They added a large 'great room' over the area where we had a deck extending out the back. They added a large room over the garage, which the young man uses as his home office. In addition, they added a full-width porch across the front. In all, they changed the living area from 2,892 square feet, to over 5,000 square feet of living space. They told us that they are so very happy living there. One day, when all of our children were in town for one of our annual golf outings, we were given a complete tour of the home. It was truly amazing to see what they had done to this home. Each of our children was thrilled to see the changes.

Before we moved to our present home, Elayne and I took a full set of pictures of every room at the Maryview Lane home including outside shots of the garden and trees the children used to play on. We did this so that the children would have something to help them remember all the fun we had when we lived there. We gave each of the children a complete album as a Christmas present the year before we moved.

What have we learned from all this? We know that, "Every house is built by some man, but He that built all things, is God." We know that money can buy a 'house,' but only the presence of The Love Of The Lord, can make a house a home. If I do not have a personal relationship with Jesus, I will never live in His "Home." Elayne and I, pray this for each of our children and their spouses and children – that they will live in a 'home' while here, and when this earthly life is over, they will live in Jesus' Home for all eternity.

54

BREAD ON WATER

"Cast your bread upon the water; after a long time, you may find it again."

(Ecclesiastes11:1)

George was a kind elderly man who lived in our neighborhood. He was especially kind to children. For many years, he taught 'shop' class in the local high school. Our children would often go over to his house to visit him. Most of the time, he could be found in his machine shop located in a special garage beside his home. One could ask him to fix anything, and most assuredly, he could do it. 'Kindness' would be one of the main qualities one could use to describe George.

Late one winter evening, Elayne and I were coming home from a meeting we had attended. It had been snowing for most of the evening, so there was quite an accumulation on the ground. As we turned the corner, from Jersey Ridge, onto 46th Street, we started down the hill, and as we did, we went very slowly to avoid sliding on the slick snow. Directly in front of us, just to the left of center, we caught the silhouette of a man, as he was walking down the hill. As we got closer, we could see that it was an elderly man, moving very cautiously. In order to keep from hitting him, I slowed the car down almost to a stop. When we were even with the man, I could see that he had his collar pulled up around his neck, to keep the snow from getting inside his coat. I rolled down the window to talk to him, and to my surprise, I could see it was George. When I asked him if he had a problem, he said that he was going home to call for help. He said his car had a flat tire and it was parked up at the top of the hill. His wife was sitting in the car, waiting for him to return. It was so cold and snowy, that he didn't want her to try to walk with him because it was very slippery. I told George that I would be happy to help him with the tire. I asked him to go back to be with his wife, and it would only take me a few minutes to drop Elayne off at our home and I'd return to help him.

In reaching the top of the hill, I could see his car. I pulled my car up to the rear of his car, so that the headlights of my car would shine underneath his vehicle. When I looked under the back of his car, I was shocked. He had tried to position the car-jack under the rear of the vehicle, but due to his age, he must have had difficulty getting the jack in the proper spot. There is a 'V' shaped slot on the frame of the car, where the jack is supposed to be inserted. Instead of putting the jack in the slot, he had placed it on the slant part of the frame seam. There was very little illumination from the streetlight, so he must not have seen the slot. The jack was on a precarious angle, just ready to slip off. First, I loosened the jack and repositioned it correctly in the slot. Then I loosened the wheel nuts holding the left rear wheel onto the car. I asked George to hold the spare tire, a little to the right of the left rear wheel, in an upright position. Ahead of time, I explained to George, that when I got the rear wheel off, I wanted George to roll the spare tire in front of me, so that I could quickly mount it on the car, before the car could slip off the jack. After jacking the car up in the air, enough so that the rear wheel cleared the street, George rolled the spare tire into place in front of me, and I placed it in position. Quickly, I put on three wheel nuts and hand tightened them loosely, to hold the wheel in place. "We got it," I exclaimed. George spoke very softly, saying, "You cast your bread on the water." As I looked up from my crouched position toward George, who was leaning over me from behind, I could only see his silhouette, outlined against the night sky. Although I heard what he said, I didn't know what he meant by it, so I asked him again; "What did you say?" Again, he repeated, "You cast your bread on the water."

"What do you mean, George," I asked him? He proceeded to tell me a story while I finished putting on the other wheel nuts and lowered the car. "When I was a young man," he started off; "I left the church after a Sunday service, to pick up my girlfriend. I was really excited at the chance to see her, so I was driving at a pretty good clip, heading over to her house. Along the way, I passed an older man at the side of the road, trying to change a flat tire on his car. He seems to be having trouble, I thought to myself. I hoped someone would come along to help him, but I knew I couldn't because I had an important date, and I certainly didn't want to be late. As I traveled along farther down the road, I thought to myself, I can't do that! I have to go back to help him. I did go back and helped him change the flat tire." So, you see, you cast your bread upon the water, and after a time, it will come to you." I understood what he meant. It was like the waves coming back to bring what had been tossed out to sea earlier.

A few years later, as I was reading in The Bible, I came across the passage telling this principle. It was in the book of Ecclesiastes 11:1, which reads: "Cast your bread upon the water; after a long time, you may find it again." That night, when it was now George in trouble, he remembered back to the time when he was a young man, and he helped an elderly man change his flat tire. Now, when he is older, another young man came along to help him change his flat tire. I'm sure, when George was younger, he didn't think this was a good thing to do only for the reason that in later years, he would be repaid. He was just listening to his conscience – helping another person in need. What did occur, is that a spiritual law kicked in, allowing The Lord to bless him at a later time, because he was acting unselfishly at an earlier time. In Acts 20:25, it is written: "It is better to give than to receive." It does not say that we will not receive. It only says that it is better to give than to receive. The Good Lord looks at the heart. Our motive should be to help without expecting anything in return. If, and when, The Lord blesses us later, and helps us to remember some earlier kindness on our part, then we can thank The Lord for His Goodness.

As I look back in our family life I can think of many times when The Lord has blessed us through someone whom we may have helped some way in the past. Some of these blessings are covered in other sections of these writings.

I am glad I stopped to ask George if I could be of help. If I hadn't, I would have missed the great lesson The Lord had planned to teach me on that cold snowy night in 1975. This incident allowed me to see a glimpse of how The Lord is 'The Great Helper.' He is always there; ready to help those who are committed to Him. I'm thankful The Lord has given me a heart that likes to help others. There is such joy in 'doing' for someone else, what that person is not able to do for himself. Later, we find that The Lord likes to surprise us with an unexpected blessing – just at the right time. For, "You cast your bread upon the water; after a long time, you may find it again."

55

LETTER FROM THE LORD

*"We have this confidence in God, that He hears us
when we ask for anything according to His will."*
(1John 5:14)

My spirit was upbeat! It was January of 1990, and the
start of a new year looked very promising. Although
my success in the insurance business, from a financial
standpoint, wasn't what would be considered the greatest,
I did have the satisfaction of having been in the business
for twenty-three years and being of service to many people.
People who were at first, strangers to me, became good clients, and more importantly, good friends.

Often times in my insurance work, I would be asked to
do something, which to me, would be a compromise of good
ethical standards. When that would come up, I would have
to tell the person in a nice way, that I could not take the particular action they wanted of me. One such situation came
up toward the end of January 1980. A small contractor client
called me and asked me to come to a special meeting he
had set up with his partner in their accountant's office. He
gave me preliminary information as to what the meeting was
to be about. Their intention was to install a special retire-

ment plan, called a Keogh plan, or HR-10 Pension Plan. This was an Internal Revenue approved plan, which allowed each partner to put up to $15,000 away on a tax-deductible basis. Since I had installed similar plans for other business clients, I was familiar with the plan requirements. At that time, my sales were at a low point, so this really sounded exciting to me. Also, the commission generated from such a sale, would be good for the Lyons family.

The phone call came to me on a Wednesday. The meeting with their accountant would be on the following Monday. This gave me ample time to research the necessary documents needed for installation, and the opportunity to select the best company to satisfy their needs. The company chosen would need to have pre-approved 'prototype documents,' already certified by the Internal Revenue Service. To lay the groundwork for this project, I first called the IRS office in St. Louis. An agent could give me the legal requirements for plan initiation. The two partners wanted to put the plan in to cover the previous tax year of 1979. From my recollection of tax-law, this was permissible as long as the contributions were paid in by April the 15th of the following year. An Internal Revenue Specialist told me that as long as the liability was established in the tax year of 1979, then the contributions could be made into such a plan up to April 15, 1980. When I questioned the individual as to what it meant to 'have the liability established' he said that the documents would have to be dated in the tax-year 1979. This is exactly what the two partners wanted to do – establish the plan for the tax-year 1979, and then pay the money into the plan by April 15, 1980. This way, they would get the tax deduction for the year 1979. The only problem in my mind was that the date of the scheduled meeting was February 3, 1980, and the documents would have to be back-dated to December 31, 1979, in order to meet the requirement of 'liability establishment' given by Internal Revenue Service.

It would be very easy to do all this. The documents are readily available from most insurance companies. The plan documents are pre-approved by Internal Revenue. After dating, and signatures, the papers would be kept on file by the business partners, which would essentially put the plan into effect. In this case, the two partners would simply keep the plan documents in their possession. The documents would not need to be filed with Internal Revenue. In review then, all we would have to do at the Monday meeting, would be to date the papers as of December 31, 1979, and sign the forms. They would have till April the15th to pay the money, and 'all is well'! This whole situation caused a dilemma for me; Would this transaction be ethical? On the one hand, the Internal Revenue allows this same approach for individuals, in that they can date the documents after the tax year but can still contribute the funds up to April 15th and still take a tax deduction for the previous year. This type of plan is commonly referred to as an IRA, or Individual Retirement Account. But, for some unknown reason, the IRS does not allow dating of documents after the tax-year in question, for a 'business' retirement plan. Of course, it doesn't sound fair, but I had to look at what would be the legal and ethical thing to do. Tax rules should be the same for either an individual or a 'self-employed' individual, but they are not. Current tax law at the time did not allow what the two partners wanted to do.

In order to decide, what would be 'right' and what would be 'wrong' I needed to get input from others. First of all, I called a CPA friend, to see what his interpretation of the tax law would be. He told me that this had come up in his practice before, but when the time came to actually pay into the plan, the people involved couldn't raise the funds needed, so he didn't have to go through with the backdating of documents. He sympathized with me because he too had a moral problem when he was asked to do the same thing. When I called my friend who is a trust officer of a bank, he told me about the same story. Bank business clients would approach him and ask him to put such a plan into effect, after the tax year had passed. His interpretation was the same as the IRS, in that the 'liability' had to be established in the tax year in question. He too said it was a tough problem, every time it came up. Although he didn't tell me which direction he went in his cases, he did say, "I'm glad this is not my problem." He said it is difficult to refuse good clients this tax benefit, if they insist on going this direction. Most of the others I checked with, said something like the following: "Don't make a big deal out of it - sign the documents - let them put the money in - and let them put the papers in the desk drawer - what's the big deal?"

For me, it was an extremely difficult decision. When I received the first phone call, I asked The Lord to help me with the decision. I told The Lord, that I didn't want to be like a 'Pharisee,' keeping the letter of the law, but missing the mark on my true responsibility to The Lord and His people. At the same time, I didn't want to do something The Lord did not approve of and thereby be a poor witness. Coupled with this, our family had some real financial needs in January and this sale would have produced about $900 in commissions. From Wednesday through Saturday, I was in prayer to The Lord, asking for His will in this situation.

Elayne, was also praying about the situation, as I had confided in her about the difficulty of my decision. She was asking The Lord to give me insight as to the right way to go. Late on that Saturday afternoon, before the proposed partner's meeting, I was in my corner office in our home, mulling over all the details of the case. I was trying to come up with an answer that would be acceptable to The Lord. Being concerned about me, Elayne sent our oldest son, Chris, into my office to check on me. Chris has a good heart, and he loves The Lord, so I went over all the details with him. At this time, he was not in the insurance business as yet. He pointed out one aspect of the case which I had not considered. He showed me that the two partners were not really escaping the income tax in question. It would be true that if they put the money into such a plan for the tax year 1979, they would get the tax deduction for that year, but when they took the money out, no matter when that would be, it would be fully taxable as ordinary income. So, in effect they would only be deferring their tax payment to a later year. Even after discussing this new aspect of the case with Chris, I still did not have peace with the idea of dating documents any date other than a current date. I was mainly concerned about 'the witness' – would it be acceptable to The Lord?

About 3:00 p.m. on that Saturday afternoon, something most unusual happened. Chris and I were still discussing the case, when our youngest daughter, Anita, knocked on the office door. As I opened the door, I noticed that Anita's eyes were opened wide. In her hand, she held a small envelope, extended toward me. She said, "This came in the mail for you, Dad." Immediately, I read the return address. It read, "GOD." At first, this upset me. I tossed the letter on my desk, saying, "That's what I need right now—someone playing with my brain!"

Chris and I finished our discussion. When he left, I continued my deliberation. Looking at the letter on the desk, I noticed that our address and the return address were both typed. I don't know why, but for some reason, I cut the envelope open, at the end, with a scissors. In my mind, I flashed back to an earlier time, when my wife and I saw a movie entitled "Oh God," starring John Denver and George Burns. I remember how corny I thought it was when the character John Denver was playing, received a letter 'from GOD.' It looked like the same thing was happening to me.

Of course, I read the letter. Here is a photocopy of the actual letter I received:

January 28, 1980

Dear Larry,

My child, I love you. I gave my only son for you
to make you clean. I created you to be as you are, and
you are lovely in my eyes. Do not criticize yourself,
or be discouraged for not being perfect in your own eyes.
This only leads to frustration. I want you to trust me,
one step, one day at a time. Dwell in my presence and
my love. Be free, be yourself. Don't allow other
people to run you. I will lead you if you let me. Be
aware of my presence in everything. I give you patience,
love, joy and peace. Look to me for guidance. I am
your shepherd and I will lead you. Follow me only.

Don't ever forget that I love you; you are mine and
I will never stop loving you, so glory in this love.
Let it flow from you, spill over to everyone, to everything you touch. Be not concerned with your self; you
are my responsibility. I will change you so gradually
you will scarcely know it. Take your eyes off yourself,
and look only to me. I lead; I change; I make, but
not when you are trying. I won't fight your efforts.

You are mine. Let me lovingly guide you. Let me
give you joy, peace and kindness. No one else can.
Stop trying to be and let me have the joy of making you
like my son, Jesus. My will is perfect. My knowledge
of you is complete. My love for you is ever present,
ever concerned, and everlasting.

Your Heavenly Father

With faith, all things are possible.

307

Here is a photocopy of the envelope:

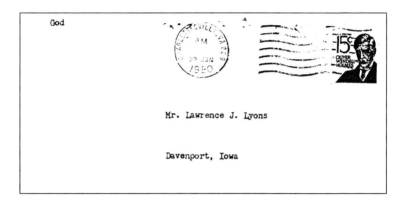

I read the letter quickly! My heart was racing! Thoughts flooded my mind. The letter was typed, so someone typed it. The letter had an actual postmark, from Charlottesville, Virginia. I didn't know anyone in that city. What is going on, I wondered? I received the letter at a point of absolute need. It came at the high point of my tension regarding this business moral decision. Then I remembered that all of scripture was handwritten by men, but those men were inspired by The Holy Spirit. I thought of the verse in Timothy, chapter 3 verse 16, which says, "All scripture is inspired of God, and is useful for teaching, reproof, correction, and training in holiness." The thought came to me that men don't just decide to start writing. Rather, they are inspired by God to put in writing, the thoughts of God on a particular matter. Could it be then, that God had inspired someone, at this particular crisis in my life, to write His feelings, when I was calling out to The Lord for answers? Did The Lord inspire someone to send me this letter"? I concluded that not only was it possible, but it was probable.

The content of this letter was very poignant and pointed. The thoughts about: "Don't allow other peo-ple to run you," "Look to Me for guidance" and "Follow Me only." These messages hit the mark. These are definitely my weak areas, as only The Lord would know. Another part that struck home for me was, "I won't fight your efforts!" Even though I try hard in everything I do, I often do not seek The Lord to see if what I am doing is in line with what He wants for me. The words were true. As I read the letter, I felt joy, peace and kindness. I truly felt the presence of The Lord. He was answering my prayers, in more areas than just the simple question of what to do in the business situation. He was giving me personal Fatherly directions, as only a Loving Father could. I felt the true peace that surpasses all understanding.

My thoughts returned to the pressing problem at hand. What should I do about the request to backdate these documents? In my spirit, I asked 'What would The Lord Jesus do? It was so simple. He would not do it. I would have to tell the two partners, "No," and look to The Lord to handle the outcome. Jesus wouldn't do it, so I won't either! I would look to Jesus to handle our financial needs.

On Monday I came to the meeting at the accountant's office. After exchanging greetings, the accountant said, "Well, Larry, what did you find out?" After my explanation of how all of this could be done, the accountant stated, "Then you will take care of this for us?" I replied, "No, I can't!" "You mean you *won't* do this for us," he asked? "I didn't say 'won't'

I said I 'can't,'" I answered. "It's a problem for me here," I said as I pointed to the right side of my head. One of the partners said, "It's a problem for me here," as he pointed to his wallet in his back pocket. "We'll get it done through someone else!"

As soon as he pointed to his wallet, I saw how wrong it would have been for me to do the backdating. It would have destroyed any witness I had built up in the minds of those present. They would have concluded, and rightfully so, that

I was just another 'phony' Christian. Wave a dollar bill in front of him and he will show his true colors!

At that instant, it was so wonderful to be able to tell them "No!" I wished I had pointed to my heart instead of my head, because it was really a problem with my relationship with Jesus, rather than a problem with my reasoning. But, I was at peace with my decision. And, I was at peace that Jesus would take care of the aspect of our financial needs.

As far as the two partners is concerned, they did find another agent to install the plan, by backdating documents, to get the tax deduction for the year 1979. They were able to put their $30,000 into a tax-deductible plan. Later, I heard from the accountant that one of their construction projects went sour, and they lost a considerable sum of money. Did they really win? Could they ever feel at peace with their decision?

Even though I did not do this specific project for these two men, I was able to fill other insurance needs for them, both personal, and business. This subject never comes up in our discussions, but I am sure they respected me for not yielding to the prospect of additional income. Two years after the incident, I was able to share this story with one of the men's wives, as we were talking about other insurance matters. I told her the details of my decision, and how The Lord helped me with my decision by inspiring someone to send me "His Letter." Today, I still do insurance work for these people, and we have a good relationship.

The experience of this decision process, and the letter I received, spoke to me very clearly. If I take my relationship with The Lord Jesus seriously, trusting Him fully in every-thing, He will teach me to ask for everything 'According To His Will,' so that I will receive what He wants me to have. This is true for any of us! I also learned that His Love for us is 'Personal' – it is 'Unconditional' – it is "Perfect – it is 'Simple and Pure' – from a Caring Father. :

Jesus loves me when I'm good,
When I do the things I should.
Jesus loves me when I'm bad,
Even though it makes Him sad.
Jesus loves me!
There is nothing I can do to make
Jesus love me less.
There is nothing I can do to make
Jesus love me more.
Jesus loves me. Yes, Jesus loves me.

The "Letter From The Lord" was addressed to me, but His Love is the same for everyone. Only those who seek Him, receive it. So, then, this letter is also addressed to you! Turn to Him and ask Him for His Hand and His Grace! In Jesus Holy Name, I pray!

56

RELATIONSHIPS

"It is better to trust in The Lord than to put confidence in man. It is better to put trust in The Lord than to put confidence in princes."

(Psalm 118:8-9)

Having a true relationship with The Good Lord is at the very heart of every relationship we could ever have with any other person. It is not possible to have an honest relationship with another person without having first an open relationship with The Lord. In His word, Jesus said, "The thief cometh not, but for to steal, and to kill, and to destroy; I am come that they might have life, and that they have it more abundantly" (John 10:10). This sounds like Jesus wants to have a personal relationship with each of us. For again, He says in His word, "I am The Way, The Truth, and The Life; no man cometh unto The Father, but by Me" (John 14:6). Again, He says in His word, "I am The Door; by Me if any man enter in, he shall be saved, and shall go in and out, and find pasture" (John 10: 9).

When Jesus was asked, "How should we pray," he didn't say, 'My Father,' but rather, 'Our Father' (Matthew 6:9,13).

Then, He added, "us...our...us...our... we...our...us...and, us." Notice, He did not say, "'my...I...mine...or me.

But how can I say 'Our' if I do not first have a relationship with The Good Lord as well as someone else? If I am not interested in other people, then I cannot have a true relationship with 'our Father,' Who is in Heaven. If I say I love God, Whom I have never seen, and do not have a good relationship with my brother, I am no more than a liar, for in His word, it is written, "If any man say, I love God, and hateth his brother, he is a liar; for he that loveth not his brother, whom he has seen, how can he love God, Whom he has not seen? (1John 4 – vs20). If I am not interested in the spiritual well-being of others, it is most difficult to approach God, Who is Holy, because God is a 'People-Lover.' God is a 'People-God.' God is interested in people; in fact, He is so interested in people, that God created us in His Image and Likeness. Scripture tells us that, "God is Love!" (1John 4:8) Love, then, is an action word, and God is an "Action God." Love isn't really love until it is given away, freely, without conditions.

Most often, God chooses to work through our prayers and the prayers of others, but sometimes He does things in our lives completely on His own. This is why it is so critical that we cultivate first, a personal relationship with The Lord Jesus, as our Lord and Savior, so that we can have a 'true' relationship with The Father and with others.

Recently, I had a situation come up that proved to me the value of relationships. On Friday, May 1, 1998, I spent the afternoon mowing the grass at home. Then, I dug out several dead bush stumps, and finished up by chopping out a dead apple tree stump. The next day, I had that sore-all-over feeling, and I thought I had the flu. Sunday, I had a fever and felt even worse. Monday, it was worse yet! The fever must have been high during the night, because when I awoke

Monday morning, I had fever sores all over my mouth and nose. Our son, Paul, brought over his children's battery operated digital thermometer to find that my temperature was at 104.3 degrees. Elayne made a doctor appointment for the next morning. The high fever lasted for three days. The doctor gave me an antibiotic to combat the fever. Every night, while I tried to sleep, I'd sweat profusely, making it necessary to change both the bedding as well as my pajamas often. During one night, I nearly stopped breathing. Elayne had to nudge me to get me breathing again. She was very concerned, and of course, she prayed for me. It turned out to be lobar pneumonia in both lungs. This was a first for me, and I waited until age sixty-eight to try it out.

The Good Lord has healed me. I am back to full strength, at the time of this writing, several months after the bout with pneumonia. I am so grateful and thankful to The Lord. But, now about relationships! During my illness, I did ask The Lord to heal me, and to rebuke the enemy in this situation. Elayne was praying for me almost constantly. She anointed my forehead with oil every night. Elayne called my sister, Angie, who lives in Molalla, Oregon, to have her and her husband Gene pray for me. Business clients called in to check on my condition. They said to let me know that they were praying for me. Elayne went to our prayer meeting on the Thursday evenings when I could not make it, and the group prayed for me. We have gone to these Thursday evening prayer meetings for over twenty years, and these dear brothers and sisters in Christ, are like family to us. A client named Sharon, sent me a card, which reads:

"Larry, I'm continuing to pray for you and your complete healing. A favorite verse of mine, which I pray for you, is, "Stretch out Thy Hand to heal and cause miraculous signs and wonders to be done through The Name of Thy Holy Servant, Jesus." (Acts 4: 30).

(signed) In Him, Sharon"

In the peak of my hurting, a client called on his cellular phone, while driving back into town, from a business appointment. It was Friday night about suppertime. He called me to tell me that he had been thinking about me for over a week, and almost called me several times. But, something seemed to always come up to distract him from calling. He decided to call me at this very time, so he would not forget again. Dick said he was wishing The Lord's blessing upon me. He didn't even know that I was sick. I told Dick that when a person's name comes to mind, it is time to pray for that person, for The Lord is bringing the name to mind for prayer needs. Dick responded, "I did man, I did!"

When I finally did return to work, the man who lives across the alley from our business, called me over to see how I was doing. Don said that he hadn't seen me for a while, and thought something might be wrong, so he had been praying for me. Isn't this amazing?

Yes, I even received cards with reminders of prayers, from JOY team members. JOY stands for <u>Jesus, Others, and You</u>, a prison outreach ministry which Elayne and I have been involved with for many years. Twice a year, there are special weekends at a local State prison, when volunteers come into the prison chapel, to share a weekend of talks and love with the prisoners. Then, on the 3rd weekend of each month, those who have made such a weekend, come for a 'Reunion Meeting.' Because of the pneumonia, I did not make the May Joy reunion. JOY team members relayed the message to me that the men at the East Moline Correctional Center were praying for me. This meant so much to me, as my love for these men is so great. I consider these men, my brothers in Christ. I received a letter from a JOY candidate, whom I met at JOY #14, in April of 1998, just before I was hit with the pneumonia. At the June Reunion, on Father's Day, he said it was okay to share this letter, so I would like to share it with you:

"Dear Larry,

May God bless you and yours. I believe you do not have the virus anymore. I believe that your children's finances are met also. I forgot to tell you, that you are to praise God in any situation that occurs. Why? Because you then allow Him to come in into whatever crisis you are in, and God is a circumstances-breaker. Yes, God inhabits the praises of His people. If I can't do anything else, I can praise God. God is my present help in time of trouble.

Now, Larry, you know and I know, that greater is He that is in me, than he of this world. (1John 4:4) I call on Him all the time. As a matter of fact, I asked His blessing on you, with all the ministering angels just waiting on your orders, to minister to you. I know, you know, and all Heaven knows, and even the devil knows, that you are the righteousness of God, in Christ Jesus (2 Cor 5:21).

Everyone knows that you can do all things through Christ Jesus, Who strengthens you (Phil 4:13). And, He will supply all your needs according to His riches in glory by Christ Jesus. (Phil 4:19)

So, I'll see you in church. Stay prayerful. And, I pray that God may give you and yours favor in every area of your lives.

Sincerely, in Christ, Melvin

This letter is so powerful. It brought me to tears. This man was encouraging me at a peak time of need, and he is in prison. The Lord was working through him to encourage me. When Melvin said, "See you in church," he meant the chapel at the prison, at the next reunion. Melvin was right. He was obedient. He prayed for me. His relationship with The Lord allowed him to love me and have a relationship with me. I did see Melvin at the next JOY Reunion, on Father's Day, 1998. Jesus did heal me, once again.

Now, as I am completing this writing, I received another card in the mail from Melvin. It's so simple, but so beautiful. It reads as follows:

"There's not much I can say, but there's one thing I can do. . . . .I'll pray for you. I was thinking about you. I pray that you and your family are doing great. Always let the Spirit of Agape Love saturate your soul. Always remember, 'Prayer is power.' Guard your heart at all cost, and The Holy Spirit will not grieve. Keep in focus 1Corinthian, Chapter 13, 'and I know, and you know, greater is he that is in you, than any circumstances, sickness, or lack of any, or any type of problem the world throws at you. And may the blessings of God almighty be on you.

See you when I see you,
Sincerely in Christ,
Melvin"

The thought that comes to mind is this: there are really only two things in life that we can do which matter. We can love one another, as The Lord commanded us to do (1John 3:23), and we can pray for one another as He asked us to do (Matt 6:9-13). When we pray, this releases the Grace of The Lord in the life of the person we are praying for, so that the person becomes closer to The Lord. As we love one another, we come closer to The Lord. Then, as we pray for one another, we come closer to The Lord, and in the spiritual process, we come closer to each other. This is relationship. This is the nourishment of life—developing relationships. This is what it means to be 'God-Like.'

Our relationship with The Good Lord is the most important aspect of our lives. The worldly person would say, "Hey, come look at me. See what I've got and see what I've done." The person filled with The Spirit of God, who has a personal relationship with Jesus, would say, "Hey, come look at Him. See what He has done for us."

Once I heard a man on the radio make two powerful statements that tell of the importance of a relationship with God. First, he said, "The greatest lesson God is teaching us is to stay close to Him." Then he said in a prayer, "I don't care where I go Lord, as long as I am with You."

57

EVERY SUNDAY

"My people perish for lack of knowledge."
(Hosea 4:6)

In 1986, I was appointed as area service agent for a prominent life insurance company, by the name of Phoenix Mutual. With this appointment, came the assignment of many 'orphan policyholders.' These are people who purchased policies from the company, however the agent who sold the insurance, is either out of the business, or deceased. Without an assigned agent, they are referred to as 'orphans.' If any policy service were needed, I would usually get a phone call. Then, I would go out to their home, get acquainted and see what service I could perform. This part of my work I really enjoyed and there was never a charge for any of this type of service.

Bill was one of these orphan policyholders. Many years prior to my being assigned as servicing agent, Bill had purchased policies on himself, his wife, and his two sons. One day he called with many questions concerning the features of these policies. I went to his home and we got to know one another. We completed the service work he wanted done. Some time after that, he called our office to see if we could help him with auto insurance. Our son, Paul, handled this coverage for him.

After that, we would see him twice a year. He would come into our office with some sort of paperwork he would want to review. When I would see him in the office, he was always polite. He seemed to be such a kind man, with such a sense of fairness. Everyone in the office really liked Bill.

In September of 1998, he called me to tell me of his wife's death. I felt so badly for him. I knew he and his wife were very close. His wife was in her mid-eighties when she died. Rather than have Bill come into our office, I suggested that I could come to his home to go over the necessary paperwork. Bill seemed glad that I offered to come to his home. Before entering his home, I asked The Lord to help me show compassion and to say the right words to comfort him. After exchanging greetings, we sat at his kitchen table. I told Bill how sorry I was to hear of his wife's death. I told him that I could not even comprehend such a loss; in fact, I didn't even want to think about the loss of my own wife, as it would be so tough without her. To this comment, he responded, "Well, we have lived a good life. I always wanted her to go first, so she wouldn't have to worry about being without me. You see, she was hard of hearing, and couldn't get around real well, so she depended on me a lot." Then he said something that really surprised me. He said, "Anyway, I'm on my way out myself!" "What do you mean, Bill," I asked? He went on to tell me that he had cancer of the liver and it was spreading rapidly. He said that the reason he had to change the time of my appointment with him, was that he had the hospice nurse stop at his home for treatment. She left just before I arrived. The hospice people only get involved when the individual is in a terminal condition. It hit me really hard to hear this. I liked Bill a lot. I was sad to see him face this situation. But, he seemed very brave about it. Bill indicated to me that he didn't have too long too live.

After we finished the paperwork regarding the death claim for his wife's policy, I started to visit with him in more detail about his condition. While he was explaining to me all the details of his different treatments, the thought came to mind that my real concern should be for his spiritual well being. I had no idea where he stood with The Lord. Oh, how I wanted to be sure of his relationship with The Lord. Even though uncomfortable, I came up with a question to start the conversation going in the direction of The Lord. "Bill, may I ask you a personal question," I asked? "Not to hurt you, but to help you – you know I wouldn't do anything to hurt you," I continued. "Sure," he said. I asked, "How are you and The Lord getting along," I asked? "Every Sunday," he exclaimed, with an inflection in his voice. "Oh, where do you attend church," I asked? "St. Anthony's, downtown," he said. "I attend the Catholic church too," I told him. "But I attend St. Paul's church, over on Rusholme Street." He seemed pleased that we had this in common, that we both attended the same type of church. Still, I was unsure of his position with The Lord, so I reluctantly pressed on. "Now, Bill, may I ask you two other questions – again, not with the idea of hurting you – I think you might be surprised at your answers," I stated. My thought was that I would ask him if he believed that Jesus was truly God, and if he believed that Jesus was raised from the dead. I was sure he would answer 'yes' to both questions, and then I would give him a scripture verse to confirm in his mind that he was saved. First then, I asked Bill if The Man Christ Jesus was truly God, made man—that He was the fulfillment of the prophecy in Isaiah, where it is written, "A virgin shall bear a Son, and His Name shall be called Emanuel," which means God is with us. His answer surprised me. Bill said, "I don't know. I never thought about it." "Do you mean that it's not possible, or do you mean that it's possible, and that you never considered it to be important," I asked him? Bill replied, "Anything's possible." When I asked him the second question concerning whether he believed that this Man, Christ Jesus, was truly dead, and that His Father raised Him from the dead, he answered simply, "There again, anything is possible." As I was about to go into other scriptures to explain the accuracy of these two truths, Bill's telephone rang. He was occupied on the phone for a few minutes. When he returned to the kitchen table to again sit down, he said, "Larry, I'm sorry, but I am going to have to lie down, I'm pretty weak." In desperation, I scrambled for what to do. I really didn't want to leave, but I could see that he was perspiring and I didn't want to cause him any stress. "Bill, let me give you these two cards," I said. Then, I gave Bill one of the ASK cards I used to witness the Word of The Lord. (Note; the content of this card can be found in one of the other sections #6, #38, and #45). Secondly, I gave him a small card which had 'the sinner's prayer' on one side, and the scripture verses on the opposite side, which would affirm the word's of the sinner's prayer. The front side of the small card reads as follows:

"Lord Jesus forgive me for I am a sinner. I believe You Lord Jesus died for me, and Your Precious Blood will cleanse me from all my sin. By faith, I now receive You into my heart as my Lord and Savior trusting You only for my salvation. Lord Jesus, help me to do Your will each day, in Jesus Name, I pray."

The back- side of the small card reads as follows:

"To heaven I am going for all eternity because Jesus, Who is God, made Man, took my place on the cross for my sins. Jesus lives in my heart, through His Holy Spirit, since I have accepted Jesus as my personal Lord and Savior."

Romans, 10:9 –13
Ephesians, 2 :8,9
John, 3:14 –17

At that point, Bill being very weak, put the cards in his front shirt pocket. As I handed the cards to him, I said, "Bill, please look at these cards!" "I will, and I'll let you know," Bill replied. I had to leave. While Bill was ushering me through the garage to the back door, I said to him, "Bill, you're a very sensitive and compassionate man and I love you." Simply, he said, "Thanks!"

Some of the things I learned about Bill during that visit, which will always remain with me. He told me that his age was 87. He said that he had 'lived a good life.' He told me that when he had cancer surgery, some two and one half years earlier, he had a visit from a minister of the church, while he was in the hospital. The minister asked him if it was okay to say a prayer for him. Bill said it was "all right as long as it doesn't start with 'Eternal Rest.'" Bill laughed. I guess the minister thought this was humorous too, since he never tried to find out anything of a spiritual nature about Bill. Bill told me also that he had a Bible – "A big one," he said.

My hope was to get back to see Bill when I got the paperwork back from the insurance company regarding the claim proceeds from the life policy on his wife's life. I first saw Bill in his home on October 16, 1998. When I went back to see him with the paperwork, it was Thursday, November 5th. Elayne and I had been to Ohio on a trip between the two visits. When we returned from Ohio, I received the claim checkbook covering the death claim on his wife. On November 5th, I returned to his home to go over the details. I was not able to visit with him because his condition had deteriorated. I was able though to talk to one of his sons who allowed me to go into his bedroom. He was under heavy sedation and I was not able to communicate with him. A hospice nurse was at his bedside.

After going over the paperwork with Bill's son, I talked to the son for awhile. His son had a great love for his father. Bill said that he came to visit him every day, and took care of all his material needs. Bill's son said that his father had composed a short statement a few days before. He read it to me. It went something like this: "Life is like a merry-go-round. It has it's ups and downs. It's been a heck of a ride this far—now it's time for me to get off, and let someone else have a turn." This made me wonder if Bill had even been able to look at the two witness cards I had left with him. I mentioned to Bill's son, that his father and I had a good visit when we were together last. I also told him that I was concerned about Bill, so gave him two cards to read when he could.

His son said, "Oh, you mean those 'Holy Cards?'"

"Yes," I said. "Bill told me that he would look at them and let me know.

Bill's son answered, "If he told you that, then he did. He's a man of his word."

Bill died five days later, on November 10, 1998. My hope is that he read the witness cards, gave his heart to The Lord Jesus and that he will be in The Kingdom when this is over. If he didn't, I'm so sad for him. If he did, I am joyful for him. Bill was open for the truth. He went to the right place, "Every Sunday." But somehow, either he wasn't listening with his heart or it was not presented in the right way, for his spirit to catch the truth of the Gospel. Bill was open, but he was uninformed. How sad, a man eighty seven years old, who was honest, frank, and yet, uninformed. Bill said it was possible. He wasn't in denial. In all those years, couldn't someone have come along who was interested enough in him, to take the time to tell Bill about The Love of Jesus? I'm sure he would have listened. Help us to take an interest in Your people, Lord in Jesus Holy Name, I pray! How it must hurt You to have to say; "My people perish for lack of knowledge!" We, who have the knowledge of the Saving Grace of Jesus, help us to be willing to share this knowledge. Can there be anything more important in life?

Note: In order to protect the identity of the family involved, I used "Bill" as the elderly man's name. That's not his name, but I hope his correct name appears in "The Book Of Life!"

About The Author

Larry was born in 1930 and lives in Davenport, Iowa. He attended grade and high schools in Davenport. After a stay in the U.S. Navy, he attended St. Ambrose University of Davenport, graduating in 1963. He worked as an engineer in industry for fifteen years before starting an insurance agency. He obtained a degree in insurance from The American College in Bryn Mawr, Pennsylvania in 1978. He worked in this family business for forty-three years and is now semi-retired, leaving his two sons and a daughter to operate it. Larry has used the insurance business as an outreach to serve people and to turn clients into great friends. Larry and his wife, Elayne, have been married for fifty-eight years, have ten children and twenty-seven grandchildren. The stories shared in this book are real life happenings with family and friends.`

CPSIA information can be obtained
at www.ICGtesting.com
Printed in the USA
FFOW05n0403300517

9 781612 154831